T0367827

A True Story of Love From The Afterlife

SUSAN H. KASTNER

Balboa Press books may be ordered through booksellers or by contacting:

Balboa Press
A Division of Hay House
1663 Liberty Drive
Bloomington, IN 47403
www.balboapress.com
1-(877) 407-4847

ISBN: 978-1-4525-5418-1 (sc)
ISBN: 978-1-4525-5420-4 (hc)
ISBN: 978-1-4525-5419-8 (e)

Library of Congress Control Number: 2012913741

Because of the dynamic nature of the Internet, any web addresses or links contained in this book may have changed since publication and may no longer be valid. The views expressed in this work are solely those of the author and do not necessarily reflect the views of the publisher, and the publisher hereby disclaims any responsibility for them.

The author of this book does not dispense medical advice or prescribe the use of any technique as a form of treatment for physical, emotional, or medical problems without the advice of a physician, either directly or indirectly. The intent of the author is only to offer information of a general nature to help you in your quest for emotional and spiritual well-being. In the event you use any of the information in this book for yourself, which is your constitutional right, the author and the publisher assume no responsibility for your actions.

All original Happi Heart artwork by Dr. Liong H. Tee ©

Printed in the United States of America

Balboa Press rev. date: 07/31/2012

CONTENTS

PREFACE

Have you ever been so much in love with someone that it hurts? No matter where you are or what you do, you can see the love in their eyes burning in your heart? It is that special kind of love that not even fairy tales can describe adequately; that will have you rise up to move mountains. You live for it. You would die to protect that special kind of love that makes you a better person just for having experienced it in your life. Those two souls melding into one are often called soul mates here in this world.

If you are one of the fortunate few to have experienced this phenomenon, then you understand what it means to lose the other half of your whole being; the emptiness, loneliness, utter despair, and intense longing to be with him or her again engulfs you day after day. To be able to touch him or her, to feel that other person lying next to you just one more time would be the greatest blessing in your now meager existence. It is all you can think about. The mundane routine of life barely intrudes into your all-consuming lonely world. Where then can you turn to seek some relief? Find some comfort? Help yourself heal?

Maybe you should consider the possibility that your loved one may not be as far away as you think. Perhaps they do communicate with you in an ongoing, almost daily conversation. It is only you that has failed to pick up your messages from heaven's switchboard. Allow yourself to consider that there may be evidence of their presence all around you, but you simply have not recognized the signs or dismissed them as purely coincidental. In a way, I am going to be asking you to learn another language: the language of the soul. You only need to allow your heart to open once more for a new kind of conversation to begin.

Consider that despite the fact that Jan's physical life on earth has ended, I have witnessed for myself the miracles and messages she has sent to us over the last three years; these conversations with heaven. Those messages from above, beyond, or through are meant to provide comfort and convey love as well as assurance that your loved one is with you and watching over you. If you believe that once the soul has crossed over it enters into a heaven filled with peace and love, you have nothing to fear in accepting a presence as anything other than a blessing in your life.

Be assured that once you have achieved peace of mind for yourself about your loved one's existence, you too may find a new sense of joy and happiness in these pages.

IN APPRECIATION

"When you follow your most precious dreams, you sing with the angels and dance with the stars." Anon

My heartfelt gratitude goes out to those who made this journey and the fulfillment of one of my lifelong dreams possible.

First, my appreciation goes to Jan who always encouraged me to develop my writing skills, just by doing something that I already loved to do.

Not enough words can express my appreciation and love for the entire Forgey clan. They have adopted me into their hearts and homes and I am eternally grateful for learning what it means to have a loving family around me.

To my parents, George and Barbara, who not only brought me into this world where I could meet Jan and Liong, but also exposed me early on to their unshakeable faith and the belief in life everlasting.

Love to you all, Susan

DEDICATION

Jan

"Don't cry because it's over,
smile because it happened."
Dr. Seuss

Thank you, Jan.

Your earthly life may have ended,
but you still live within each and every one of us;
until we are able to meet up with our angel again.

CHAPTER 1

How Do I Even Begin?

"Dearest Jan,

My life took on meaning when I found you. For all my personal faults and shortcomings, I want to tell you on this 56th anniversary of my existence in this lifetime that I love you. I want you to be with me – this lifetime and if ever there is any next lifetime – for I may then be a better person for you.

Liong
April 1, 2000"

This love letter from Liong to Jan on his birthday is but a small glimpse into the life and love Liong and Jan shared here on earth. The steadfast love experienced between Jan and Liong is the very foundation of this story. Over the eighteen years of their life together, they shared a love that was unstoppable and unshakable. Even when Jan was in her final days, when asked if there was anything that needed to be done, she smiled and simply said, "Liong will take care of it."

It is not often you find a couple who had such total trust in one another. No doubts plagued their relationship; no angry words were ever spoken. In fact, everyone who knew them can attest to the fact that theirs was a life of harmony, love, and abundant happiness. To know Jan and Liong was to know love in its purest form, and they exemplified the very definition of what soul mates are.

If this story is to have any deep, meaningful impact on you, it is important for you to understand who Jan and Liong were in life together. That bond that they shared is what makes this story so impactful. Too often in other books, you are presented with dry, static information, usually reduced and isolated into single encapsulated events. Even though the "wow" factor may still be present in the event being told, often it does not give you any useful information that you can apply to your own life, your own situation, with any lasting satisfaction or insight.

My relationship to this project is that I knew Jan for seven years before she passed and I have known Liong for over sixteen years. I am blessed to say that they were and still are my friends. I felt that their story was an important one to share, showing what is possible. Even if this book only brings comfort to one more person struggling with grief, I have succeeded.

Now it is important to make this point clear before we go any further: I am not a psychic, psychologist, psychiatrist, member of the clergy, or any kind of authority or expert on death or the afterlife; nor even a professional writer for that matter. So you will not find any expert opinions, conclusions, or religious dogma anywhere in this book unless it is something that was written down by Liong in his journal.

I have read other after-death experience books, and in some cases, I almost felt the writer needed to find some justification or corroboration for what they were writing. Without some "official" recognition or authority, what they felt, perceived, or experienced was not legitimate in its own right. There was always a point-of-view spin attached to the experience, whether it was religious, psychic, or psychological. This book will not contain any elaborate spinning of the information to any particular point of view. It will simply be a presentation of the events that have taken place between June 5, 2008, and June 5, 2011. I am relying entirely on your heart to hear what is true.

This book is written as a testament to that sustaining love that has continued on even after death. It should be noted that Liong started writing his journal simply as an outlet to share his thoughts on what life had become after his angel passed away. It was to be his journal of memories, thoughts, and feelings about their life together. Instead, it evolved into a written record of experiences, in many forms, of Jan's continued presence in his daily life. As you get further into the story, you will see that over the three years since Jan's passing, the volume of entries grew from only a few pages in 2008 to an almost daily record by 2010.

Needless to say, it would be almost impossible to write about every single time Jan has made her presence felt because of the sheer volume of material available. Therefore, I chose to group some of the events contained in the journal into categories to better illustrate the dynamic communication patterns between Jan and Liong or Jan and other important people in her life.

Another reason for writing this book was to fill in a gap that Liong was not able to find for himself after Jan's passing. We both read a multitude of books written by psychics, psychologists, spouses, and near-death survivors, and then some more. All of them dealt with either a single event or a few events that were of short duration. There did not seem to be any books out there that dealt with an ongoing, almost daily communication with a loved one who had passed away.

I asked people if they would read this kind of book or if they thought a book like this would help others deal with their own loss. Every time I received positive affirmations to my query. Everyone believed, or at the very least wanted to believe, their loved one was still somewhere close by their side.

I actually started discussing with Liong the possibility of writing a book in October 2009, and thankfully he agreed. His only conditions were that I had to use the contents of the journal with limited editing, and I also needed to continue contributing to Jan's scholarship fund at Colome High School annually. Naturally, since the conditions were so reasonable, I quickly accepted his terms.

To add flavor to our story, a little understanding of the Chinese culture is required, as it plays an important factor in the coming pages. For those of you that do not know, the Chinese are a very superstitious people about the souls of the departed. They will take great pains not to offend the spirit of anyone who has departed this world. It is important for them to honor their deceased loved ones by burning candles or incense, making offerings as a token of respect, mostly of favorite foods, and honoring their memory. To that end, it is also the custom to mourn the loss of a loved one for a period of three years. It seemed, therefore, a perfect timeframe for the book to cover the first three years after Jan's passing, signifying that Liong's traditional period of mourning had come to an end.

Actual passages are used from the journal as written by Liong at the time. You will see a drastic contrast in his writing style when you compare his love letters to Jan and the entries in the journal. The love letters are full of passion and affection, whereas the journal is completely devoid of these elements. The sharp contrast in writing styles reflects the emptiness I have seen in Liong since Jan's passing.

For those of you that want to follow the linear chain of events as they evolved, the entire journal has been included in the latter half of this book. You can follow the progression of events as they unfolded. I would caution you not to be fooled into thinking that every significant event in the journal has been included in the first half of the book. There are many more examples of Jan's communications contained within the journal's pages for you to consider. I tried to select a balance of small, medium and large manifestations in each of the categories to show that the magnitudes of the communications are not all the same. Just as in life, there are highs and lows in everything, including the afterlife. At Liong's request, the only things that have been omitted from the journal are passages that do not show any communication from Jan or are of a sensitive nature to friends and family members.

With all of that being said, I ask you to sit back, put your feet up, grab a cup of your favorite reading beverage, and prepare to be amazed.

CHAPTER 2

Let Me Introduce You To...

To walk by Jan and Liong on the street, you would probably ask yourself, "How in the world did those two people ever get together?" I am sure to the casual observer they would have appeared as an extremely odd couple. Jan was fair skinned, five foot three inches tall, and almost as big around when I first met her on my birthday in January 2001. Liong is Chinese, five foot six, and slender. Perhaps that is one of the reasons this story is so appealing, because of the diversity of our dynamic duo.

Jan and Liong

Jan and Liong

Liong often talks about the day he first met the love of his life, Jan: "I was playing blackjack at the Golden Nugget in downtown Las Vegas. Jan was dealing blackjack at the next table. When I looked over at her, she was staring at me. Then she flashed me a big smile. I got up and moved to her table. On her name badge was the town where she was born. It said Winner, South Dakota. So I said to her, 'Where is Winner, South Dakota?'

"Jan replied, 'You wouldn't know even if I told you. It's a small town of only four thousand people. Where are you from?'

"I leaned over the table toward her and said, 'I'm from Loser, California.'"

They both laughed about that meeting for the next eighteen years.

In actuality, Liong Hian Tee's birth in Manila, Philippines, was as dramatic as it could get. He was born into a poor Chinese family during the height of World War II while the United States was conducting a bombing raid over Manila on the night of April 1, 1944. The electricity was cut off in Manila by the Japanese because of the air raid, and his father had to cover the windows with blankets before lighting candles to illuminate the room. Since the city was under blackout conditions and bombs were exploding all around, Liong came into this world in a very dramatic way. He even jokes that is why he is such a romantic person even today because he came into the world under candlelight. Coincidentally, it was also the Year of the Monkey in the Chinese calendar. That might give you a few clues about his nature.

By American standards, we would have called him a precocious child. Liong was the fourth of seven children and the second son. According to the stories he tells, he always had a crusader spirit and a mischievous nature, whether it be with his family or his many friends. In fact, he believes he was a knight in an earlier life. Of course some members of his family say it is because Yong-Yong, his eldest sister, dropped him on his head as a baby.

Just like any good knight, he never allowed anyone to bully him or his siblings and friends, even if they were bigger or stronger. That even included some of his teachers. If he did not like them, he always found ways to make fun of them in front of the class. And as far as he knows, he is the only one in his school that ever graduated as valedictorian of his class with a conduct D grade. Yet, among his family and classmates, he is still the one that they all remember. Liong was known for always getting things done, even though sometimes his father would mockingly ask him, “Is it legal?”

Despite all the antics of his youth, Liong’s family was always a top priority to him. Realizing the many sacrifices his parents had to make to provide him with a home, food, and clothing, he did all that he could to help his mother and father. Never wanting to be a burden to his family, he learned early in life that he would have to rely on himself to get ahead, even if it meant selling mismatched socks as “the new American fad” in front of his father’s store to earn his pocket money for the movies as a schoolboy.

Unlike Americans who were raised to go to school and get a good job, Chinese children were taught from a young age to own their own business, even if it was only a food cart on the corner of the street. You were considered a failure in their society, at the time, if you worked for others. This notion of not wanting to work for others combined with his crusader spirit and sharp mind enabled Liong to pursue diverse opportunities wherever and whenever he could find them.

After graduation from high school in Manila, he attended the National Cheng Kung University in Taiwan, a sister university of Purdue in Indiana. Even before he had completed his senior year, Liong had already received a scholarship offer to attend the University of Wisconsin-Madison. However, he could not leave Taiwan without making his mark there as the first foreign student to graduate at the top of his class in 1967.

While attending the University in Taiwan, Liong rented a room from the Lu family, whose patriarch happened to be the warden in charge of all military prisons in southern Taiwan. Colonel Lu liked Liong so much he asked Liong to become his godson. When Liong's parents went to Taiwan for a visit, Liong's new godfather told his father, "It's a good thing Liong has the heart of a Buddha; otherwise, he could be a very bad person if he wanted and he has the intelligence to lead bad people." I am certain this was not the kind of glowing endorsement from a person who had dealt with military prisoners since World War II that Liong's father wanted to hear.

Upon completion of his bachelor of science in mechanical engineering, Liong went onto Wisconsin where he earned both his Masters and PhD in mechanical engineering in three years. After graduation, he continued on at Wisconsin as a post-doctoral fellow in the mechanical engineering department. For a short time, he consulted with the paper industry and completed a grant study for the United States Department of Defense.

In the early 1970s, Liong decided to return to the Philippines and was asked to serve as a technical consultant to the Philippines National Housing Authority with the responsibility to jumpstart a manufacturing complex. When the political climate started to change in the Philippines, Liong decided to return to the United States with only four hundred dollars in his pocket.

Between 1986 and 1991, Liong pursued his dream of being a business owner. He utilized his many skills and experiences and worked as an insurance agent at Prudential Insurance, became a real estate broker in California, and finally became the owner/operator of a medical clinic and medical laboratory business in Los Angeles.

At this time, Liong was riding high and the world was in the palm of his hand. What better way to celebrate success in life than to spend a few days in Las Vegas?

Elinor, a good friend and coworker of Jan's from the Mirage Hotel and Casino, wrote in a note to Liong on June 12, 2008, "To know Jan was to know Jan loved Liong." And according to Jan herself, she and Liong fell in love as soon as their eyes met over that blackjack table at the Golden Nugget casino.

Jan Marie Forgey was as opposite to Liong as you could possibly imagine. She was born in Winner, South Dakota, in July 1958 to John and Lucy Forgey. John was and still is a Black Angus cattle rancher. Jan was the third of six children and the oldest girl in the family. Growing up in a small ranch house with four brothers and a baby sister, taught Jan early to be self-motivated and thrifty. Ranch life is not an easy one, for those of you who have never experienced it. Yet, to know Jan, you understood she would not have traded it for any other kind of life. She was a ranch girl and proud of it.

To know Jan was to also know how much she loved her family. Naturally, because she lived in a remote area and there were not too many other entertainment options available, she spent many happy hours playing Cribbage with her dad and cards with her mom and their many friends. Of course, it depends on which one you talk to as to who won the most games.

As with any child from a small ranching community growing up in the sixties and seventies, she did her turn at 4-H, raising two lambs and a baby steer and taking part in country fair cooking competitions, for which she won a couple of ribbons. Even at an early age, Jan developed her lifelong love of cooking and especially baking.

Jan started her first seven years at school in a one-room school house, which her two older brothers, Steve and Neil, and her two younger brothers, Danny and Dale, also attended. It was not until the eighth grade that Jan actually started attending a regular school in nearby Colome, South Dakota. After graduating from Colome

High School in 1976, she attended Black Hills State University in Spearfish, South Dakota, just outside of Rapid City.

Always a hard worker, when Jan arrived at school, she unloaded her belongings from the car into her dorm room, loaded her new classmate Linda Lyons into her car, and drove into town. When Linda asked her where she was going, she simply said, "To look for a job." They pulled into the local Pizza Hut and thus began Jan's lifelong love affair with Pizza Hut pizza. Her friend and roommate, Linda Lyons, even remarked at Jan's memorial service that they ate a lot of pizza that first year.

Until graduating with a degree in business in 1980, Jan worked in Spearfish in an insurance agency and babysat for friends and some of her professors. In late 1980, after graduating, she moved to Casper, Wyoming, and worked in a toy store before securing a job as a bookkeeper at the Four Way Pipe Company, where she earned the nickname "Miss Five Ways." Always a social person, Jan was able to build up enough experience to become a freelance bookkeeper.

Naturally, with all this innate talent as a people person, Jan managed to find the time to introduce her brother Steve to his wife Shirley and her brother Danny to his wife Lyn.

One day in 1987, Jan up and decided she was going to move to Las Vegas. She began her career as a pit clerk at Caesars Palace as well as being a part-time dealer at the Golden Gate in downtown Las Vegas. She even tried a stint as a standup comic. Her first full-time dealing assignment was working the graveyard shift at the Barbary Coast on the corner of Flamingo and Las Vegas Boulevards. By 1989, Jan was a premiere dealer at the Golden Nugget, where she met Liong the following year.

Jan transferred to the Mirage in 1997, which according to her was "the best casino on the strip!" Jan was quite content and loved her job and coworkers so much so that she stayed at the Mirage until just before her passing in 2008, stopping only because she was no longer physically able to go to work.

So when exactly did this eternal love affair begin for real? Soon after their first meeting, Liong was assaulted by two muggers in the backyard of his home in Los Angeles on Thanksgiving evening in 1991. One of the muggers hit him in the head with the butt of his gun and then fired a shot at him as they were running away, the bullet creasing Liong's stomach. Naturally, he refused to go to the hospital.

After the paramedics wrapped him "like a mummy," as he claims, he told himself, "I'm not dying without knowing the angel I met in Las Vegas."

That was a tricky matter, however, as Liong did not know Jan's phone number. He took a chance and called the 411 operator in Las Vegas and asked if she was listed.

At that same time Jan was in a bad relationship and was speaking on the phone with her college classmate and friend, Linda Lyons, who was then a flight attendant living in Phoenix. She was crying to Linda; asking her where her "wonderful world" was. She even had the Louis Armstrong song, one of her all-time favorites, playing in the background. When she heard the call waiting beep on her phone, she placed Linda on hold and switched over to find Liong on the other end, calling her from Los Angeles that Thanksgiving evening.

Jan quickly switched back to Linda saying, "That Chinese I was just telling you about is on the other line!" From that moment on, she never had to ask where her wonderful world was; he was right there on the phone.

Over the next eighteen years, life was magical for both Jan and Liong. Every day was an adventure and every moment a dream come true. As one of her coworkers and friends told Jan, "You are a modern Cinderella."

The following love letters exchanged between Jan and Liong show that their love found no boundary in time. As is true of all of Jan's love letters, she never wrote a date on any of them because as she once told Liong, "Our love is timeless."

> "My dearest Jan:
>
> If the pens in my hand are the keys that can unlock the doors to your heart and soul, then I thank God for

giving me this precious gift, for it grants me access to see a kindest heart and purest soul. A person like you will always be blessed. I thank you for being my friend, my love, my soul mate.

Love,
Liong
April 8, 2000

I bought you some of your favorite coconut cakes. Hope you enjoy them."

"Liong!!

You are my dream!! See? Dreams do come true. Words cannot describe my love for you. You make my world colorful every minute of every day. This Thanksgiving and every day around it, I am most thankful for you! You make my 'happi heart' sing!!

Love you Baby –
Jan"

CHAPTER 3

The Golden Years

Over the next couple of years, Liong went back and forth between his home in Los Angeles and Las Vegas to be with his angel. He would also fly Jan to some exotic spot for a romantic getaway, surprise her with a cruise, or get tickets to the Kings hockey games or seats at a Lakers basketball game. It was during this time that I first met Liong through a mutual friend while I was living in Los Angeles.

In 1996, Liong's father became seriously ill and Liong decided he needed to return to the Philippines to be with his parents to see to their needs. He ended his business in Los Angeles, packed his bags, and never looked back on that part of his life.

Yet, even while Liong was gone, Jan's soul was still connected to him. She told me that she was driving down Spring Mountain Road on her way home from work when she was overcome with great sadness and started to cry. She just knew something had happened to her baby. Later that day, Liong called her to say his father had passed away. By the middle of 1997, a few months after his father's death, Liong returned to the United States once again. This time, however, he was returning home to Las Vegas to have his angel always by his side.

This became the best of times for Jan and Liong. With Liong in her daily life, Jan blossomed and her creativity grew. Three of her great passions were calligraphy, collecting inspirational sayings, and collecting and baking sugar cookie recipes. Jan was gifted with several types of artistic talent, in fact. She could make candles and bath salts, and she was drawn like a magnet to pretty paper. As a result, she took scrapbooking classes, collected stickers and rubber stamps, and had a treasure trove of different edging scissors. In a moment of divine revelation, she came up with the idea to calligraphy her sugar cookie recipes on pretty premade recipe cards and give them away as gifts packaged with a cookie cutter or cookie scoop.

Jan's friends at work loved getting her gifts at Christmas. In fact, they loved them so much they asked her to make more so they could buy them to give away as gifts. Her Christmas business was outstanding and she could hardly keep up with the demand. Yet she knew she wanted to do even more. How great would it be to do what you loved to do and make money at it at the same time? So, here was the birth of her Happi Hearts business.

Trying to test herself further, Jan went over to a friend's house to try her hand at watercolor painting. Her first drawing was a beach scene, which she proudly presented to Liong upon returning home. He looked at the picture carefully and said, "You haven't quite finished it." Where upon, he proceeded to take the watercolor paints and brush, and with a few strokes, he added in shorelines, clouds and footprints in the sand. Jan was mesmerized by the transformation of her crudely painted picture. She looked at Liong and said, "I didn't know you could paint."

Life transformed again in that moment. From then on, all Jan had to say was, "Honey, I need a painting of two little girls in the field," and Liong would paint them for her. Jan loved telling her friends and family, "Liong paints what I dream." Liong would spend hours painting whatever Jan requested. He would have to go to Office Depot to make copies or to have them reduced before they could be transferred onto her recipe cards. Jan would calligraphy a recipe on the card then package it together with a cookie cutter or cookie scoop. As you can imagine, this was a slow process for her and she knew she could not possibly make it into a profitable business, even if she was having fun.

It was right around this time that I moved to Las Vegas over Thanksgiving weekend of 2000, thanks entirely to Liong. At that time, Las Vegas was booming and Liong had told me that it was a place people went to start over. Las Vegas was definitely the place where I needed to be. Going with what my car could hold, I made the move from Los Angeles, initially living in the spare bedroom of my friends' house.

Since I did not really have a place of my own and definitely not a lot of space, I asked Liong and Jan if I could set up my computer in their spare bedroom. Neither one of them had any objections to my request. I would go over to their home to work on my computer in the evening, answering ads in the paper while I was looking for work or to access information that I needed for an interview.

On a couple of occasions, Jan would come into the bedroom and watch me work on the computer. After a couple of weeks of this, Jan called me one day and asked if she could "mess around" on my computer. I had no objections and I told her how to turn it on over the phone and walked her through the startup operation. I also told her that she did not need to worry about crashing my computer; that was the best way to learn how to use one.

A couple of days later I was over at the condo working on something and Jan came in the room to get one of her gift sets out of the closet. The closet in the second bedroom, by the way, was jam-packed with plastic tubs filled with cookie cutters, cookie scoops, candles, gift bags, all kinds of paper, and knickknacks of every quantity, size, and color. I asked her what she was doing and what all the knickknacks were for. Jan was more than happy to oblige my query. She told me all about her Happi Hearts business and how Liong painted and she wrote calligraphy by hand on each recipe card and so on. I frowned a little and said to her, "That must take a lot of time." She sighed and said yes and wished she could do it faster. I thought for a moment and said, "I may have a program here on my computer that could help you."

Jan quickly pulled up a chair by my side and said, "Show me."

That is when I introduced Jan to my graphics program used to create newsletters, gift cards, scrapbook pages, recipe cards, and stationary, etc. I showed her the option for creating recipe cards and how to insert text and the multiple font choices and pictures to make a finished product that could be printed out. I explained to her that it was possible to scan and save the pictures Liong drew directly into the computer so that they could be used over and over again. Her eyes went wide. I could see the wheels turning in her mind. Little did I know I had just given Jan the missing link for Happi Hearts, Inc.

Within two weeks, Jan had purchased a computer and a top-of-the-line color LaserJet printer. With only a few more training sessions, her little base of operations expanded exponentially. Liong was having a hard time keeping up with her requests for paintings. She asked him to paint snowmen, butterflies, birds, buffalos, dogs, rabbits, lemonade stands, teapots, tea cups and saucers, cookie plates, little children, and the list went on and on. Liong gladly painted whatever Jan asked for. To him it was a labor of love.

As time when on, Liong's paintings became larger, even more detailed and vibrant. Jan's sister Lisa, who also lived in Las Vegas, sewed pillows with the Happi Heart artwork printed on it as well as special Happi Heart aprons. Jan even came up with a series of magnets and dishtowels. Now she had the means to mass produce her Happi Heart collections and was fully armed to do business. Her first line of attack was going into all the small home boutique and gift card stores. Jan's innate ability to make friends with everyone she met aided her in obtaining her dream. She now had a new mission in life: bring happiness to everyone through her Happi Hearts.

Around 2004, when Jan's grandniece, Elexis, was doing show-and-tell in her kindergarten class, she brought in several small fossils taken from a hill to the side of John and Lucy's ranch in South Dakota. Lexi referred to the place where Grandpa John discovered her fossils as "Ivory Hill." Jan was fascinated with this description, as she knew that in 1919, the complete skeletal remains of a full-sized Gomphotherium, a prehistoric four-tusk elephant, had been found on that very hill on her family's ranch. Those remains are now on display at the American Museum of Natural History in New York.

Intrigued with the idea of this small, four-tusk elephant, Jan began writing a short children's story called "Tusk," about how the little Gomphotherium ended up on her father's ranch 10 million years ago. She told everyone she met about her story and had Liong paint all the characters in vibrant detail. Soon they had me involved to write a full-length version of the story for possible publication. With both of her passions for Happi Hearts and Tusk to keep her busy, Jan's life was full with all sorts of possibilities for the future. Life was very good.

CHAPTER 4

The Diagnosis

In early to mid-2002, Jan made a commitment to slim down and she organized a Weight Watchers group at the Mirage Hotel and Casino. As part of that pledge to herself, she started walking every morning for three hundred and sixty five days a year, rain or shine. With weights in hand, she marched around her neighborhood getting fit. Much to her satisfaction, the pounds started coming off and she was feeling great. However, her tummy never quite disappeared as much as it should have. She even commented on a few occasions that her stomach was hard to the touch, which she could not quite understand.

Then in the summer of 2003, Jan awoke in the middle of the night in incredible pain and she began vomiting. Liong was worried because Jan never got sick. She had never taken a sick day in twelve years of working at the Mirage. Her pain worsened to the point where she asked Liong to take her to the emergency room. During the exam, the doctors discovered a large tumor on Jan's ovary, and she was referred to a gynecological oncologist. Within a few weeks, Jan found herself in Desert Springs Hospital undergoing surgery to remove a twenty-five-pound malignant tumor from her ovary.

Jan's doctor was comforting and seemed to know what he was doing and assured her that he had gotten everything out. He saw no reason for her to undergo any follow-up chemotherapy at that time. Feeling pretty good, Jan enjoyed her three-month, forced recuperation by spending her time happily in front of the computer working on her Happi Hearts business and talking daily on the phone to her family and many friends.

The neighbor downstairs from Jan and Liong is a wonderful lady named Jean. In fact, Jean and Jan moved into their respective condos within a month or so of each other and over time, a deep friendship was formed. Jean visited Jan every day for a laugh, a little gossip, and a root beer float. Despite being in her late seventies at the time, she would spryly climb the stairs to visit her dear friend. There was not a single visit that Jean did not offer to bring Jan whatever she needed or to run any errand for her "precious angel."

Every single week that went by, at least one or two of Jan's coworkers and friends visited to see her and bring her treats. As you can see, Jan was quite happy and pampered during her blissful recuperation. She almost regretted having to return to work at the Mirage after being spoiled by Liong and her many friends.

By 2006, Jan had placed her Happi Heart product line in about fourteen local Las Vegas area stores and was also selling her Happi Hearts products on the Internet. The state of South Dakota featured Jan's work at the capitol building in Pierre for distinguished entrepreneurs from South Dakota. In Las Vegas, Jan's Happi Hearts made the front cover and featured story in the *Country Register* newspaper in the June/July 2003 issue.

Cover of the Country Register

Jan's biggest Internet sellers were limited edition copies of paintings Liong had created of all the MGM properties on the Las Vegas strip. You could see the mechanical engineer in him at the forefront. For example, if you look at his painting of the New York-New York Hotel and Casino, I swear you can count every single window on every single floor because the detail is so exact.

Jan standing in front of her Happi Heart display

Liong's original watercolor of the New York-New York Hotel and Casino

It was in mid-April 2006 that I moved into the second bedroom of Jan and Liong's condo. Once more my life was in shambles and Jan and Liong were there to help me get back on my feet again. It was only meant to be a temporary arrangement for a couple of months. However, in the late autumn of 2006, Jan started coughing. It was not bad at first, but it was a persistent cough. After a couple of weeks, Jan began complaining of not feeling well and being very tired most of the time. At first, the symptoms resembled the flu and she went to her regular doctor to get some medication. Unfortunately, nothing seemed to help. By now, not only was her cough worse, but she was having trouble breathing. Upon returning to her doctor, she was sent for a blood test.

The results were not good. Jan's CA-125 protein test, a marker for ovarian cancer, was up over two hundred. An average, healthy female should only have levels between zero and thirty-five U/ml. Jan's worst fears had come true: her ovarian cancer had returned. As if that was not horrible enough, she was beginning to swell up like a plump grape. Jan returned to her original oncologist, and they began considering different types of chemo treatments. Her doctor also told her that it was the sacks that surround the lungs that were filling with fluid and would have to be drained. This is what was causing her difficulty in breathing.

To alleviate the swelling, every week for the next several months, Jan had to go to a radiology clinic and have the fluid drained off her lungs in a procedure call a thoracentesis. The radiologist uses an ultrasound machine to locate the engorged sacks and then inserts a long needle into the patient's back to reach the lung to draw off the fluid. Needless to say, it is a very uncomfortable and sometimes painful procedure to endure. However, Jan always met the challenge bravely and managed to make everyone around her in the room smile and feel good about what they were doing.

As for the chemo treatments, at first Jan decided to take part in a clinical trial testing a new ovarian cancer drug. Unfortunately, after several weeks of no significant changes in her CA-125 levels, she and her doctor decided it would be better for her to continue with the more established chemo treatment. This meant, of course, suffering through the usual side effects of losing her hair, vomiting, feeling nauseous, and having a general lack of appetite.

Not letting her self be daunted by this prospect, Jan had her hairdresser, Kathy, a school friend from Colome now living in Las Vegas, shave her head. I must say that even without hair, Jan was still the sunny and radiant person I had come to love and cherish as a good friend. At that time, nothing seemed to be able to stop her, and her doctor and friends marveled at her continually happy disposition. She even continued to work at the Mirage. Her favorite boss, Brian, allowed her to work a shorter week to make allowances for her chemo treatments.

When it appeared that the thoracentesis was going to be a perpetual treatment, since no one could explain where this fluid was coming from let alone stop it, the radiologist suggested a procedure to Jan that involved draining the sacks around the lungs and injecting a powdery substance into the sack. This would in essence burn the lining of the lungs and prevent the fluid from returning permanently. All of us crossed our fingers because we knew what it was costing Jan physically and emotionally to have to keep going every week for the procedure.

Many of you know that expression, "Be careful what you wish for, you may get it; just not the way you expect it." Well, this was the case with Jan. Yes, her lungs stopped filling up with fluid. However, the fluid just found a new destination in her abdomen. Instead of a needle in the back every week, Jan now had to have one or two in the tummy. But at least the pericardiocentesis procedure was not as painful or uncomfortable as the one into the lungs.

By the fall of 2007, between the new chemo medication and the pericardiocentesis, Jan was beginning to feel a little better and her CA-125 levels were going down slowly. It appeared everything was working. Yet, she was still weak and her energy was easily sapped; the perpetual swelling up did not help either.

Just after having undergone a "debulking" surgery in early December 2007 to remove any tumors in her abdomen, Jan's doctor's assistant called her on the phone one day to inform her that her doctor was no longer going to see her and that she had to find a new doctor for her chemotherapy treatments elsewhere. This seemed like a rather cold-blooded thing to do, and Jan was very devastated by the news. After all, she had been with this doctor for almost three years. After some time, Jan did manage to speak to her doctor. He said his decision was based on the fact he did not think he could do anything else for her. He preferred to do the surgeries required but leave the follow-up care to someone else. He did, at least, refer Jan to another cancer treatment center in Las Vegas.

With all of her medical records in tow, Jan delivered them to the new cancer center and made her appointment to meet with their team of doctors to plan the next steps in her treatment. As you might expect, the group meeting went well and she left with a very positive attitude. Her next appointment was just before Christmas 2007 with the doctor assigned to her case that was going to tell her what kind of chemotherapy they were going to be using.

For those of you who have had to either go through this cancer treatment process yourself or be with someone who has had to go through it, have you ever found yourself asking the questions, "Where in the hell do they get these doctors from? What kind of unfeeling bastards do they accept into medical school?"

Jan's new doctor was a female with no bedside manner whatsoever. She walked into the exam room, told Jan that her previous doctor was inept and that he had completely mishandled her case, and that she was going to have to start from scratch with everything. In a matter of minutes, the new doctor reduced Jan to tears. Naturally, you can imagine how Liong felt about this change of events. Besides feeling totally helpless, he was livid with the abruptness and cavalier treatment his angel was receiving, and he demanded that she find a new cancer center. He was not going to allow any doctor to upset his angel like that again.

In early January 2008, Jan chose another cancer center. However, even after several rounds of chemo, nothing seemed to be helping. Still no one had an answer to where the fluid was coming from, and even though her CA-125 levels were hovering around sixty, Jan felt herself getting weaker. As a consequence of her failing health, in February 2008 Jan stopped working at the Mirage.

By mid-March 2008, Jan told Liong she did not have the strength anymore to work on her Happi Hearts. That admission broke his heart. Finally pushed to her limit, Jan demanded that her cancer doctor give her a referral to the UCLA Medical Center in Los Angeles, California. You would have thought she was asking for a free ticket to the moon at the way they dragged their feet in accommodating her request.

As March was coming to an end, Jan had to move into Lisa's condo which was located on the ground floor of the same condo complex, as she could no longer make it up the stairs to her second floor condo she shared with Liong.

It took a couple of weeks, but Jan finally got her referral to UCLA. After making several phone calls to UCLA to get her appointment set, we made our plans. I took a couple of days off work, and with all her medical records in hand; I drove Jan and Liong to Los Angeles for her appointment with Dr. Robin F. Eisner, MD, PhD, in mid-April. Dr. Eisner was and still is the chief of gynecology and gynecologic oncology in the department of obstetrics and gynecology at UCLA Medical Center.

By this time, Jan was using a wheelchair, as she did not have the stamina to walk any more than a few steps. I wheeled Jan into Dr. Eisner's office and waited with her. I do not really believe either one of us knew what to expect. Jan was, as usual, very upbeat and optimistic. For my part, I was holding my breath with an unexpressed hope that he would part water and make her well with a wave of his hand. Even now I find it hard to write about this chapter in Jan's life. Thinking of that appointment with Dr. Eisner now, three years later still makes me weep in both sorrow and intense anger.

Dr. Eisner was certainly a far more personable doctor than some others that Jan had to deal with. He walked in and sat down in his small office for our meeting. He asked Jan to tell him her history. Jan explained the basics of her case since the first diagnosis in 2003. The moment she stated that there was no chemotherapy at that time, the doctor stopped her immediately and asked her to confirm what she had just said. When she did, he sat back in his chair with a look of utter disbelief and said, "It's standard procedure to follow up all ovarian tumor removals with chemotherapy. I can't believe they didn't do anything." I was stunned and I was sure Jan had to be as well.

After a few seconds, Jan replied very softly, "That makes me sad."

"Sad?!" I turned to her in disbelief and said in a raised voice, "Jan, you should be as angry as hell!"

She just shrugged her shoulders and continued with her medical history for the doctor. We both had an opportunity to ask questions, and I specifically asked about the fluid buildup and where it was coming from. Without batting an eye or pausing for thought, Dr. Eisner told us, "That's a byproduct of the cancer cells reproducing."

It was so simple an answer, yet none of the doctors in Las Vegas had been able to tell us that! My God, were there no computers or telephones in their offices that they could not have found that out earlier? Were their egos that big that they could not ask for help if they did not have an answer?

Jan asked him, "Then why are my CA-125 levels so low?"

Again without hesitation, he said, "All that means is that the ovarian cancer has mutated into a different form of cancer that does not leave that particular protein marker in your blood. So, the CA-125 is no longer a viable measure of the cancer you have now."

Yet again I asked myself why the Las Vegas doctors never thought of that or even mentioned the possibility of Jan having a different form of cancer. Was there some kind of medical conspiracy to cover up the apparent overwhelming stupidity amongst the cancer doctors in Las Vegas?

Dr. Eisner continued. "What we have to do now is determine what chemotherapy to use. We may have to try a few different ones to find the right combination for you." He asked a few more questions and then said the words that gave me incredible hope. "We have a roundtable here at UCLA. The roundtable is made up of a group of doctors from all areas of specialization that get together once a week on Thursdays. We have doctors specializing in radiology, livers, lungs, hearts, gastro etc., and when we have an interesting case, we present it to the roundtable and we all discuss it from our particular medical perspective. That way all factors are considered in the discussion when determining a course of treatment. What I would like to do is present your case at the roundtable on Thursday next week, and then we'll coordinate with your cancer doctor in Las Vegas as to what we recommend for your treatment."

I felt myself exhale for the first time since arriving in Los Angeles. There was still hope, and the doctor seemed to believe Jan still had a chance and that he might be able to fix the mess created in Las Vegas.

Both of us left his office very encouraged. This was the first positive news we had received in a long time.

After we returned to Las Vegas, Jan, Liong, and I sat at the kitchen table discussing the trip and the doctor's prognosis. Both Liong and I were taken back when Jan remarked, "Honey, you have to know there is no cure for me." Liong just looked at her, surprised by her admission. Neither he nor I could say anything.

Actually, Dr. Eisner did not get to present the case for two weeks, and then it took another week to ten days to get everything set up with Jan's local doctor's office. So it was not until the third week in May that Jan went for her new chemotherapy treatment. Disaster! Almost immediately Jan had an allergic reaction to the drugs and had to be taken off the drip within a matter of minutes.

Like the trooper she was, however, Jan returned the following Monday and was given another new drug. This time she was able to tolerate it with no seriously bad side effects. This particular chemotherapy treatment was going to require her to go seven days in a row for about an hour each.

As if the daily chemotherapy was not enough, Jan still had to be taken that same day to the radiologist's office to go through her weekly pericardiocentesis treatment. This time around, however, she insisted that she and Liong wait for her attorney to go to the radiologist's office in Henderson so that she could sign her advanced directive paperwork.

Upon returning home that afternoon, she asked her sister Lisa to go out and buy things that she had enjoyed as a child: a Salt 'n Nut Bar, canned peaches, pudding cups, and a can of sloppy joe mix. Jan went and lay down on her sister's bed. Liong went in to lie down with her, holding her and stroking her hair. Both of them fell asleep.

Sudden movement a few hours later awakened Liong. Jan was sitting on the side of the bed and saying, "Jesus, why are you doing this to me?" She turned to look at Liong. For the first time in all their years together, Jan was looking at Liong, but she was not seeing or recognizing him. Again, she repeated her query to him, "Jesus, why are you doing this to me?"

Liong has often remarked that in eighteen years, Jan had never spoken that way before. She had never gone to church during their time together, and it seemed very strange to him that she should now be calling out Jesus's name. She lay back down on the bed and seemed to go back to sleep. Liong was perplexed but felt sure that it must have been a dream and she would be alright in the morning.

However, the following morning around seven, Jan sat up in bed and asked the same question, "Jesus, why are you doing this to me?" Liong walked around to her side of the bed to help her stand, but instead, her legs buckled underneath her. She slipped to the floor and sat there at the side of the bed, unable to move.

CHAPTER 5

The Miracles Have Only Just Begun

The phone rang early at seven fifteen that Tuesday morning. A frantic Lisa was telling me Jan had collapsed on the floor and was asking me what she should do. My response was immediate. "Call 911 right now. I'm coming over."

One of the great advantages of living in the same condo complex is that I was standing in Lisa's condo in less than fifteen minutes. When I arrived, the front door was open and I found Lisa and Liong in the bedroom on either side of Jan, trying to pick her up off the floor. Upon entering the bedroom, Jan looked up at me and smiled and said, "Hi there!"

"Hi yourself! How are you doing?"

Jan looked bemused but did not give me an answer. It was almost like she was intoxicated.

I asked if they had called the 911 operator. Liong told me no, that he was going to try and drive her to the doctor. I stopped him immediately and said this was beyond a doctor visit; she needed to go to the hospital and we were going to need professional assistance. I dialed 911 and asked for the paramedics to come. Thankfully they were there in less than five minutes with an ambulance right behind them.

When we arrived at the hospital, Jan was already in the emergency room. She was semiconscious and saying things that made no sense. Liong and Lisa took turns being with her. We felt it was important to have a familiar face around when she woke up. My job was to be the runner, fetching items from home, getting local fast foods, keeping friends and family informed what was going on, or doing whatever was needed while they kept vigil.

Lisa and Liong called John and Lucy and told them to fly down to Vegas to be with their daughter. Hours passed while doctors ran tests and took readings. Jan would wake up for a few minutes at a time then go back to sleep.

Finally, in the late afternoon of Tuesday, the doctor talked to Liong and Lisa. Just when we thought things could not get any worse, the doctors diagnosed Jan as having suffered a stroke in the left hemisphere of her brain. From that point forward, Jan was no longer responsive to anyone, including Liong.

It was late in the evening on that Tuesday that John, Lucy, Neil, and Danny landed at McCarran airport. Lisa had gone down to meet them and transported them straight to the hospital, where Liong informed them of the situation. The news was devastating for them. They spent a few hours with Jan, just talking to her and touching her face and hair in between shedding a few tears. Finally, Lisa drove them home so that they could get some rest.

All day Wednesday, the hospital ran more tests and monitored readings. Jan was completely out of it. Friends and coworkers visited and offered their support to the family; many of them broke down in tears at the sight of Jan so lifeless. In the early evening, the doctor laid out the situation to Liong, offering no alternatives to what they thought.

"By tomorrow morning, you have to make your decision to put her to sleep because she is not waking up," is what Liong was told succinctly. He asked the doctor what would happen if she did wake up; what would her life be like? The doctor stated unemotionally that if Jan recovered, she would be paralyzed on the right side of her body and would most probably have suffered irreversible brain damage.

After the doctor left him, Liong leaned over his angel and whispered in her ear not to worry, that he would take care of everything for her. He also told her that it was alright if she wanted to go to her eternal home. But if she could, he asked her to return to those that loved her so that she could say good-bye to her family and friends and they could say good-bye to her.

Liong stayed behind after everyone left. He called me at around 11:00 p.m. to let me know what the doctor had said. I immediately called Jean downstairs and the both of us drove out to Summerlin Hospital, arriving just before midnight. When we got there, Liong was alone in the room with Jan. She seemed to be resting comfortably. It was after 1:00 a.m. before Jean and I returned home.

With a heavy heart, not knowing how he could find the will to make such a drastic decision, Liong left Jan's room. The nurse assigned to take care of Jan was a Filipina and she sympathized with Liong, having lost her own brother to cancer. She insisted that Liong go home and get some rest as he was ready to collapse. She would be there the whole night to watch over Jan. Liong gave her his phone number to call him in case he needed to go back. With that, he left the hospital to go home for the sleepless night ahead.

Liong is not religious in the sense of aligning himself with a particular belief, but he does follow many of the Buddhist teachings. One of the principal beliefs of the Buddhists is that you do no harm to other living beings. You can imagine then the struggle he was facing that night; not just being the one deciding to let her die, but also knowing he was letting go of the other half of his soul.

At six-thirty the following morning, Liong's phone rang. On the other end of the phone was Jan's nurse. His heart sank for a moment expecting the worst, but instead the nurse said, "This is the nurse, and guess who wants to talk to you?"

Thinking that it was a doctor about to get on the line, Liong was flabbergasted when a very familiar voice said to him, "Honey, where are you?" His beautiful angel was talking to him on the other end of the line. He was literally speechless for a few seconds before answering her, "Honey, I'll be right over."

Liong got to the hospital in record time. He found Jan in her room, sitting up in the bed, waiting for him. He uttered a prayer of gratitude to the heavens and went into the room and sat by his Jan. Given the circumstances, it seemed inconceivable that this was the very morning he was supposed to decide to put his beloved angel to eternal sleep.

During the course of the day, doctors came and went. One doctor asked Jan to raise her right arm and she did without any trouble, making a fist in the air like the champion she was. He asked her if she could move her legs, which she did without hesitation. Yes, there was some loss of movement on her right side, but it was very slight. With time and a little rehabilitation, it would disappear. This was truly the first miracle.

On the flip side, however, Jan's memory was affected and she was having trouble with names of people and objects. Everyone's except Liong, that is. She always remembered Liong's name.

They did try to give Jan another MRI, but she became so agitated that she tried to crawl out of the machine and they had to stop. She made Liong promise her that she would not have to do anymore MRIs, and he agreed.

While she was in the hospital, I suggested to Liong that he take over the compact disc player with a collection of Jan's favorite songs and also some of her Happi Hearts to help jog her memory. He took my suggestion and played several of their favorite songs and showed her several of her Happi Hearts. She seemed to recognize them, fingering them softly.

When she got to the "Silent Night" Happi Heart, Liong started to sing, with Jan joining in on the sing-along. Unexpectedly, Jan turned to Liong and said, "I will be there this Christmas." Just so you know, she was there, but that will be discussed later in another chapter.

"Silent Night" Happi Heart

After a couple of days in the hospital, Jan was transferred to a rehabilitation center. Liong had tried to keep her at the hospital so that they could do the pericardiocentesis right there. However, the insurance company, in their infinite wisdom, insisted that she be moved to a rehabilitation center. It did not matter if transporting her back and forth caused her pain or distress. It was cheaper for the insurance company and that was the most important thing.

The facility was brand new and situated on the edges of Las Vegas. Being a newer facility, it took into consideration that family members might want to spend the night with their loved one. Naturally, Liong moved into her room to help her eat and wash and to make sure she never woke up alone during the night. Lisa and Lucy went over during the day to relieve him for several hours at a time. I, too, would do relief work from time to time, but mostly I was the runner. If Liong, Lisa, Lucy, or John needed anything from the house or if Jan requested her favorite 7-Eleven slushy in the middle of the night, I was on my way.

Jan made remarkable progress at the rehab center. So much so that John decided to return home to South Dakota. In many ways, it did not even seem like Jan was sick at all. In fact, Liong even commented that Jan seemed like her old self, before she had gotten sick. She seemed to have rewound time ten years. Naturally, it did not take Jan long to charm all the duty nurses and attendants, wrapping them around her and Liong's fingers. Liong was even able to sweet talk them into giving Jan a larger room that contained a small kitchen area.

Jan's hairdresser, Kathy, was only too happy to go to the rehab center to cut Jan's now unruly hair. The rehab center even gave Kathy permission to use their on-site beauty salon to make it easier for both of them. Jan was like a kid, totally enjoying her short ride down the hallway in her wheelchair for her personalized hair appointment.

Others came as well. Daily, Jan received visits from many of her coworkers at the Mirage. She recognized quite a few and it was like Cinderella holding court with her closest friends. Those that came covered almost every aspect of the casino operations, from cocktail waitress to pit bosses, dealers all the way up to the vice president of casino operations. It was during one of these visits that one of her dealer friends brought along a handmade "thinking of your/get well" quilt. Hundreds of squares were filled with pictures of her coworkers so she could see and remember all of her friends at the Mirage. Cards and flowers were everywhere in her room, with more arriving daily.

Mirage Quilt

Some may find it hard to believe, but good casino dealers can often form lifelong friendships with regular customers at the casino. This was certainly true of Jan. Over the years, many came to Las Vegas just to play at her table. One such friend was John, who was, at the time, the president and CEO of Allied Waste based in Phoenix. When he heard Jan was sick, he flew out to Vegas just to visit her in the hospital.

Another good friend was Andy, a public relations man for the Miami Dolphins football team's fan magazine. Andy made two trips a year to Las Vegas and always played at Jan's table. He happily swung by to wish her well. In fact, Andy was the last visitor that Jan was able to acknowledge with a wink when he left.

Despite all the progress made with Jan's rehabilitation, she still needed to go back to the hospital for her pericardiocentesis. Since her arrival at the center, it had been almost two weeks since her last one and she was severely swollen and very uncomfortable.

CHAPTER 6

The Crossing

The most remarkable thing that made this time so magical at the rehab center was that Jan had no memory of being sick. She was in good spirits and was like her old self again. Everyone who stopped by marveled at her sunny disposition. Things were going so well, in fact, that Lucy returned to South Dakota on Saturday, May 31.

Then, as if out of the blue, we were brought back to reality. On Sunday, June 1, Jan started to complain about not feeling well. The insurance company had already made arrangements to transport her back to Summerlin Hospital on Monday for her pericardiocentesis procedure. Liong tried everything humanly possible to have the procedure done on Sunday at the rehab facility but to no avail.

Liong wrote a full account in his journal on December 29, 2009, recalling that last trip to the hospital. He had never told anyone before what was weighing on his heart that day.

> <u>December 29, 2009</u>
> ". . . Jan was transferred from the Rehab Center back to Summerlin Hospital for her pericardiocentesis; drawing off her fluid buildup inside her upper body. While being taken by the ambulance that was there to pick her up, Jan told Lisa, 'No more.'

While waiting in the ER at Summerlin Hospital, Jan repeatedly told me, 'Don't let me suffer, don't let me suffer.' I looked at her and promised her I wouldn't. On June 4th, Jan was not communicating. I had instructed the Doctor to give her morphine, a pain killer, continuously. She was having a hard time breathing. On the morning of June 5th, Jan's blood pressure started dropping slowly but steadily. I had told her the night before, upon seeing her breathing difficulty that it was, 'Okay for her to go now and be without pain. Be at peace, everything will be taken care of.' Jan's breathing became increasingly difficult as the morning went on. Her blood pressure kept going down.

Everybody, Lucy and the others went down to the cafeteria. Lisa was sitting by herself in the lobby. John was dozing off in the chair next to Jan. Jan opened her eyes. I shouted to John, 'Quick, John, Jan wants to see you!' I reached for her eyeglasses because I knew Jan couldn't see far without her glasses. I put on her eye glasses. I dialed Lisa to come quick. With her eyeglasses on, Jan looked at me and at John, and tears started coming down from the side of her eyes. I wiped off the tears. Jan tried to talk, but her throat was bubbling with fluid. Tears came down again. Jan shut her eyes.

Lisa came running in. At this time, Jan opened her eyes again, looked at Lisa, John, and me. Tears came down again, and then she shut her eyes and left us to be with God. In the 18 years that we shared, the only times that I saw Jan shedding tears were times when she was happy or touched by kindness. I had never seen her cry because of pain or sadness."

For those of us who were downstairs in the cafeteria, Lucy's phone rang about ten after twelve. It was Lisa, telling us to get back upstairs. All of us jumped up, leaving our trays and food right on the table, and ran to the elevator. However, by the time we got back to Jan's room, she had already left us. I could not believe it. It did not seem real somehow that such a wonderful person was no longer there to share life's adventures and her infectious laughter with the rest of us. We all counted on her for providing us with an abundance of happiness.

I remember walking directly across from Jan's room to the nurses' station. I looked at the nurse right in front of me and simply said, "She's gone," and then I returned to Jan's room as we all said our loving good-byes to that beautiful spirit.

Liong began writing his journal that day.

> June 5, 2008
> "Jan finished her journey on Earth; she went HOME first. Now I travel my journey on Earth without her. That one fateful day when we found each other; we looked deep into each other's eyes and saw love. Right then our souls embraced and became one forever. I knew then that I will never travel alone. Jan will always be by my side."

I definitely concur with Liong's assessment that this is actually the beginning of our story. Liong is not alone in his steadfast belief that Jan has and is staying by his side. Many of us have seen for ourselves and have also been touched by Jan's spirit since her passing.

Jan's cousin Keith in Wyoming, for instance, was home alone on the morning of June 5. He swore to his family that he heard Jan's voice calling his name loud enough that he turned around to see if she was there.

In fact, right there at the hospital, Lisa had her own experience. She was sitting in the elevator lobby talking to family on her cell phone. Suddenly, as she describes it, she felt a strong energy pass through her body. It was warm and loving and then it was gone. At that moment, she jumped up and said to herself, “She’s going to do it. She’s now with the two most important men in her life.” Just then her phone rang. It was Liong telling her to go back into the room right away. When she got there, John and Liong were leaning over Jan, and Lisa was able to catch her eye just before Jan passed.

CHAPTER 7

First Signs

Liong was living in the Philippines when he had a dream that he later shared with Jan.

> December 10, 2008
>
> "As I was reading in bed and watching the Lakers play the Suns at 9 p.m., right now I smell banana again, Jan is here with me. A surging thought rolled into my mind. I remember shortly after meeting Jan, I told her that many years ago when I was still in the Philippines, must be in the late 70's or early 80's, I had dreamt about being in a faraway place and I saw a chubby girl dressed in black. I walked towards her and she looked at me and smiled. I told Jan that she looked just like that girl. Chubby, same smile; a smile that I haven't seen on any other human being I've set eyes on. I told her it must be destiny that we meet . . . ."

Even before meeting her in person, Liong felt connected to a chubby girl somewhere far away. One of the more interesting aspects of their relationship was the detail. Jan could tell me where they ate dinner, what they ate, what she was wearing, what Liong was wearing, and the music they were listening to on many of their getaway adventures. This was especially true during the early years of their relationship.

The same is true for Liong. In fact, he recalls that Jan was wearing a black uniform when he met her for the first time at the Golden Nugget. When they went on their first date at the Rio Casino and Hotel, she was wearing a black shirt and jeans and carrying a black purse. Jan liked black so much that when Liong asked her to pick out new furniture for her apartment, she selected an all-black set. It was not until she discovered that Liong painted and her passion for Happi Hearts intensified, that she lightened up and made pink her new, all-time favorite color.

I am making an assumption here that most of you reading this book have lost someone close to you, whether it be a spouse, parent, sibling, close friend, family member, or god forbid, a child. Desperation to rationalize and understand that death of a loved one drives humans to find answers like no other phenomena I can think of. It is an all-consuming desire; an imperative to gain an understanding of where they are and how they are doing before any thought of returning focus back to this life can even be considered. I am sure we all know someone who never fully made it back from that limbo existence after suffering a devastating loss.

If you are to have any meaning come out of the reading of this book, you must be open to believing that our loved ones are still near at hand. I spent a great deal of time telling you about Liong and Jan's history. I did this so that you would come to know both of them as three-dimensional people. I wanted you to be familiar with their habits, humor, and extraordinary life together so that you would see and hear them as real people, not just characters in a book. That is what makes this book so different from all the others out there.

Based on what friends and family members have intimated to me, every single one of them believes that the soul survives. Is it, therefore, so hard to believe that Jan remains connected to Liong even though she is a little further away right now? After all, he dreamed about a chubby girl, dressed in black, and Jan was without a doubt the lady in black (and chubby) when they first met.

Almost immediately after her passing, events started happening that were completely inexplicable. Well, perhaps some could be explained, but when you stop to consider the sheer volume of events, their frequency, and the preciseness, it gets harder and harder to just dismiss them all as completely coincidental.

Liong's journal, in fact, documents that it did not take very long before Jan started sending him messages and signs. Those signals took on a variety of manifestations, but they were all methods that he would be able to recognize.

> June 9, 2008
> "Dreamed about Jan in bed looking like old days; chubby and rosy cheeks. When I asked where is the doctor? Who is going to give you the shot? She said, 'What doctor?'
>
> I said, 'Well, you are not well, honey!'
>
> 'I am okay.' – Jan.
>
> 'But . . .' – Liong.
>
> 'It never happened; forget about it, it never happened.'"
>
> Then the following day he experienced another dream.
>
> June 10, 2008
> "Early morning; I was still half asleep, felt a warm glow next to my face. The image of Jan appeared vividly in my dreamlike state. Smiling, just like before, dressed in a lace gown; face glowing with an aura. I said, 'Thank you honey.' She shook her head with her contented smile then slowly faded away."

Coincidence, wishful thinking you say to yourself? It could be. None of us would have disagreed with you at that time. However, the following day got a little more interesting and a little harder to explain away. Keep in mind while you read the entry below, since getting his first cell phone, Liong's phone was only set on ring, never on vibrate.

> June 11, 2008
> "I went to Gold Coast. My cell phone showed two missed calls. I got out of the Gold Coast. I called Lisa to see if she did call. Lisa didn't. I called Susan, she didn't call. So I decided to go to the Orleans for lunch. Arriving at the 3rd floor parking garage, got down from the truck, my cell started buzzing. I looked at the display. To my surprise, the name Jan appeared with her cell number. I answered. Only heard a loud booming voice, but made no sense what it was. My first thought was that I must have lost Jan's cell and someone is using it. But I remembered well that her cell phone was on the table at home. I went home to find the phone on the table. I checked her phone; there was no record of a call being made. I listened to my message. It said the voice mail was received at 12:37 p.m. Susan got home after work. I told her what happened. She didn't believe it. So I pressed my cell phone for the record of the call from Jan's cell. Susan saw it. It said call was made at 12:36 p.m. I called back at 12:37 p.m. How did it happen? I don't know. Maybe it's Jan's way of letting me know she is okay and happy."

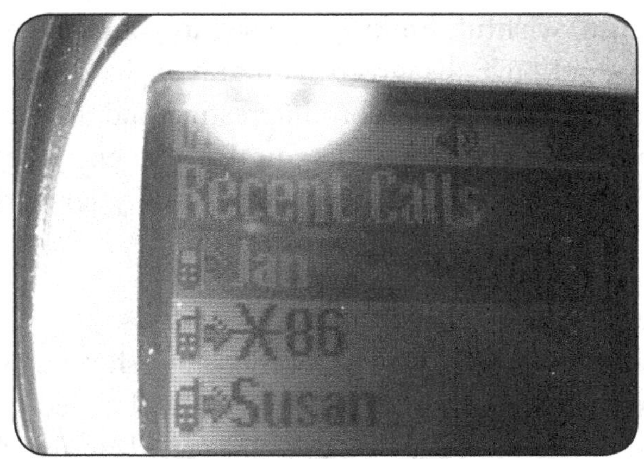

Cell phone photo of Jan's call after she passed

I know when Liong called me at work that day, he was very excited. Without even saying hello, he asked me, "Do you have Jan's cell phone with you?"

It seemed like an odd question, but I said, "No. I'm using my own phone."

Liong went on in a rush that he had gotten a phone call and it showed Jan's name and number on his display. Wow! What could I think? At first I thought it was a case of wishful thinking on his part. Yet I knew Liong is not a "wishful thinking" kind of guy. He is totally grounded in reality. However, I also know Liong is technology challenged. I thought for sure there had to be an electronic explanation that I would discover when I got home that night.

When I did get home that evening, I looked at Liong's Verizon Kyocera phone. There was clearly a display of Jan's name and phone number received at twelve thirty-six in the afternoon for that day under the missed calls list. Now there was no disputing his experience. Here was physical evidence that should not have existed. I tried taking pictures of the phone and the display, but they did not turn out very well. This marked the first in what was to become a very long string of unexplainable and mysterious events for us to ponder.

We were not able to pick up Jan from the crematorium until late the following week. By that time, Liong said he needed to get out of town for a few days for a small mental break from all the daily grind stuff he had to take care of with Jan's passing. Taking advantage of his timeshare membership, we booked a suite at a very nice club in Indio, California, only a few hours' drive from Las Vegas.

Liong had purchased a pink backpack with wheels and a pull handle. As would become our custom from then on when going on a trip, he placed Jan's urn, lighter, tea candles, and candle holder into this backpack. We loaded the car with our precious cargo and headed out to California for the weekend.

> June 14, 2008
> "Susan and I drove to the Indio Wyndham Resort. I just wanted to get away. That night the room lights turned on and off by itself 3 times. I just said, 'Jan I know you are here. Come sit down and watch TV with me.' While leaving the room for dinner, Susan noticed the light in the kitchen turned on again. I guess Jan is playful with me like the old days."

After checking into our suite, we sat back to relax for a while, watching the television before we headed out to dinner. As we were sitting in the living room area watching television, the hallway light between the front door and the kitchen area turned on while both of us were sitting on the couch. I asked Liong, "Did you see that?"

At the time, Liong had not noticed anything and I just wrote it off as being a fluke in the electrical system. Upon our return to the room from dinner, it was now finally cool enough for us to go out and enjoy the Jacuzzi for an hour. When we got back in the room, I sat in the living room watching television while Liong was in taking a shower. I got up and went into the bedroom to ask Liong a question. Just as I got inside the bedroom doorway, the light directly over the entrance to the bathroom door flicked on. I had not turned on any light switches and I could still hear the shower running in the bathroom so I knew Liong had not either. I turned around and left the room immediately, waiting until Liong came out to tell him about the second lighting anomaly.

One of the many advantages to a timeshare is that there is a washer and dryer in each suite. This suite's laundry closet was directly across from the entry into the kitchen area. After cleaning up, we dumped our wet clothes into the washing machine and turned it on. Again, we perched on the couch in the living room to watch a movie we had brought from home. Not five minutes later, the light directly above the laundry closet door turned on by itself. This time even Liong saw it, and we were both convinced that Jan was there playing games with us. One light you can write off as a fluke, maybe two, but not all three. Perhaps the more remarkable fact about this whole situation was that neither one of us was unduly upset nor frightened by the thought that Jan was, in fact, our travelling companion. It just seemed right somehow.

Now if you want to assert that it was all coincidental, Liong and I went back to the Indio timeshare in November 2010. You would be right in guessing what happened over two years later in a completely different part of the complex.

> <u>November 19, 2010</u>
> ". . . Arrived at Indio 8:25 p.m. Went to turn on the TV in the living room. Susan said that the light above me just turned off. There were many lights in the room, I didn't notice it. I looked up, the light was off. So I flipped the switch a couple of times. Nothing happened. I went into the bedroom to unpack. When I came out, I noticed the light is now on! The lights turned on and off the last time Susan and I came to Indio Resort – one week after Jan's passing. I must have logged it in my journal in 2008.
>
> 8:36 p.m. the light above the TV went off again. 8:41 p.m. the light turned on again. I decided to get up on a chair a few minutes ago to rotate the light bulb to see if the light bulb was loose. It wasn't loose and the light didn't come on. Now it came on by itself!

> 9:37 p.m. chatting with Susan while watching TV. We talked about Lisa going home to South Dakota to be with John and Lucy. I said Jan knew that I, a city man since childhood, would not be comfortable in a small town like Colome. This is why Jan stated in her last writing that she wants to be with me until the time I pass, and then we will both go back to Colome to be with John & Lucy. And this is also the reason Susan and Lisa were with me all this time to make sure they both understand our wishes. I jokingly said, 'What if Jan had asked me to go back to Colome? I guess I might have to open a Chinese restaurant there and name it the Sitting Duck Restaurant since everybody knows Sitting Bull.' The lights flashed instantly after I said it. Just like old days when Jan and I would laugh heartily with each other's jokes. Susan saw the lights flash also, and she said, 'Jan, you are here!'"

Then there are those occasions when Jan just likes to play little games with our psyche. Perhaps she is just testing her ability to control electronically based devices, or maybe it is just another one of those coincidences that happens in life; either way the timing was impeccable.

> June 27, 2008
>
> "Susan came home. I was thinking about the song Jan and I had listened to years ago while going to Solvang. My mind has been quite forgetful after her passing. The air conditioner suddenly started fanning out warm air, not cool air. I got up to check it. It was putting out warm air. I had adjusted the thermostat to 76° F. It was working prior to this. Susan complained about the house being hot. The house temperature was at 82° F. I waited for an hour, still no cool air. So I decided to call an air conditioner repair service. Susan suggested a company; she said her company used

> their service. I called, went thru the whole procedure of listening to what the company does, what charges are depending on 1-hour, 2-hour and 4-hour windows. Then answering questions as to what is wrong with the air system. I told her a 2-hour window would be okay. After a few more questions, she put me on hold to contact their service guy for an appointment for tomorrow.
>
> Just when I was holding, I told myself, the song is 'I Will Miss You When You Go,' by George Hamilton IV. It was the song that I told her years ago in the car that I hope this is one song we never have to play for each other. I started to look for the CD. At this point I felt the air turning cool. I got up and true enough the air has turned cool after almost one and a half hours of running without coolness. The air system has never done this since we serviced it couple of years ago. The girl came back on the phone. I cancelled the appointment. The air has been working till today."

You might ask what all this fuss is about with this one isolated incident. I myself would ask the same question. However, this very same thing happened exactly three years later on June 28, 2011. Not only did the air stop blowing cold, but the temperatures were exactly the same; the thermostat was set at seventy-six degrees Fahrenheit and the inside temperature was eighty-two degrees Fahrenheit. If you are wondering, yes, the cold air did come back on about an hour and a half later. Also keep in mind that the first occurrence was at Jan and Liong's condo and the second took place at my new house. Is this just another case of random chance? Let us keep going and see what else happens along the way.

Not all of Jan's first signs were as literal as the phone call or the switching on and off of lights. Some of the messages came through in less dramatic ways. One of these methods is through sudden, random, and sometimes communal thoughts. Liong has experienced several of these sudden, random thoughts. Again it is all subjective, but the number of times that this has occurred seems to defy the laws of probability. These random thoughts could be for almost anything, such as buying a particular item, doing something in a different way, or having premonitions about members of the family. They can occur to individuals or to two or more people at the same time.

One of the more significant group thoughts occurred while we were on vacation in South Dakota. Lucy's washing machine had died a day or two before we arrived in Colome. Yet, when the three of us were separated, we all seemed to have the same thought at the same time and without any prior discussion.

> October 20, 2009
>
> "I was driving John's pickup following John's tractor this morning. A thought popped into my mind that Jan wants me to get Lucy a new washing machine. Her old one conked out. After getting home, I called Lisa and asked how much it is going to cost to repair the old washer. Lisa said that she and Susan had just decided to chip in half of the cost of a new washer half an hour ago; just about the time the thought from Jan came to me. So I told Lisa about Jan's wish, and I put up the balance of the washer as a gift to John and Lucy."

At the moment Liong called Lisa, she, Lucy, and I were all standing at the checkout where Lucy had just ordered her new washer and we were waiting to schedule the delivery.

When it was determined that Lucy's washer could not be repaired, we had gone back in the store so she could pick out a new one. Lucy knew which machine she wanted, but she was hesitating because it was expensive. The thought just came to me that I should chip in for it and was reaching for my wallet. Before I could even get it out of my purse, Lisa had already pulled out two hundred dollars from her pocket and was handing it to Lucy. Is this yet another coincidence?

If it only happened once, perhaps, but with Jan there is always more to come.

To clarify a little more, these random thoughts seem to come out of nowhere, without any prior consideration, and usually when you are relaxed and not thinking about anything else. Sometimes you will even say to yourself, "Now what made me think of that?" Be assured someone out there may be trying to send you a message.

> March 24, 2010
> ". . . Lisa came into the bedroom, told me that when she saw the three bananas on the dining table, she had the idea of making banana nut bread – Jan's pride. She had been making banana nut bread since she was a child for a 4-H contest, came into mind. Interestingly, Susan came home, looked at the bananas, and asked Lisa if she has Jan's banana nut bread recipe. Did Jan put that idea in their heads?"

If you do manage to hear and take action on your random thought, you may receive a confirmation of some kind with a second sign. It is also possible for you to experience multiple signs during the same incident, as evidenced by the following entry.

> April 6, 2009
> "Honey Jan, it's been 10 months since you left. I miss you more than ever. Things have been happening the way I thought it to be. Sometimes ideas just pop into my mind, and I know it was your wish. I followed every idea that came into my mind. It seems you have a hand in all the good things that had happened to your loved ones. I try to take good care of them as you asked me to. Today I smell it so strongly. When I saw the bouquet of pink roses and small pink carnations, I just had to get it for you. At this writing, the smell I have been used to is coming on so strong. Honey, I know you are with me right now. I love you."

As you can see from the passage above, another form of communication, besides the random thoughts from Jan, is through smell. I know it sounds a little weird, but it has been a significant signal from Jan to Liong, especially when she is very happy. In fact, it was one of the first signals Liong received from Jan. Every morning for nearly two years, Liong would cut up a banana for Jan because her doctor had told her that her potassium levels were low. Many times since her passing, Liong will smell bananas. It is Liong's belief that he smells bananas when Jan is trying to tell him she is happy.

The first journal entry that actually mentions the smelling of bananas is on December 6, 2008, even though I know Liong smelled bananas almost from the beginning. Lisa and I gave Liong an early Christmas present that first year without Jan. It was a ticket to go see the psychic John Edward at the Flamingo Hotel and Casino on December 6, 2008. Liong wrote a very lengthy journal entry later that day about his experiences and observations. He even made a list of the most important things he got out of the show. On that list, he mentioned smelling bananas.

10/15/08 Visa 8723859437175.00 Saturday
Flamingo_Conl
FLAMINGO HOTEL
PRESENTS
John Edward
FLAMINGO SHOWROOM
DATE: 12/06/08
11:00 AM SHOWTIME
Seating Begins One Hour
Seating Prior to Show Time
Guests are part of a larger audience,
thus no one attending the seminar
is guaranteed a reading
NO REFUNDS / NO EXCHANGES
L.E.T. Included
SECT: A Front
TABLE: 22
SEAT: 6
Susan
Kastner

Ticket stub to the John Edward show

<u>December 6, 2008</u>

"... 3. That senses like smell, light etc. indicate your presence. I could tell that you were at the show with me because I could smell the smell of bananas halfway thru the show."

Many times Liong has asked me, "Do you smell something?" Unfortunately for me, not once have I been able to say yes. However, I have no doubt that he can smell bananas and that Jan is letting him know she is happy and by his side. Further in his journal entry of that day, he also found a little peace with Jan's passing.

> December 6, 2008
> ". . . 5. I am more relaxed now, more convinced that you, Jan, are now happy and without pain. As John Edward said, don't look at someone's passing as losing a battle to cancer. Think of it as her winning the battle over the disease that overcame the physical part of her soul, because now she is well and living in another form."

Six months later, marking the one year anniversary of Jan's passing, Liong still shared that view with even more certainty.

> June 6, 2009
> "One year ago, God extended his hands to Jan. Come home now, my angel. Jan took his hand and she had no more pain or suffering.
>
> Jan had told her brother Danny before her passing, to not grieve for her, for her life was full now. Thank you, Jan, for feeling that way; because my life was also full after 18 years of being with you.
>
> The pain of losing you, the hurt when I miss you, are as deep today as it was one year ago, and I know the pain and hurt will continue for the rest of my conscious life on earth. My only consolation and joy is that you have been showing me signs that you are

> still with me and watching over me. Please do not stop doing so because it is what keeps me going on with life. When the time comes, I know you will be there waiting for me. The other day, Monday, June 1st when Susan was wheeled into the surgery room, I sat down in the lobby. I shut my eyes and saw you at my left side right away. This time you were surrounded by a fog like mist, and I saw wings behind you. I asked you what are they, and you just smiled. Yes, my Jan is an angel, and because she is an angel, I know she will be waiting for me. I love you Jan."

As I said earlier in the chapter, if all of this is coincidental, I guess you as the reader are going to have to make a decision whether you believe that your loved ones that have passed on can and want to let you know that they are there. I know for myself that when I tell people about some of the incidents in this book, every single one of them said they believed in these kinds of phenomena.

To that end, I would ask you open your mind a little further. Further in the sense that, I would like you to consider that over time it is possible to cultivate a daily conversation with your loved one who has passed. What I have shared with you up to this point are just individual examples. However, the real power in this book is that by the time of this writing, Liong's conversations with Jan have developed into a daily dialogue. It did not happen right away. Just like a fine wine, it took time to mature and develop into the full-bodied flavor and fragrance of a vintage wine. And like any connoisseur, you have to train your mind how to understand your senses; to see, hear, smell, feel, and correctly interpret what might already be in front of you. To recognize the signs your loved ones are leaving for you takes patience, a mind at peace, and a loving heart open to receiving those messages.

In order for you to fully appreciate how this development came about, I must introduce you to the single most important and effective tool in Jan's arsenal of communication both before and after her passing: the cell phone.

CHAPTER 8

Evolution: The Cell Phone

A cell phone is a very innocuous piece of equipment. A simple communication device, once the size of a small shoebox, now has been downsized to the size of a lady's makeup compact. The cell phone is technology at its finest; versatile, portable, and still a very powerful instrument that can fit comfortably into the palm of your hand.

Why does this little piece of technology play such a key role in our story? Over the last three years, the cell phone has been the chief source of communication between Jan and Liong. From the first message three days after her passing, when Liong received a call showing Jan's name and cell phone number on the display, to the writing of this book, the blinking lights have become an almost daily occurrence. You might ask what is so unusual about a cell phone flashing. To begin with, the cell phone in question has no service.

Let us examine how the cell phone flashes have evolved, beginning just after Liong's attendance at the John Edward show at the Flamingo.

> <u>December 07, 2008</u>
> "I have to write this down early in the morning before I forget. Last night I took my usual half a pill of

Tylenol p.m. to sleep. Jan took half a pill for a long time. It was 12:00 midnight. My mind just wouldn't rest, thinking mainly about Jan; about what was said and asked in the John Edward show. Next thing I know, looking up at the clock, it was already 2:15 a.m. So I decided to take another half of the P.M. pill. I turned on the dresser light, cut a pill in half, put back the scissors and turned off the light. I reached on the left side of the dresser where the water bottle is; the cell phone was next to the water bottle. I was leaning up a bit to grab the water when the cell phone in front of the water bottle lit up with only half of the crescent moon shaped green lights. Then the light went off. I knew I wasn't seeing things because any light in the dark appears to be very noticeable, and it was color green, not red.

I thought that it might be because there is a message from Lisa or Susan. I checked and there were none. I told myself there was no way the light could have come on. Even if the charger was on, it should be two of them, not just one. So I plugged in the charger, the two red lights came on and stayed on for a while charging, then turned green. Two of them, not just one, and at that time, I smelled the smell of bananas again. I knew then it was Jan letting me know she had pulled one on me again. I love you Jan."

I looked on Samsung's website and pulled up whatever I could find about the a630 model. When I could not find anything specific about flashing lights, I clicked on the "Contact Us" button and submitted a request for technical support to send me an answer. Additionally, I checked out their Frequently Asked Questions (FAQs) section. Under the FAQs, I did find a reference to, "Why does my cell phone flash?" However, it only made references to receiving incoming calls or charging the phone. Even then, it still only specified flashing red lights. There was no mention of flashing green lights at all. To date, I have never received a reply to my query from Samsung

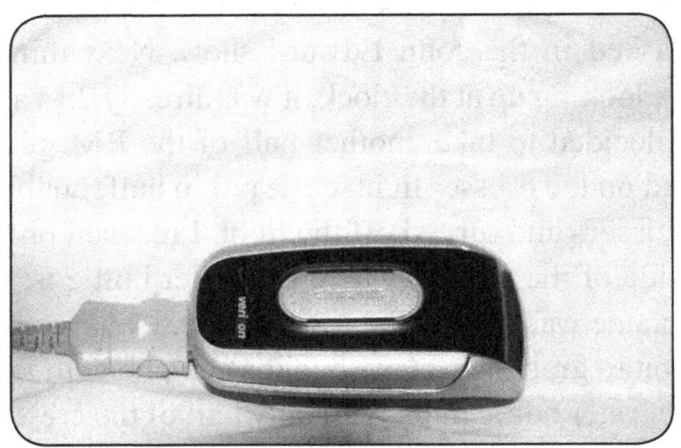

Samsung SCH a630 phone

A similar flashing incident with the phone was repeated again just a couple of weeks later.

> <u>December 30, 2008</u>
> "12:14 a.m. about 10 to 15 minutes ago, I came into my bedroom. My cell phone was, as usual, on my dresser to my right. The room was dark. I pressed the TV remote control to turn on the TV. Before the TV lit up, I was reaching for my cell phone to check if there were any messages. The green lights on cell phone, both crescent lights, lit up briefly then shut off. The cell phone was not being charged. I checked the phone for messages and there were none. I asked Susan when the green lights should come on. She thought that when there was a call to the phone, the green lights would come on. I told Susan to call my phone from her cell. The red lights came on, not the green. I know if I plug in the charger, the red lights come on during charging. When it is fully charged the green lights will come on until the charger is unplugged, then the green lights would go off. Is Jan

letting me know that she is home? If so, the only things that happened today related to her . . . ."

In order for you to understand the full significance of the cell phone, let me give you a quick recap on the history of the cell phones involved. When I moved in with Jan and Liong in 2006, I was using the Samsung cellular phone model SCH-a630 from Verizon. Jan was using the Verizon Motorola Razor model 3Vm cell phone, and Liong had no cell phone at all. When Jan started getting weaker in the early spring of 2008, Liong decided he needed a cell phone so that Jan could reach him instantly. Wanting to keep it as simple as possible, we got him the basic Kyocera model KX444. It was on this phone that Liong received that first call from Jan's cell phone three days after she had passed away.

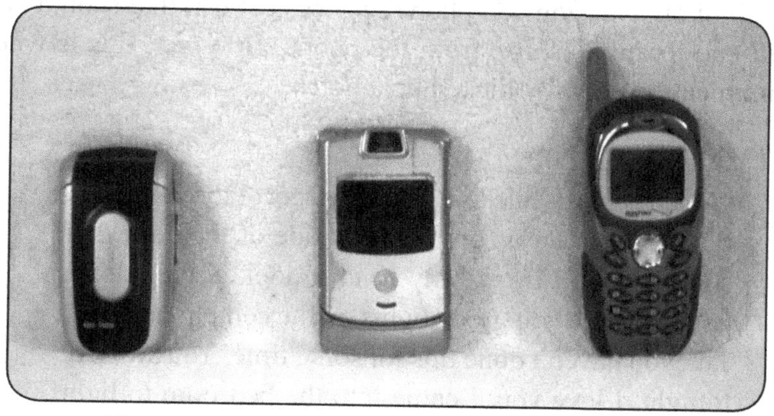

The three phones used by Liong, Jan, and Susan

A little over a month after her passing, Liong and I went to Verizon to get the service changed since three phones were no longer necessary. I kept Jan's Motorola Razor and her phone number. Liong thought his Kyocera phone was too big to carry in his shirt pocket, but he liked my Samsung for its compact size. So we eliminated his Kyocera cell phone and transferred his cell phone number over to the Samsung a630.

The Samsung a630 is a flip phone. In the center of the front cover of the phone is an elongated, oval-shaped, silver medallion with the Samsung name imprinted on it. Around the edges of this silver medallion are two thin, elongated half-crescent bands that light up. When the phone receives a call, the bands flash red. If the phone is charging, the bands stay red until the charge is complete, when they turn green in color. It is to these two bands that we refer to as the flashing or blinking lights on the phone.

Just over a year after Jan's crossing, I found myself in the fortunate position of being able to purchase a home in Las Vegas, moving in at the beginning of August 2009. Around that same time, Liong suggested that I transfer the cell phone service into my name. Company regulations prevented me from keeping the Verizon numbers because the account was still listed under Jan's name. I chose to go with a different cell service all together. Now, not only did we get new cell phones, we also got new cell phone numbers in September of 2009. With all of our Verizon cell phone services cut off, that should have put an end to any flashing from the phone. However, this is where communication actually kicked up a notch.

> October 12, 2009
> "At 5:03 p.m., while I sat down in front of the computer, the cell phone was on my right side of the desk. For some reason I turned my head to look at the phone, and I saw the two green lights on the cell phone blink. Jan, you haven't done this for some time. You are here tonight. I love you. I came into the bedroom to light incense. I love you Jan, thank you for doing this again. But honey I am changing cell phones, but I will keep the old one with me, and I will keep it charged. Maybe you will now do something with my new cell phone? We shall be going home to Colome this weekend to see our headstone. I know you are thrilled and happy that we will be going home to see John and Lucy. Danny, Lyn, Skylar, Dawn and baby Elise will be there also."

I can almost hear what you are thinking right now: these are just some random signals being sent out over the network that all cell phones receive regardless of the account activation status. Believe me when I tell you we have all considered that possibility. Unfortunately, that theory does not hold much water under the circumstances because the phone never flashes at the same time of day, the same number of times, or even on the same days of the week. During the last three years, there have been numerous occasions when the phone has stopped flashing all together or flashed in rapid succession. We are also sure that it is entirely coincidental that on many of these occasions it turned out that something was happening simultaneously to either a family member or friend of Jan and Liong's. Several of these occurrences will be illustrated in the following pages. Therefore, please keep in mind that when you factor in all these variable nuances what the mathematical probability is that could explain the flashing phenomena.

One such example happened shortly after changing our cell phone services in September of 2009. Liong, Lisa, Toni, and I made a trip to South Dakota in October to see the new headstone that had been installed in the Colome cemetery. It was during this trip that the significance of the cell phone started to manifest itself.

> <u>October 21, 2009</u>
> "Trip to Rosebud Casino: Went to Rosebud with friends of John and Lucy, 4 couples. We arrived at Rosebud Casino around 5:30 p.m. I went to the Bingo Hall and took out the cell phone. Told Jan that this is the place where we last had hot dogs, the green lights started blinking every 5 seconds or less. I showed it to Lisa, Susan, John, Lucy and Connie. Jan must be happy and excited for the blinking didn't stop until we left the casino. The Verizon wireless service had been disconnected by 10/19.
>
> When I first arrived at Rosebud Casino, while walking through the main casino with Susan, I heard a voice

calling, 'Liong.' I turned and nobody was around. A few seconds later I saw Lucy walking away around 15 ft. away. I walked over and asked Lucy if she had called me, Lucy said no. Well, did I hear Jan? Because after that is when I went to the Bingo Hall and the green lights started blinking."

Another example of the continuous flashing occurred when Liong returned to Manila the following month upon the death of his mother. Liong's mother had lived with Jan and Liong for six months in 1999 during which time she and Jan became very close.

<u>November 12, 2009</u>
"Took my cell phone with me. Couldn't contact Jan since I last got a phone call from sister Yong-Yong about Mama's passing on 11/10 in Manila. Rushed back to Manila on the first available flight via Asiana Airline. All along the journey I glanced at the cell phone periodically without any message from Jan.

Arrived in Manila at 12:15 p.m. While waiting in line at Immigration, I had the urge to take the cell phone from my pocket; the green lights blinked immediately. It kept blinking and I finally timed the intervals of blinking at approximately 5 seconds apart. Yong-Yong and family took me to lunch. Finally arrived at the mortuary, Arlington Memorial Crematory, at 3:30 p.m. I checked my cell phone; it was still blinking at the same pace, much like the time at South Dakota at Rosebud Casino. Shut my eyes; saw Jan, same appearance as when Mama was with us in Las Vegas in 1999 or 1998? Mama was with her, so was Papa. They were all smiling at me. As much as I was sadden by Mama's passing, I am comforted by their union and they all seemed happy together.

It is now 7:00 p.m. I am home at Yong-Yong's to take a shower; the phone hasn't stopped blinking since 12:15 p.m."

Between November twelfth and seventeenth in 2009, while Liong was in Manila, the cell phone blinked every four to five seconds. It did not stop until just before he boarded his return flight to Los Angeles. What also makes this phenomenon remarkable is that Liong could not charge the cell phone because the Philippines uses outlets of two hundred and twenty volts; not the customary outlets of one hundred and ten volts used in the United States. Despite the fact that the phone flashed continuously and he never turned it off, the phone never ran out of a charge during those six days.

Another example of the continuous flashing happened when John and Lucy visited Las Vegas in February 2010. The lights flashed over ten times while we played cards. In April of that year, the phone flashed twenty-two times within one hundred and three minutes, when Liong received a call from our old neighbor Jean that one of our former neighbors had passed away and another one only had a short time left. After that, the lights only flashed a few more times before stopping.

When Jean herself was undergoing hip replacement surgery on October 6, 2010, the phone flashed fifty-five times during the entire ninety minutes while Jean was on the operating table.

The very next month, Liong got a personal message of his own.

<u>November 7, 2010 – Sunday</u>

"Woke up in the dark, went to the bathroom. Came back to bed, the lights started flashing nonstop between 2:52 – 3:03 a.m. I counted 116 times within 11 minutes. It hasn't done that since I was in Manila for Mama's cremation. What was Jan trying to tell me? Maybe I will know in due time"

It was not until the following day that Liong remembered something significant.

November 8, 2010 – Monday

"12:15 p.m. just struck me that last year at this time Mama was rushed to the hospital on 11/7 and passed away the next day, today. Is this why the lights flashed nonstop the morning of 11/7, when Jan met Mama again on the other side?"

You may believe that these types of phenomena would dissipate over time. On the contrary, they have continued on stronger, more frequently, and more precisely. For my birthday weekend in 2011, Liong took me to the Grand Canyon in Arizona. Jan showed us she was with us all the way.

January 27, (2011) – Thursday

"TRIP TO THE GRAND CANYON AND SEDONA

I positioned the cell phone in the glove compartment in front of my seat so that I can see the lights if they flash.

While on US-93 the CD was playing, 'I'll Miss You When You Go.' I was about to tell Susan that was the song playing when Jan and I were vacationing in Solvang. Before I said it, the lights flashed at 11:21 a.m. Memories, Jan still treasures them!

The lights flashed 27 times starting at 11:27 a.m. while we traveled on US-93.

11:31 a.m. Susan said she wonders what Jan will do when we reach the energy vortexes in Sedona. Right after that, the lights flashed continuously 42 times. The flashes stopped for a minute, then started again. I showed the flashing cell to Susan.

At 1:53 p.m. the flashes stopped when I told Susan about what Lisa felt at the time of Jan's passing. I always feel sad and lost when this thought enters my mind. I guess Jan feels the same way."

My birthday continued on with many confirmations of Jan's ongoing presence.

<u>January 28, (2011) – Friday</u>
"It's Susan birthday. We went to the lobby for breakfast at 8:14 a.m. I placed the cell phone on the table in front of Susan. The lights flashed continuously in front of Susan. Jan was wishing Susan a happy birthday."

She flashed throughout our tour of the Grand Canyon. However, the most sensational part of the day started after completing our Grand Canyon tour.

<u>January 28, (2011) – Friday</u>
". . . While driving us backed to the Holiday Inn Express, the tour guide asked where we are heading after Grand Canyon. Susan told her Sedona. The tour guide said 'Oh! You are going to Oak Creek Canyon.' Right then the word 'creek' stood out in my mind. I remember having a dream months ago where Jan told me she was going to a place with water, a place with the word 'creek.' Could it be Oak Creek Canyon? Sedona? The energy vortexes? I will have to check my journal when I get home.

2:52 p.m. entering the winding road to Sedona, the sign, 'Oak Creek Canyon' showed up and the lights started flashing. The mountain road was only two narrow lanes. It was a very winding road. Susan was driving only 15-20 miles per hour. The lights flashed all the way. It stopped only when we got off the winding road into Sedona. I counted 53 flashes during the 18 minute drive."

January 29, (2011) – Saturday

"No flashes since entering Sedona yesterday afternoon. After breakfast, we set out for the Boynton Canyon Vortex. While searching for the Vortex, the driving instructions said to look for a 'T' sign. We arrive at a 'T' sign, and the lights flashed twice. We are on the right track. The lights flashed 3 times when we got to the parking lot to start hiking up the trail to the Vortex. I told Susan, 'Don't let anyone tell us she is not here with us,' and the lights flashed instantly.

As Susan and I walked uphill on the trail, half way up, I was worried about Susan not being able to complete the trail. It was uphill and a red dirt trail, not even easy for me, more so for Susan. I asked Susan if she wanted to turn back because the downhill could be even more difficult on her knees. Susan said without hesitation, 'I am here with Jan, I can make it!' She did. We placed a red rock on the tree limbs at the peak of the Vortex. When Susan placed hers, the lights flashed 3 times. I asked, 'Jan is this where you came to?' The lights flashed.

While coming down the trail I told Susan, 'Jan would have loved to walk this trail with us.' I remember when we were walking on the hills at John's ranch with John. It was getting late in the day. Jan was just so happy, her 'simple happiness of life,' as she coined it. The lights flashed right then.

We got back into the car. I said, 'Thank you Jan for coming on the trail with us;' the lights flashed at 11:18 a.m."

As promised, Liong did go back through his journal to find out when he had dreamed about the Jan going someplace with water and the word "creek."

> February 1, (2011) – Tuesday
> "Was in the computer room and suddenly remembered to check out the dream I had months ago about Jan telling me that she was going to a place with water with the work 'creek' in it. I went back thru the diary. Found it on August 12, 2010, where Jan said she was going to a place where there is water and a place with the word 'creek' in it. This was five months ago. Sedona is in 'Oak Creek Canyon.' There is water around Sedona. The Boynton Vortex is on 'Old Creek Road.' Coincidence?"

In the Introduction, I mentioned that family was very important to Jan. Even from the other side, Jan still continues celebrating their successes. Take for example her brother Danny's recent success at his cattle auction.

> February 15 (2011) – Tuesday
> "Susan had a stress test appointment in Henderson. Drove her to the doctor at 10:30 a.m. When I came home, decided to cut a banana for Jan, haven't done this for some time. I put the banana on Jan's altar. Came into the computer room, put the cell in front of the computer screen. The green lights started flashing. It was 11:33 a.m. It must have flashed continuously at least 40 times! I started wondering why? Is there something that made Jan flash this many times?
>
> Suddenly remembered that Danny and John were having their bull sale at the auction this morning. I called John's home, no answer. Lucy's cell, no answer. Lucy finally called me back at 2:10 p.m. She was

very happy. She told me that Danny and John sold their entire herd. Neil was also home. Now I know why Jan was so happy. I told Lucy about the flashes. Lucy giggled, 'Oh! That girl of mine!' Jan, you are the greatest!"

The list goes on and on and on. In fact, I have counted over four hundred references to the cell phone flashing documented within the journal. They run the gamut of just a single "good-morning/good-evening" flash to flashing during a song, specific question, shared memory, or joke or alerting us to problems somewhere within the family.

One of Jan's favorite pastimes was to watch football or basketball games with Liong. Jan always liked to share in Liong's victories and celebrated them by waving her fist in the air, yelling out "Yes!" on great plays or ultimate victories. Even now she continues to celebrate with Liong during football or basketball games by flashing the cell phone lights on a touchdown or great play (but only for the team Liong has bet on, of course).

This is but the tip of the iceberg, because as of now, their electronic communication has evolved so far that Liong can ask Jan specific questions and she will flash an answer back to him within seconds. Consider that statement for a moment. Liong has asked Jan questions like, "Honey, are you here with me now?" and the cell phone will flash instantly. I have seen this for myself; I do not need to take Liong's word for it. I am a witness as are others beside myself. Perhaps you say it is just an atmospheric anomaly; like I said in the beginning, it is for you to decide.

Despite all this evidence Liong has collected over the past three years, he still sometimes questions the meaning of the flashing lights.

<u>January 27, (2011) – Thursday</u>

"I know people might say that the flashes are just flashes; maybe electronic or telecommunication glitches, etc. I have lived for these flashes the last 2 years and 7 months. They have become a big part of my life. There are the flashes that just occur regularly these days without my thoughts, actions, or words. I regard them as Jan's messages to me that she was here with me. Then there are the flashes that responded to my thoughts for her, and then the flashes that respond to my questions to Jan, and last but not least, the flashes that occur instantly to circumstances involving our past lives together. After the last 31 months, to me and others who love Jan, there are no more doubts that my Jan is with us and watching over us, more than she ever did before her passing."

CHAPTER 9

It's Only a Coincidence

Much of this book focuses on the communications between Jan and Liong. However, one should not assume that the entire extent of their conversation is only limited to a flashing cell phone, the smell of bananas, or the ability to sense her presence. Jan's manifestations, if you are open to believing that these are not just random coincidences, include a gamut of expressions. What are these other forms of expression? Examples that will be examined here cover animals as well as aural, physical, and very extraordinary coincidences.

Our neighbor Jean planted Callistemon trees, also known as Bottle Brush trees, outside the front door of her condominium. The upper branches reached a height just below the kitchen window sill of Jan's condominium. Jan loved her view of the trees with the bright red flowers. In particular, she loved to watch the hummingbirds feed off the tree brushes, and Liong painted many hummingbirds as part of Jan's Happi Hearts collection. She admired their graceful beauty and their ability to hover without effort. Several times the birds would fly up and stare at her through the window before flying away. After she passed away, the hummingbirds did not come to the condo window anymore, at least not that we ever saw. However, once we had moved into my new house that changed.

August 22, 2009

"I stood in the backyard of the new house thinking about Jan. How happy she would have been here in this house that she had chosen. Just two days ago Lisa commented about having to tell the hummingbirds that used to visit Jan outside of the condo's windows that Jan had changed addresses. Just when I entered the house and was closing the screen door, out of nowhere, a hummingbird appeared in front of my eyesight outside the screen door. The little bird just stayed there for maybe 5-10 seconds staring at me, then flew away. We have been here for almost two weeks and never saw a hummingbird. Was it Jan's wish? Did she send the little bird here?"

June 13, (2010) – Sunday

"The lights flashed at 8:19 a.m. Decided to get up and mow the lawn. Two hummingbirds appeared in front of me. Looked at me for a while then flew away. The last time I saw a hummingbird at home was last August when we first moved in. Jan loved the hummingbirds. She always watched them outside of our condo's windows."

April 28, 2011

"Susan left for work. I was standing in front of the front lawn. Suddenly a little hummingbird appeared out of nowhere. Looked at me then flew away. It's been a long time since a hummingbird came to me. Jan loved hummingbirds. A message from Jan? There are no red flowers in the front lawn."

April 30, 2011

"Jean is coming for lunch today; first time since she had her hip surgeries.

Lights flashed at 10:36 a.m. Jean arrived at 12:30 p.m. and had a nice visit with her. As Jean got into her car to leave, and Susan and I were in the driveway, a little hummingbird flew in front of me and Susan. Susan quickly told Jean. Jean had tears in her eyes. She believed her darling Jan had sent her a message."

Even though Jan had grown up on a ranch surrounded with cows, pigs, chickens, dogs, cats, and sheep, she was not an animal lover. Her heart was totally dedicated to the house, cooking, collecting recipes, and especially to the people she loved. Lisa, Jan's sister, on the other hand is a devoted dog lover and has owned dogs almost her entire adult life. Lisa's dog, Buddy, died unexpectedly in December of 2007 which, as it turns out, afforded Jan the ability to move in with Lisa for the last few months of her life.

Recently, completely by coincidence of course, Lisa related the following story to me.

<u>Late April 2008</u>
"When we knew she was leaving us, I told her she had to walk Buddy for me when she got there. She told me, 'I'm not going to walk your damn dog.' I told her, 'You have to 'cuz he has to pee.' So she said, 'Fine . . . I will walk your damn dog!'"

Please understand Jan never had any kind of affection for animals. She was a lover of people, first, last, and always, although she understood and accepted Lisa's adoration for her pets. Yet, it seems she seriously heeded Lisa's request and sent her a special visitor soon after her arrival on the other side.

<u>June 7, 2008 (Saturday)</u>
"On the Saturday night after she passed away, when I was sleeping, Buddy jumped onto my bed. He was so real. I was touching him. I asked him if we needed to go for a walk so he could pee.

> And then he just looked at me and jumped off the bed and two big doors opened and a gold light came through and he went into the light."

Just a few months after Jan's passing, Lisa made the decision to get another dog. In September of 2008, before Lisa even had time to go to the pound to look for a new pet, a coworker at the Mirage said there was a small puppy that had been abandoned that was available if she wanted it. They further enticed her by saying that if Lisa did not take the dog it was heading to the pound that very afternoon.

Naturally, Lisa was noncommittal when she heard about the puppy. However, the moment she saw the small dog, it was love at first sight for both of them. Dakota was immediately installed into his new home and became ferociously protective of his new mistress like most small dogs do. It was just another of those small coincidences that when Lisa took him to the veterinarian for his first checkup, the vet determined Dakota's birthday as being June 5, 2008. Even at the moment of her death, Jan was sending Dakota to be Lisa's new protector, and we all took this as a sign of Jan's continued and active presence in our lives.

Dakota

Another form of communication that I suspect everyone has experienced is hearing your name called but no one being around who could have said it. I know it has happened to me and I have dismissed it as being my imagination. However, on three separate occasions Liong has heard someone talking to him. The first time was on our trip to South Dakota when we went to the Rosebud Casino on October 21, 2009, for dinner and an evening of fun as mentioned in the previous chapter.

The second occurrence was almost a year later.

> August 13 (2010) – Friday
> "Went to Smith's, saw a beautiful bouquet of daisies, etc. in a very cute Happy Face vase. Got it for Jan. As I was putting the flowers next to her urn, I could swear I heard a small voice say, 'Honey.' I turned to look. There was nobody at home at the time."

Ten months later, Liong was at a nearby casino playing a few coins when a very familiar voice called to him.

> May 2, 2011
> "I went to the library. Stopped by Smith's and got a pot of lovely pink flowers for Jan. After that, I went to Arizona Charlie's, decided to play a few hands of video poker. No sooner did I sit down to play when I heard, 'Honey I am home.' I turned and looked around; there was nobody within 15 feet of me. I cashed out and came home."

A similar type of sensation to the aural is the physical manifestation that I assert most people have experienced but again write it off as just their imagination or nervous system playing tricks on them. I know from my own experience on several occasions that I have felt someone sit down on my bed after retiring. There is also the feeling that someone has actually touched you somewhere on your body. Liong has had both of these experiences.

March 1, (2010) – Monday

"At about 1:30 p.m. while reading, 'The Survival Files' by M.E. Allen, just after Lisa came into the room to tell me she is going to the grocery, I felt a slight pull of the bed spread to the left side waist portion. I thought it was Dakota who came up on the bed. I turned and it wasn't. Guess Jan was telling me that Lisa is coming along fine."

December 6, (2010)—

"Last night I woke up a couple of times. I felt so warm. The space outside of the place where I was lying felt cold. Once I woke up feeling a pinch on my wrist."

In fact, Liong is not alone in feeling these manifestations. Toni, Jan and Lisa's cousin, was at the house in July 2011 and found herself in the unfortunate position of getting sick. After she showered and went back out into the living room, she told us that she felt a hand patting her on the back of her right shoulder while she was in the shower. She was very clear that she was facing the shower head and there was nothing hanging behind her that could have caused the sensation. Liong, Toni, and I were totally convinced it was Jan giving Toni comfort.

There really is no adequate way of explaining the next category other than as a group of very extraordinary coincidences. Yet, as seemingly random as they are, there is a personal significance attached to each of these manifestations that relates directly to Jan.

November 27, 2009

"The thought that Jan must be with me made me go into the bedroom. I have always tried to maintain a lit candle all the time for Jan. Entering the room I noticed the candle had split into unusual shapes; a bigger heart shape had been formed with a bright color forming the heart and at the back side, two little hearts were formed. The inside of these three hearts was black in color. I called for Lisa and Susan to come quick and see it. They came into the room, looked at it, and rushed out to grab their cameras. Some pictures were taken. It was quite a sight. Attached is my drawing of the configuration of the hearts. After that, I came back into the bedroom and told Jan, 'Thank you for the message of love to me, Lisa and Susan.' Suddenly the three hearts burst into a bright glow and were gone after the glow. I took a picture of the candle after that burst, which shows the candle now burning normally with the wick in the center of the flames."

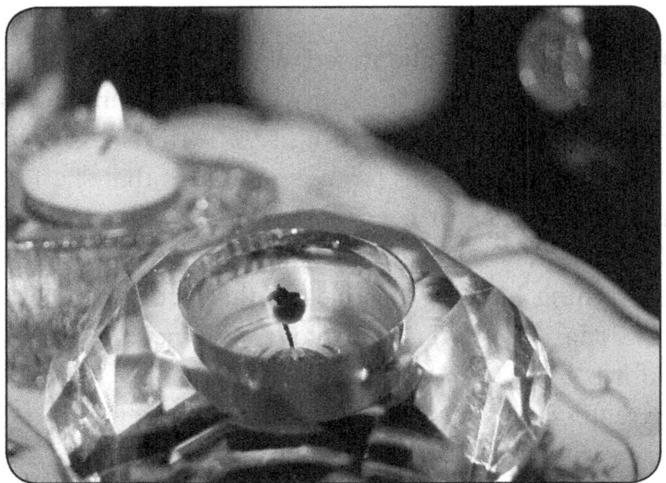

Three-heart burning candle wick

Normal burning candle wick

If once was not enough, the three hearts appeared again.

April 13, (2011) – Wednesday
"I went to the library this afternoon, and then passed by Smith's to get a pot of yellow tulips for Jan. When I came into the bedroom with the tulips, the candle appeared to look different. I took a close look at the flame, and the wick had split up into three heart shapes. I remember the same happening some time before – going back to check on the journal. Yes, it did happen on 11/27/09, the day after Thanksgiving in 2009. I am glad that Jan is happy with the sign."

As mentioned previously, the importance the Chinese place on honoring their deceased loved ones is not considered a duty but a matter of honor and respect. For those of us in the West, one of the more common Western traditions is to burn candles for the departed, whereas the Chinese burn incense.

After Liong's mother passed away in November of 2009, Liong set up a small shrine, as is the Chinese custom, in his room to pay respect to his mother. Besides the incense holder, he placed a small, glass tea candle holder in front of her picture. This same tea candle holder had also been used in front of Jan's shrine. What happened with the candle was something of a surprise for Liong.

> <u>December 29, 2009 – Tuesday</u>
> "First, a couple of weeks ago, after I shut off the TV set and was ready to go to sleep, I heard the clear sound of something falling. A popping sound followed by the sound of an object falling and hitting something. I thought I had knocked over something on the dresser, over my head, when I reached up to pull a pillow from under my head to place down at my feet inside my blanket; a ritual. I ran my hand over the spaces around me and didn't touch anything. I disregarded it and went to sleep. The room was dark as I had turned off the battery operated candles by Jan and her tea candle lights had been blown out. I had placed a tea candle light in a glass holder on top of the plastic casing that made up Papa and Mama's altar earlier, and had lit a candle. That candle had burned out long before I went to bed.
>
> The next morning while I was lighting the candle for Jan and turning on the little night light for Jan, while getting the incense from next to Papa and Mama, I suddenly noticed some splintered glass on the cabinet. I looked and the glass tea candle holder had actually split in half with the burned out tea candle base still sitting in the half broken holder. The other half had fallen off the plastic casing of Papa and Mama. The splintered glass was on the cabinet and on the floor. I had used that glass candle holder for Jan since Jan passed. I had taken it from the condo to the house. I just couldn't explain how it could split up in half when the candle wasn't even burning? I told Susan and Lisa

about it. Was it Mama, or Mama and Jan, or Papa, or Mama and Jan that caused it to split?"

It was not until later that day that Liong remembered something very important about his mother. She did not like burning candles. Perhaps that was her way of telling him not to burn any more candles for her.

According to the *American Heritage Dictionary,* the word "serendipity" means "the faculty of making fortunate and unexpected discoveries by accident." Even if you are not familiar with the word, perhaps you have had the experience of finding something that you have lost, misplaced, or just plain forgotten about at precisely the right moment that you needed it. I want you to consider the following journal entries and ask yourself if you believe they are all just cases of serendipity or if there is a guiding hand out there watching out for us.

<u>September 20, (2010) – Monday</u>
"Susan and Lisa were going through some old stuff in the garage. They found a book with Jan's dedication to me. One of her lines said, 'Are you really a spy?' That was one of our jokes; she always liked it because of the James Bond movie, 'The Spy Who Loved Me.' Susan and Lisa were asking me about another line Jan wrote, which they don't understand. I explained it to them.

Susan was not feeling well tonight, so we didn't watch a movie like we do regularly every night. So I came into the bedroom, switched on the TV. While going through the channels to find one that I might like to watch, right there on channel 344 was, 'The Spy Who Loved Me!' Coincidence or was it my Jan being playful again? 11:19 p.m. lights flashed; I guess it is goodnight Jan."

December 21 (2010) – Tuesday
"No signs. Lisa called Susan this morning that she had gone shopping alone in Mitchell. She was sure that Jan had been with her. She was trying to find something for a neighbor, going around the store, her eyes caught a vase with a favorite quote of Jan's – the right gift! If Jan was shopping with Lisa, then I don't expect any flashes today."

December 22, (2010) – Wednesday
"7:00 a.m. lights flashed. Jan is home. Got up from bed and went into the computer room, gathered up yesterday's newspaper, then went into the living room to light up the Xmas tree. While bending over to press the light switch, a small brochure fell out of the newspaper. I picked it up. The big print on the front page is "SHOPPING." Jan is telling me that she was with Lisa yesterday – shopping!"

Shopping flyer

December 24, (2010) – Saturday
"Lisa had made some of her home-made noodles for me. She called to say that when she opened the cloth used to cover the noodles for drying, the noodles appeared in a heart-shaped arrangement. She sent me a picture thru the phone. This happened on the day Lisa went to Mitchell shopping. Amazing!"

Lisa's heart-shaped noodles

Besides hearts being her favorite shape, let me remind you that pink was Jan's favorite color.

January 21, (2011) – Friday
"Today is Jean's 83rd Birthday. Went to Chinatown to get a birthday cake for her. Also picked up some of Jean's favorite port buns. Just so happened that there was only one pink decorated cake in the bakery."

How is that for five separate but specific acts of serendipity? We talked about *The Spy Who Loved Me*, and the very same movie just happened to be on TV that night. Lisa went shopping and found the perfect gift with one of Jan's favorite quotes on it, and she was sure that Jan was with her. What about Liong picking up the shopping flyer that had fallen out the newspaper dated the very same day that Lisa was shopping with Jan in Mitchell, South Dakota? Or what about Lisa making homemade noodles and having them turn out on the drying towel in the exact shape of a heart? Then, of course, there is the bakery having only one cake for sale and it just happened to be pink in color. Again I ask you, what are the chances of all of these incidents being mere serendipity?

Your natural disbelief could have you asking, "How can you possibly believe that Jan is sending so many random signs?" It is funny, but for those of us who watch all these events take place, we say just the opposite: "How can you possibly disbelieve that Jan is sending so many signs?" In fact, we take her presence so much for granted now, that when she does not communicate daily, we wonder what she is up to and where she has gone. In time she always lets us know. That is just her way of doing things now.

CHAPTER 10

Healing

There is a sneaking suspicion in the back of my mind that the title of this chapter conjures up images of snake oil salesmen and holy roller revival meetings. I am pleased to say that there is nothing that dramatic here. No one is going to try and sell you anything at the end of the book or offer you free tickets to the next tent show in your area. Despite the stereotypical images created when using the word healing, there have been many recorded cases of individuals who have been healed from some malady or other, and Liong is no different in that regard.

When Jan was in her final two weeks of life, Liong was beside her continuously the entire time. He was both sleeping in the rehabilitation center and taking care of her needs virtually twenty-four hours a day, or he was staying by her side after she was transported back to the hospital for the last time. Naturally, two weeks of nonstop stress took its toll on the human body. After she passed, his body was one massive ache and pain. Imagine his surprise when he woke up on the fifth day after Jan's death.

> <u>June 10, 2008</u>
> "Early morning; I was still half asleep, felt a warm glow next to my face. The image of Jan appeared

vividly in my dreamlike state. Smiling, just like before, dressed in a lace gown; face glowing with an aura. I said, 'Thank you honey.' She shook her head with her contented smile then slowly faded away.

My legs have been hurting since her passing. Every morning the calves felt painful to walk on. This morning I got down from bed, I felt no pain in my legs at all."

Additionally, Liong and other members of his family have had a long history of stomach acidity and ulcers. Liong has taken strong antacids for the condition most of his life. Imagine his surprise again, just over a month later, when the following happened.

<u>July 15, 2008</u>
". . . and then I saw a bright light emitting from the wall in the living room from the place where I hang the picture of an angel sleeping among the flowers and birds. The frame and mat are now used for Jan's picture to be taken home next week.

Then I felt the left side of me brightening up with light. Not the left forward side which would be from the TV. The light disappeared shortly and I got up to talk to Susan who was working on the DVD. Before I turned into the living room, I had to rush to my bathroom. Did I vomit! I didn't think there would be anymore to vomit after the two previous times I vomited. I didn't eat anything. But so much dirty stuff came out.

After this, I felt so much better. Took a hot bath and Susan showed me her first draft of the DVD then I bid her goodnight and went to my bed. This morning

I woke up, the bad feeling in my chest and stomach which I have felt every morning since Jan left me, had disappeared. I felt good . . ."

Notice in the two journal entries above that each healing was preceded by the appearance of a bright light or glow that had no specific source. As a side note, in addition to the above journal entry of July 2008, Liong has not taken any antacids in three years and no longer suffers from any significant stomach problems.

Just for a twist, Jan will sometimes use physical aches and pains to make her presence felt. There have been a few occasions where Liong has experienced an ache or a pain in exactly the same locations Jan felt discomfort. I like to think of these moments as her way of kicking him in the butt when he questions why she does not seem to be sending him signs of her presence.

> <u>Jan 22 – 2009</u>
> I have been asking Jan repeatedly since 1/18 why she has not given me anymore signs that she is here with me. This early morning, my right foot hurt so intensely that I woke up. It hurt badly when I tried to bend my right foot and toes. I tried to do my push-ups and it was difficult because my right foot could hardly support the push-ups.
>
> This afternoon, a notion suddenly came into my mind, "You silly, Jan has been trying to tell you she is here since 1/18. She has been giving me the signs by the candles burning out prematurely, like the first few months. I have been so sad missing her that I did not notice that those were the signs she gave me. Well, the foot hurting acted like a switch. I went to Jan and told her that I now realize that she is now here all this time since 1/18. After that my right foot stopped hurting. It was her right leg that went away from her in her last days.

On the other side of this coin, however, sometimes there is a price to pay for your loved one being near you. Liong has always been much attuned to the spiritual world around him. Many times he has sensed when a friend is in trouble. Take me, for instance. I was living in Los Angeles and my life was not going well at that time. In fact, I was being evicted from my apartment and had nowhere to go. Out of the clear blue, Liong, who was already living in Las Vegas, called a mutual friend to go over to my apartment to get my new phone number. Fortunately, I was there when John showed up. After giving John my number, I waited for Liong's call. Two hours later my phone rang.

The first words out of Liong's mouth were, "I just had the sense you were in trouble and I needed to call you." Never were truer words spoken. The really amazing part of this is that I had not seen or been in communication with Liong in any way for over three years; not since he returned to the Philippines to be with his dying father in 1996. I was in trouble to be sure and it was because of that phone call that I moved to Las Vegas to start my life all over again. Both of us still marvel today, eleven years later, at what prompted him to make that call.

It is because of this hypersensitive spiritual awareness that Liong can sense Jan's presence around him. Unfortunately, when Jan is close by for any length of time, his blood pressure will rise significantly.

> <u>July 28, (2010) – Wednesday</u>
> "Birthday of my Jan!
> Woke up at 5:22 a.m. and lit the lamp Lucy gave me. Sang happy birthday to Jan and meditated to her. Told her how much I love her and miss her. Cut a piece of her favorite red-cake. Lisa made it; Jan had asked me to have Lisa make it, and then served my Jan a cup of coffee. The lights flashed brilliantly in the darkness at 5:29, 5:55 and 6:24 a.m. The banana fragrance filled the air the whole morning and afternoon.

Had a bit of difficulty breathing. Took my blood pressure at 4:24 p.m. It was high – 151/91. My B-P has been running around 123/80 the last two months. Why this high today? Tested it again tonight; still the same.

Went to Ping-Pang-Pong, Jan's favorite restaurant with Jean, Susan and Lisa to celebrate Jan's B-day.

No flashes tonight, but the fragrance is still filling the room tonight."

<u>July 29, (2009) – Thursday</u>
"Woke up at 6:45 a.m. Tested my B-P – 125/67. So what happened yesterday?

Fragrance still strong in the room this morning. Lisa talked to John. According to Lisa, John told her that he had forgotten about Jan's birthday. Well, Jan woke him up Tuesday and he suddenly remembered the next day, Wednesday, is Jan's birthday. Guess Jan didn't want her beloved Daddy to forget!"

Liong is a very intuitive individual. I mention this because he seems to be tuned in on what is happening with his family and many friends, no matter where they are. Sometimes, if the situation warrants it, he sends Jan to watch over those people in their lives who need special attention or healing. Take for example the following four entries.

<u>August 17, (2010) – Tuesday</u>
"Lights flashed at 5:20 p.m. Felt very sad the whole day, can't find a reason why. Told Susan I was just so sad."

August 18, (2010) – Wednesday

"Woke up still feeling very sad. Went to the casino to pass my time.

6:25 p.m. got a call from Lusing. Informed me that sister Yong-Yong had a bad fall in Manila, and was hospitalized with a cracked vertebra. She was in awful pain the whole evening. Sister Yong-Yong is not someone who complains about pain. The pain must be severe. My heart aches so much. She loves me and Jan so much. I talked to Jan right away, to go and see Yong-Yong, to take care of her, to lessen her pain. Jan loved Yong-Yong very much."

August 19, (2010) – Thursday

"Since 6:25 p.m. last night, after talking to Jan about Yong-Yong, the cell didn't flash the whole night. 8:15 a.m. received an email from Phillip that Chai visited Yong-Yong. She is now doing better and the damage is not as bad as first diagnosed. Thank you, Jan."

Oct 6, (2010) – Wednesday

"Jean is having her hip replacement surgery today, so I was expecting Jan to be home.

Came home at 1:46 p.m., lights flashed at 1:48 p.m., then 2 times at 1:51 p.m.

Jean's surgery started at 2 p.m. The lights flashed: 2:02, 2:04 (3x), 2:07 (3x), 2:08, 2:10, 2:11 (8x), 2:12 (3x), 2:13 (5x), 2:14 (2x), 2:15 (4x), 2:31, 3:31 (4x), 3:32 (6x), 3;34 (5x), 3:38, 3:41, 3:42 (3x), 3:44, 3:45 and 3:46 p.m.; 55 times between 2:02 – 3:46 p.m. Jan is really watching over her 82 yrs. old neighbor.

I came into the bedroom at 11:52 p.m., said goodnight and the lights flashed at 12:09 a.m. Goodnight honey."

October 18, (2010) – Monday
"John having surgery at 5:00 a.m. Vegas time. Got up to go to the bathroom, came back to bed at 4:58 a.m., lights flashed brightly in the dark. 5:19 a.m. lights flashed again.

10:24 a.m. Lucy called to inform me that John's surgery went well. Lucy told me that the other day Jaycee, Jan's nephew, found a heart-shaped green pepper in the yard. They all think that Jan was there looking after John. I believe so; Jan loved her Daddy very much. Came into bedroom at 11:53 p.m., said goodnight to Jan. Lights flashed at 12:08 a.m . . . ."

When Jan is watching over her family, Liong knows not to expect any flashes. However, when they come, he appreciates every time she acknowledges him. Sometimes when he asks for a special visit, she appears to him in his dreams.

March 8, (2011) – Tuesday
"Had a hard time sleeping last night. Still awake a 2:59 a.m. Asked Jan to please come into my dreams; haven't dreamt about her for a long time. Fell asleep after that. Woke up at 7:40 a.m. and remembered clearly that I dreamed about meeting Jan in a park. I looked at her; held her heavenly face in my hands and asked, 'Is this true? I am so happy!' Jan replied, 'Don't you think I am happy too?' I woke up feeling happy; been a long time since I woke up this way. Thank you, Jan.

I was on the phone with Susan talking about Jean's surgery tomorrow. She has to be at the hospital early at 5:30 a.m. I told Susan I offered to take Jean to the hospital but Jean said that Dane had already told her he will drive her. The lights flashed. It was 3:30 p.m.

By the way, my aches and pains of the last few days had disappeared this morning after I woke up feeling happy. The lights just flashed while I am writing this at 4:01 p.m."

What is to say all this is Jan's doing versus it just being coincidental? Honestly, I can tell you that the more we have come to believe that Jan is here with us, the more things happen to confirm that belief. It is no longer wishful thinking to us; it is the genuine realization that she is here and we have given her the opportunity to remain an active participant in our daily lives.

Oct 7, (2010) – Thursday
"Last night I told Susan something I had kept to myself for the last 28 months since my Jan's passing. I told her that all throughout the five months of Jan's ordeal before she passed, I did not feel any sadness or sorrow. There was no notion that my Jan was leaving me. The hurt only came after her passing. This has been eating me up inside. Today, as I was reading Sylvia Browne's, 'God, Creation, and Tools for Life,' on page 102:

'We meet a soul, outwardly like any other, and get a feeling that this one has wound its way to find us. You know there was a preordained reason that you were to come together for that brief moment, or for whatever time you are together, and we have a sense that we are home. That is what going 'Home' feels like – that

> fleeting euphoria . . . We will spend our time down here, see the sights, then go Home.'
>
> Yes, I think those five months, we knew deep inside, that my Jan was going 'Home.'"

I have read in some books that when you hold on to your loved one, you keep them bound to this earthly plane. However, in those books I have read the message as being based on a selfish need born out of intense grief to maintain their existence. I am pleased to say this is not the case here. Yes, we mourn Jan's passing, but the life we are experiencing now is based on bringing happiness to all of Jan's friends and family members, not on some morbid sense of overwhelming loss. Love is what is here with us today, and who is to say that love cannot transcend this three-dimensional earthly plane of existence?

CHAPTER 11

He's Not the Only One

Recognizing that Jan was a very social person who cared deeply about her family and many friends is the foundation upon which this book gains meaning. Perhaps one of Jan's favorite quotes from Willa Cather best expresses my meaning: "Where there is great love, there are always miracles." It is that quality of being with and loving people that makes these events so personal and touching. Who Jan was in life is who she continues to be after death.

Jan so enjoyed visiting with her extended family and many friends. Her cell phone was her lifeline to the outside world and her instrument of choice to reach out and touch the lives of others. Even after death, Jan continues to reach out to many of those same family members and friends to let them know she is close. Jan has found a way to remain in touch.

> July 21, 2008
>
> "Rosie the cocktail waitress visited Jan at the rehab center 4 days before Jan passed away. Rosie met Lisa at the Mirage. She asked Lisa how Jan is doing, not knowing that Jan had passed away. Upon learning that, Rosie cried. Lisa comforted her by showing where Jan is now resting comfortably at home with

> Liong in her study room. Lisa showed her the picture of Jan's urn. Lisa had taken the picture off her cell phone. After parting with Rosie, Lisa heard her cell phone beep. When she looked at her cell phone, the picture of Jan's urn came on the cell phone again. Jan, are you telling Lisa that you were there when the picture was shown to Rosie?"

What Liong did not make clear in his journal entry was that Lisa had actually deleted the picture of Jan's urn off her cell phone. To this day, Lisa has no idea how the picture reappeared on the phone for her to show to Rosie that night at the Mirage, or why her cell phone beeped at her with the picture coming on her screen again. To us the explanation is easy; we know it was Jan making her presence felt.

On our first trip to South Dakota for Jan's memorial service, a few accounts of contact were shared with Liong by other family members, all showing that Jan is keeping her eye on her loved ones. For Dale, her brother, Lyn, her sister-in-law, and Kathy, her sister-in-law Clarice's sister, these events were as real as if Jan had been standing right in front of them.

> <u>August 3, 2008</u>
> "These are events told to me while I was in South Dakota:
>
> Dale mentioned one day he felt the presence of Jan at his house. He was alone and he definitely felt Jan was there with him.
>
> Lyn said one night while she was still awake, she felt someone had blown air against her lips. There was no air movement in the room, but she was positive someone blew air on her lips, much like Jan would always do to play tricks on her.

> Kathy, sister of Clarice, Neil's wife, told of a dream in which she saw Jan telling stories in front of some children in heaven."

Intuition, especially feminine intuition, has taken a hard knock in the last couple of decades. Yet intuition is our first line of defense in keeping ourselves out of harm's way. I suggest you should never take your intuition, senses, or dreams for granted. There may be messages from your loved one if you just look, listen, feel, or see.

If you have any doubts about receiving messages while you dream at night, please consider the following two passages. To help clarify one point, the Kim referred to in the July 12, 2008, passage is Lenora's daughter, thereby making Kaleen, in the September 22, 2008, passage, Lenora's granddaughter.

> <u>July 12, 2008</u>
> "Again, this week I had told Lisa that I had a dream and I was holding up a baby. I didn't tell her that the baby had dark colored skin. Could it be that Jan was telling me that Kim's daughter is pregnant with a black baby? We'll wait to see if this is true!"

> <u>September 22, 2008</u>
> "Today Lisa told me that she had forgotten to tell me that her brother had told her a couple of weeks ago that Kaleen, the granddaughter of Lenora, is pregnant with a black baby from her black boyfriend. I went back to check in this little notebook, on July 12, I had told Lisa and Susan of my dream about holding a black baby. I guess Jan was really telling me about it back on 7/12. Jan, I know you are still with me and taking care of me and the people you loved. I miss you so much."

Family first was always Jan's credo. She was the biggest cheerleader in the family, and I believe all the Forgeys would agree that Jan was the hub of the family. She loved staying in touch to celebrate victories, small or large.

> <u>November 4, 2008</u>
> "Called Danny tonight to congratulate him on his being elected to County Commissioner of Tripp County, S. Dakota. He said when it was announced that he had won the seat, his phone rang, no number, just one ring and nobody was there. He said he knew it was Jan's call to let him know how happy she was. Danny had kidded her about being his campaign manager. I can hear her saying to Danny, 'Way to go!'"
>
> <u>December 19, 2008</u>
> "Coming home from the courthouse, I met with Lisa. She asked me if I had telephoned Kristine in July. I said I couldn't have telephoned her because I do not even know her last name to find her number from Jan's phone book. I had wanted to give her the Akita notebook Jan had made for her years ago and didn't even follow up on it. Lisa said Kristine wants to know because Jan's phone number appeared on her cell last July. I know I did not call her. If this is so, then Jan must have done it, just like her number appearing on my cell phone last June."

Liong returned to the Philippines in May of 2009 to attend the celebration of his mother's ninety-third birthday. His mother was almost totally deaf at this point and rarely spoke to anyone. For health reasons, he had instructed his family not to inform his mother that Jan had passed away. I spoke with Lusing personally about this incident, and she confirmed everything that Liong said as being 100 percent both accurate and true.

May 14, 2009

"I came back to Las Vegas from the Philippines on 5/12. On the morning of 5/12, when I went in to see Mama before leaving, Mama looked at me, and to the surprise of Lusing, who was in the room, Mama said to me, "You are leaving today. You are alone now, take care of yourself. Call me when you get home, but call me when there is no one around. I will go to see you . . . ."

Mama has lost her hearing for many years. Nobody told her (how?) that I was leaving. Nobody told her about Jan's passing last June. Did she really know that Jan had passed by using the word 'now?' How did she know that I was leaving that day? She did not acknowledge Seng or Lusing the days when we were all there. The maid taking care of her even said she was speaking in English some time the second day I was there. The only person she would speak to in English was Jan???

When I was in Honolulu on May 6, I truly felt Jan's presence with me. When I shut my eyes, she would appear to me looking like the way she looked in 2002, when she took Lucy to Honolulu as Employee of the Month at the Mirage. She was at her heaviest at the time, so that should explain how she appeared to me. My brothers do not believe in my communication with Jan. They think it is just me missing her. I guess if I believe in Jan, that is enough for me, for I truly miss her so much – day and night."

Lusing and Mama were not the only Tee family members to have an experience with Jan. Liong's nephew Stephen and his family live in Illinois, near St. Louis, far removed from Las Vegas. All the way out in the heart of the Midwest, Jan still found time to pay them a couple of visits.

> July 13, 2009
> "Stephen called me yesterday as he and family are coming to Vegas this week. He told me that he dreamed about being here at the condo and seeing Jan fixing breakfast. Then Jan talked to him about the Strip and that she doesn't need to go with them since he knows Vegas very well now. She also said to him, "I am no longer working." Stephen said the dream was so vivid. I told him Jan was always appreciative of his help since she was first diagnosed with the tumor back in 2002 or 2003. Jan is a person who appreciated every little love and care given to her."

> October 2, (2010) – Saturday
> "Noticed a call from Stephen at 5:32 p.m. last night. Called Stephen. Stephen told me that Rollie and Joy are in Illinois visiting with them. Rollie was fixing his computer and Jan's picture appeared on the screen. Rollie didn't know why it came on. Jan loved my nephews. Stephen was very helpful to her during her ordeal. Jan must just want them to know that she remembers them and was saying hello."

Even from the other side, Jan still has a fantastic sense of humor and enjoys playing jokes on her friends and family. She continues to play practical jokes on her sister Lisa and her cousin Toni.

> October 22, 2009 (Thursday)
> "Tonight Lisa and Lyn were preparing dinner; Lisa unconsciously threw away a bowl of mushrooms cut by Lyn. They were all laughing and Lisa said she didn't even know that she had dumped it into the garbage. I was watching TV in the living room. Well,

I shut my eyes and Jan appeared. She was laughing like her usual happy self and told me that she made Lisa do it."

<u>November 4, 2009</u>
"Took Susan to Summerlin Hospital at 11:00 a.m. Coming home, Lisa was preparing lunch. She had a text message from Toni, Jan's cousin who drove us to South Dakota on the last trip. Toni said that last night she was alone with her grandfather, who is sick; she heard Jan's voice calling her name, then the usual 'giggle.' Toni was working at Spring Valley Hospital when Jan had her first surgery in 2003. It was then that Toni met Jan after losing touch with the Forgey family for a long time."

<u>November 9, 2009</u>
"Lisa received a text message from Toni that she saw Jan last night, early this morning, at around 1 a.m. Jan must have been in Lake Havasu to see her before coming home."

Jan was her daddy's little girl, and when John and her brother Danny had a successful bull auction, she had to let them know she was celebrating with them.

<u>February 17, (2010) – Wednesday</u>
"The last time Jan flashed the green lights was Monday early morning 2:11 a.m. I missed her so much that I tried hard to meditate to get a message from her. Tuesday morning till today, I was not able to feel her. Feeling a bit low. Then this afternoon Lisa told me that Danny had a good sale of his cattle at the auction in South Dakota. So did John. Lisa also said that Danny mentioned to her that after he made the sale, his cell phone rang. It said, 'Restricted No,'

and nobody was at the other end. Danny felt that it was Jan. This also happened the night Danny got elected as County Commissioner of Tripp County. I told myself no wonder Jan was not here. She was busy in Winner with Danny and John."

The following year, when Danny and John had their bull sale, Jan again found the time to stop by and pay them a visit.

February 15, (2011) – Tuesday
"Came into the computer room, put the cell in front of the computer screen. The green lights started flashing. It was 11:33 a.m. It must have flashed continuously at least 40 times! I started wondering why? Is there something that made Jan flash this many times?

Suddenly remembered that Danny and John were having their bull sale at the auction this morning. I called John's home, no answer. Lucy's cell, no answer. Lucy finally called me back at 2:10 p.m. She was very happy. She told me that Danny and John sold their entire herd. Neil was also home. Now I know why Jan was so happy. I told Lucy about the flashes. Lucy giggled, 'Oh! That girl of mine!' Jan, you are the greatest!"

In August of 2010, Lisa was at a crossroads in her life. She knew she was no longer happy in Las Vegas and was contemplating moving back to South Dakota to be nearer to her family. Just as she always did, Jan found a way to bring Lisa some welcome reassurance while she grappled with her decision.

Early August 2010
"When I decided to move home, one night I was praying that it was the right decision; and while praying, Jan's face was right there smiling at me. And

I knew if I opened my eyes she would disappear, but I had to open them just to see if I could see her for real. But, of course, she wasn't there."

This same type of reassurance was also given to Melissa, Jan's niece, right before she gave birth to her second baby.

<u>October 8, (2010) – Friday</u>
"Melissa, Jan's niece had a baby on Monday. It was an induced birth. Melissa told Lisa that prior to her going to the hospital; Jan had come to her assuring her that everything will be fine. Jan loves the family."

<u>November 15, (2010) – Monday</u>
"So much to write today.
7:16 a.m. just got a call from Lisa; John is in the hospital. He was in a lot of pain and was undergoing tests to find out what may be the problem. I lit incense, telling Jan about her Daddy.

7:21 a.m. called Lisa. Lisa said Lucy swore that somebody was at home last night, that she heard footsteps in the hallway.

9:27 a.m. the lights flashed, and Susan called to say that Doctor didn't find any major problem with John.

I have been smelling the smell of cookies the last two days. Jan baked the best cookies. She often baked cookies for her friends at work, and they liked them very much; I do not like cookies. So I decided to call Lucy at 3:24 p.m. Lucy answered the phone. They had just gotten home. I told Lucy that Jan wants her to bake some cookies for John, John loves cookies. Well, John said that Lucy had promised to bake him cookies but didn't. Lucy said she will today, and she again told me that she heard footsteps in the hallway last night.

4:00 p.m. told Jan that Lucy is going to bake cookies for John and the lights flashed instantly at 4:01 p.m."

CHAPTER 12

Truth Is Stranger than Fiction

Although I consider everything that has happened over the last three years to be amazing, there are some incidents that rise above the others and need a category all their own. They are those "gotcha" moments that are so much harder to explain than any of the others and cannot possibly be called coincidental. Some may take your breath away; others will have you saying "wow!" Either way, they are pretty awesome.

It had been decided shortly after Jan's passing that a memorial service would be held for her in her home town of Colome, South Dakota, on the weekend of her birthday at the end of July. Liong had many pictures of Jan taken throughout her life, and he wanted to put some kind of presentation together to show during the service or reception.

I volunteered to make a DVD presentation. Knowing absolutely nothing about how to do it, I plunged in with both feet. The first step was to scan each photo Liong selected into the computer. Step two was to take the photos and create customized slides with the photos and captions Liong had written, and then add in some special effects. Next I had to assemble the slides in the moviemaker program that came with my computer. After the slides were placed in order, I laid in the transitional wipes between the slides and finished up the movie portion by adding in the chapter headlines and title cards that were to appear during the show. The final step was to add a musical underscore to complete the presentation. Naturally, we used some of Jan's favorite songs as the score for the slideshow. Sounds relatively simple, right?

My adventure of making the DVD is not very well documented in Liong's journal, amounting to no more than a passing reference to a burned-out tea light candle.

> July 22, 2008
> "Last week when Susan was finishing up the DVD, she was typing a quote on the 'Sister' drawing, one of Jan's favorites, I told her that Jan is very particular about this drawing and the quote she chose for it. Susan said its okay; she had to finish the DVD. While she was typing a quote of her choosing, I was standing behind her, I turned my head and saw the tea candle light had died.
>
> With that I told Susan, 'I think Jan doesn't want another quote on her Happi Hearts.' I went into the room and looked thru the Happi Hearts, found the Happi Heart with the sister drawing; gave the quote to Susan. I re-lit the candle. It burned the whole evening without dying again."

"Sister" Happi Heart artwork

This entry does not even begin to explain everything that was going on while I was making the DVD. For instance, the tea light burned out on several occasions not just once. Be assured there was no air movement in the condo office, no windows were open or fans blowing. The candle would just go out for no reason. It got to the point that I did not even question why it happened; I just took it to mean that Jan was not happy with something and that it needed to be changed. When the changes were made, the candle always remained lit.

My biggest problems occurred when I was trying to lay down the music. I timed out the length of the recordings, splicing them together so that they faded in and out evenly with no noticeable transitions. When I played the entire movie back, however, the musical segments had mysteriously moved for no reason at all and were no longer synched up with the slides. Another problem that coincided with the moving slides was the movie getting stuck on either the same slide or song.

I tried rearranging the songs. It did not matter. I even went so far as to recreate the slide from scratch and re-rip the song from the CD to the computer. It made absolutely no difference. The movie jammed on the photo of Skylar and the Steve Miller song. The perplexing part was that the picture was no different than any of the others I had done. And as I said, all of the songs were burned directly off the original compact discs and played normally when I was using the media player. Ultimately, I changed the picture and eliminated the song all together. Naturally you can guess what happened. After those two changes were made, the tea light remained lit the entire time and the movie played without a hitch.

However, this pales in comparison to what was happening to Liong around the same time.

> <u>July 21, 2008</u>
> "I came home from the dentist at 12:30. There is a message from Sav-On to pick up a prescription drug. Went over to Sav-On. The nurse said there is no drug for Tee. I thought the dentist had called in the other day for my painkiller. The other nurse recognized me and said it must be for Jan. I looked at her and said, 'Jan? Who called in?'
>
> She looked at the bottle of cough medicine and said, 'Doctor Davidson.'
>
> Well Jan hadn't seen her since January. What made her call in for Jan? Jan, are you kidding around with me?
>
> Talked to Lisa about this – Lisa said remember every time she was going home, she always ordered some cough syrup to bring home to Dad and Mom. So, she did it again. But how did she make her doctor call in for the cough syrup?
>
> How did she send the prescription on the pharmacy's computer?"

Perhaps someone out there can rationally explain to me how Jan's prescription for cough syrup was sent to the computer at Sav-On Drugs on July 21. At that time, she had been gone for over six weeks and had not even seen her regular doctor for several months before that. Perhaps this was Jan's first attempt at manipulating electronic equipment.

Moving into late autumn, Liong had to go out to Stephen's vacation home in Henderson to replace a light bulb. The mechanical engineer got some welcome assistance from his angel.

> <u>October 30, 2008</u>
> "I went to Anthem at around 1 p.m. to change the burned-out light bulb at Stephen's house. Knowing that it works on a light sensor, but not remembering that it was high up where I could not reach. Also, if I climbed up, stepping on the pipes to cover the light sensor, I won't be able to see the lights if they come on or not, to find out which one needed to be replaced. I hung the blanket over the sensor; jumped down and walked over to the corner to the garage. The lights were not on. While thinking that I may have to give up and come back at night, I turned and saw the lights come on. The left garage light was out. Then they all went out again. I walked to the side of the garage and saw the blanket lying on the ground. I backed up the truck, changed the light bulb then climbed up again to put the blanket over the sensor again to check if the replaced bulb was working. Well, the lights never came back again. I waited for a while to see if there was a time delay for the sensor. Nothing happened. Just then the cell phone rang and a (506) area code number came up. Three different 506 numbers have come up in the last two months. I went to Susan's office and asked her to dial the numbers. They said the numbers did not exist???

Honey Jan, did you make the lights come on so that I could know which bulb was out? Are the 506 numbers your way of letting me know you are with me? Oh, and I received a text message last month, saying, 'Hey baby.' The other one, the last couple of days when Lisa and I were on the way to Casper, Wyoming, read, 'Sun to shine, thank God for Jesus,' from Cynthia. I knew it cannot be from Cynthia, Susan's friend, because she doesn't believe in Jesus; she is a Jew. Too bad I had Lisa erase the text message because I would like to know who sent it. Jan???"

One thing I would like to say before continuing with the next installment is that there are a plethora of incidents throughout the journal regarding the CD player or the cell phone flashing on specific songs, especially between the periods of June 2010 to June 2011. This is part of that fine-tuning I referred to in earlier chapters. Jan will consistently flash during Celine Dion's "Power of Love," Tina Turner's "The Best," Louis Armstrong's "What a Wonderful World," and The Righteous Brothers' "Unchained Melody." She has a way of making the CD player stop on specific songs or play a different song than the one selected. As I keep telling Liong, "Why ask why? Just go with it. She picked it for a reason, so sit back and enjoy it."

If you will recall in chapter 5, I mentioned that Jan said she would be with us at Christmas, after she and Liong sang "Silent Night" together at the hospital. Well, she did not forget her promise, and she did not disappoint us.

<u>December 7, 2008</u>

"I put on Jan's favorite Xmas songs by Johnny Mathis for her. I went into the room to watch football. When I came out, the music had stopped. I was surprised because it wasn't that long that I was in the room. I looked at the player; the disc had stopped at no. 6, which never happened before. I looked at no. 6 then at no. 5. The last song that was played was, 'I'll

> Be Home for Xmas.' Somehow Jan had stopped the player after no. 5. I remember what she told me days before she passed at the hospital when I showed her the Silent Night Happi Heart, one of her favorites. I started singing 'Silent Night' and Jan sang with me. Then she said to me, 'I'll be there this Xmas.' Jan, maybe you are reaffirming your promise to be here on Xmas. I love you Jan."

It is like I said before; Jan can make electronic gadgets do her bidding. I guess that includes computers too. The best part is that it was not just Liong's computer that was affected.

> <u>December 24, 2008</u>
> "Dearest Jan, I know you are home. I have been smelling the usual banana smell since yesterday. It was particularly strong last night.
>
> I left the computer on the picture of you looking at me with so much love and joy. I tried to turn off the computer many, many times and it wouldn't turn off. I left it there for half an hour. I tried to turn it off again and still wouldn't turn off after many tries. I know you are home. You won't let it turn off until I am sure you are home. Honey, I miss you so deeply. It still hurts very much when I miss you.
>
> Lisa, Susan and I had a Christmas meal at 3:00 p.m. Jan, of course, had her share of good food with us. We decided to turn off the power at 4:15 p.m. I left and came home at 6:30 p.m. Susan turned on the computer, this time the computer behaved like usual. No more not turning off on the photo of Jan & I.
>
> Lisa called Susan and me shortly after she went home at 4:00 after the Xmas meal. She said she turned on

her computer, and the same thing happened to her computer; the computer wouldn't turn off. Jan was with her also."

Liong's nephew Stephen is a doctor who lives in Illinois and comes out to Vegas a couple of times a year. As was mentioned previously, Stephen was very helpful to Jan in deciphering medical reports and terminology, and she appreciated his assistance very much. So it came as no surprise to us that she continued to practice her sense of humor on him as well.

February 15, 2009

"While at the Silverton Casino, I noticed a voice mail at approx. 3 p.m. It was Stephen's message saying he was returning my call to him at 2:30 p.m. I was very sure that I did not call him at 2:30 since I was having lunch with Lisa and Susan at Johnny Rocket's at 1 p.m. Then I proceeded to play video poker. I checked my phone to see if I had called him and not remembered. There was only one call when I called him to tell him about my car license numbers for registering with Anthem. I talked to him. So there can be no mix-up of any sort. I didn't call and there was no record of a call on my cell.

At about 3:30 p.m., I had an urge to take out my cell phone from my jacket. As I held my cell phone, the green lights flashed in front of me, but only the upper half light. Thinking about it afterwards, I guess Jan must be telling me it was she who left the phone number on Stephen's cell phone. The green light was to let me know that she was there with me and that she did it."

February 17, 2009

"Stephen called me yesterday morning before they left Las Vegas. I told him I had tried several times to call him yesterday and that I did not call him at 2:30 p.m. yesterday. He said his cell phone had shown that I called at 2:30 p.m. He also said that his cell phone was not working properly all afternoon soon after that.

'Strange.' he said.

Well, Lisa then told me that yesterday when she called John and Lucy. John said to Lucy, 'It's Liong, let me answer the phone.' His caller ID showed my number.

Lucy then asked Lisa, 'Why are you using Liong's phone?'

Lisa said, 'I am using my own, Liong is not even here . . ???'

I guess my Jan was having fun that day with everybody: Stephen, John, us. 'Way to go, baby!' as Jan always said. Love you, baby."

The next incident was not logged into Liong's journal but instead comes from Lisa, Toni, and myself. Toni had volunteered to use her Nissan Pathfinder for our trip to South Dakota in October 2009 to see the headstone. She introduced us to her TomTom GPS system, named Richard, who spoke to us several times during the trip. Richard got so annoying that she turned him off, and for the return trip to Las Vegas, Toni never turned her GPS system on at all.

It was during our return to Las Vegas from South Dakota that one of the more spectacular events took place. As is our custom, we bypass Salt Lake City and instead cut through Provo Canyon, as it is a much prettier ride and has far less traffic. We crossed out of Wyoming into Utah on Interstate 80 and were moving closer to Salt Lake City. Toni asked, "Does anyone know the exit we have to take for Provo?"

As soon as she finished her sentence, Richard's voice came on and said, "Route 189, Heber City, one mile."

All three of us did one of those cough-laughs in stunned amazement. Toni said over and over again that Richard had never even been turned on since leaving South Dakota. How could he turn himself on like that? Lisa said what we were all thinking: "That's Jan!" This was truly the most amazing demonstration of Jan's electronic prowess to date. Unfortunately, Liong missed all this because he was wearing headphones, listening to a football game on my portable satellite radio.

This next journal entry, I have to say, is my favorite. Of course, after you read Melissa's email you will understand why. Originally I was going to entitle this chapter "That Creeps Me Out," in honor of my boss Bob. When I was telling Melissa's story to my coworkers, Bob walked out of his office and said, "Susan, you've got to stop talking about this stuff." I was taken back and asked him why. "Because I believe in this stuff and it creeps me out," was his emphatic response. Again, I was taken back. I thought about what Bob said and could not understand his horror of hearing this wonderful story. Jan had been gone for over a year and a half, and with every sign she had given us, I, for one, looked forward to her communications because they made all of us happy. It was like receiving a letter from a long-lost friend who only had good news to share. Each sign was a blessing and there was nothing to fear because only love was present in her communications.

After we returned from South Dakota in late October 2009, Liong had me send out via email photos of his and Jan's headstone to members of both of their families, showing them where he and Jan would spend eternity together. Two days later he received this email from Melissa, Jan's niece in Casper, Wyoming.

Jan and Liong's headstone

Fw: RESTING PLACE

Melissa & Shad

To Liong Tee, Lisa Forgey, Teneil–work
From: Melissa & Shad
Sent: Tue 11/03/09 4:15 PM
To: Liong Tee; Lisa FOrgey
Cc: Teneil

2 attachments (total 690.9 KB)
View slide show (2)

I wanted to pass a little story about these photos to Liong.
When we received these photos the other night I had Vincent on my lap, as he likes to watch me check email. He also likes seeing the pictures on the computer, well we opened this email and I was just looking at the email not saying anything, and Vince says "Momma look . . . Jan", I said what? he then replies "See Jan, and chuckles" I asked him where

do you see Jan? And he pointed at her yearn . . . . so I asked him again . . . . where is Jan hunny? and he repeated the pointing at Jan's yearn and said "See Jan" with a smile on his face. So I asked him does Jan come and play with you, does she visit? "Yeap he says", "play trucks" hmm . . . . She works in mysterious ways! Take care, Love you
Melissa

Melissa's e-mail gave Liong great comfort and confirmation that Jan is sending us messages. Liong's journal entry reflects the hope and continuing wonder at the many manifestations that Jan uses to play with all members of her family.

November 03, 2009

"In another two days, Jan will have been away from me for 17 months. I decided to have a new notebook to record our connections. This morning's email from Melissa, Jan's niece in Casper, was both comforting and heart-warming. To know that Jan has visited little Vincent and played with him. To know that a two year old boy would not know how to make up a story; and also that Vincent never intellectually was able to know Jan when Jan held him in her arms in October 2007, opened the door to a whole new way of looking at departure from life, from his/her earthly physical body. I now firmly believe that my Jan is happy, playful, loving as she was on earth, and that we will eventually be together again. She has not left the family she loved, and she has not left me.

Jan holding baby Vincent

Read email from Melissa. Lifted the spirits of everybody in the family who knew about this. Jan was in Casper October 2007; Vincent was only a baby in her arms. Jan loved to see Vincent's photo on the internet, up to the moment of her passing. She called Vincent her little 'Viking.' Jan's favorite football team in life was the Minnesota Vikings. Vincent is only beginning to talk recently. How amazing. How heartwarming. My Jan is making the rounds to everybody she loved.

This photo was sent to me on August 21st, 2008 when Vincent was 1 yr. old. He is now 2 yrs. and 2 months old. The back of the photo says, 'To great Uncle Liong, Go Vikings.'

Vincent (one year old)

Attached are Emails:
1. I sent photos of the Headstone at Colome cemetery to family members on 11/1.

2. Melissa returned an email to me on 11/3 regarding little Vincent and Jan.

3. Teneil email to me on 11/3 regarding Melissa's email.

RESTING PLACE
Teneil Forgey

To Liong Tee, Lisa Forgey, Melissa & Shad
From: Teneil Forgey
Sent: Tue 11/03/09 4:36 PM
To: Liong Tee; Lisa Forgey; Melissa & Shad

WOW THAT MAKES ME CRY, KIDS ARE WONDERFUL AREN'T THEY! I HAVE NO DOUBT SHE PLAYS WITH HIM! SHE HAS GOT TO LOVE IT AS MUCH AS WE ALL DO! I MISS HER BUNCHES. SOOOOO . . . . DID WE EVER FIGURE OUT WHO IS PREGNANT?????? LIONG YOU BETTER BE FOR MAKING HER TELL US ALL!
LOVE YA ALL

> TENEIL
>
> Amazing? Miraculous? Comforting? Believable? – Yes!!!
> 4. Picture of me and headstone in Colome.
> Emails from Liong Tee to Steve & Shirley on 11/l, Melissa to Liong Tee on 11/3, and Teneil to Liong Tee on 11/3 said it all!
>
> p.s. Is this the baby, Vincent, that I dreamed about some time ago; that Jan was telling me she was playing with baby Vincent?"

Yes, we would all really appreciate a rational, scientific explanation for how little, two-year-old Vincent knew who Jan was and that her remains were located inside an urn sitting in front of the newly installed headstone. I have heard it said that children can often see things that adults cannot because their minds are not cluttered with scientific facts saying that it cannot be.

After Lisa moved home to South Dakota in October of 2010, she recorded a very unusual phenomenon again with the headstone at the cemetery.

October 25, 2010

"Lisa went to visit our headstone after arriving home and she texted a picture of the headstone to Susan. It had rained overnight. Lisa went back to the cemetery this morning. The rain had stopped. The headstone was dry except for a rain stain inside Jan's heart – it was the shape of a person! There was no stain on my side or anywhere else. Lisa took a picture and texted it to Susan. She texted, 'Nobody can tell us she is not here!' I will ask Susan to print the photo. People who love and miss each other should see this. Your soul mate never left, and if she had a pure soul, God will grant her the ability to visit her love ones anytime, anywhere. The many and regular events over the more than two years since Jan's passing should convince everybody that their soul mate will be around to take care of them and their loved ones.

Came into bedroom at 11:37 p.m. and said goodnight. The lights flashed at 11:39 p.m. Goodnight, honey, and thank you for the sign on the headstone. It brought a lot of comfort to your loved ones."

Headstone with shadow

At the turn of the twentieth century, the "hourglass" figure of a woman was considered the ideal silhouette. As you look at the photo of the shadow, you really have to marvel at the symmetry of the figure. It had rained the night before and this image was on the stone the following morning. Yet, as Liong points out in his entry, his side of the heart did not have any kind of marking on it. It has rained and snowed many times in Colome, South Dakota, since the headstone was placed there in September of 2009. However, the figure on Jan's side of the headstone had never appeared before, nor has it re-appeared since. The stone has been checked and there are no cracks that would account for the shadow appearing. Perhaps this is Jan's way of looking down the hill and watching over her parents' house, or maybe it was a welcome home message to her sister Lisa.

If the silhouette image is not enough to impress you of Jan's dexterity in leaving messages for her family and friends, here is another example from times gone before to express her presence. It was customary back in the eighteenth and nineteenth century for visitors to leave a calling card when stopping by to say hello to friends and neighbors who may or may not have been home at the time of the visit. Never let it be said that old traditions die, as evidenced by our next journal entry.

> <u>January 27, 2011</u>
> "Before leaving for Arizona, received an email from Shirley. The email explains it all. Amazed is what I felt. Almost 23 years and my Jan still brings memories to her loved ones. Shirley was her favorite sister-in-law."

> <u>January 27, 2011 (Thursday) Shirley Email</u>
> "Now Liong I have something that happened today, that was so special and I couldn't wait to get home to tell you about. We are having some work done in our office with our heating and cooling and workers are coming in and out. They moved our copy machine

out away from the wall and found a business card underneath the copy machine and put it on top of the machine. When I went to the machine to make a copy, I saw the business card and it was a card with Jan's name on it. It was her business card when she worked for World Wide Travel. I was so surprised and amazed. It had some things written on it and a date of 4/24/87. Trying to think back, I do believe my boss at the time may have did some business with Jan. It made my day and I felt her near. I am sending you a picture of the card. It is in really good shape. I will save it and give it to you in July unless you would like me to send it to you now. I have several of my Happi Hearts hanging in my office and I enjoy looking at them and keeps me close to her in my mind."

Jan's business card from 1987

The thoughts that keep coming to mind are: what are the odds after twenty-four years of being lost underneath a copy machine that 1) the card is found, 2) it is in excellent condition, and 3) it just happens to be from your loved one who has gone beyond this lifetime? I mean, really, what are the odds of that? If you were in your own home it would be far easier to explain away, but not at the office with countless numbers of cleaning crews, machine replacements, and servicing. In this case, it is just too hard to believe it was only a coincidence and far easier to believe that Jan was stopping by to visit Shirley before going on to her next port of call.

When certain types of electronic anomalies happen, it is so easy for us to say that it was just a fluke. Just how many flukes does it take to become a noticeable pattern? We have already discussed in this chapter alone nine flukes: 1) the problems in putting together the memorial DVD; 2) a bottle of cough syrup called in by her doctor almost six weeks after her passing; 3) sensor-operated lights turning on in middle of a bright autumn day so that Liong could change a bad one; 4) several incidents with the CD player either playing a different song than the one displayed or stopping for no reason on a particular song; 5) Jan's picture showing up on the computer that would not turn off; 6) a return phone call for a call that was never made; 7) a GPS system that turned itself on and answered a question within seconds of being asked; 8) a two-year-old boy who knows and plays with Aunt Jan and was not old enough to remember her; and 9) a mysterious shadow in the shape of a woman's silhouette which has never been seen before or since. So I ask you again, how many flukes does it take to make a consistent, recognizable pattern before you believe that it is possible for the other side to communicate with us? And we are still not finished.

> April 22, 2011
> "The lights flashed good morning at 5:34 a.m. The thought of going to South Dakota without her kept bothering me. I put in the DVD Susan made – Remembrance – A chronicle of Jan's life. Tears began flowing after the first view of baby Jan. The pain of missing her is still deep. After watching the DVD, I simply collapsed mentally. Clicked on the CD. The song of Perry Como, 'And I Love You So' came on! I had clicked on the CD countless times. This is the second time this happened. The last time was when

it played The Three Bells; had to check when that happened.

I turned and looked at the disc indicator. It showed disc #1, the first song is, 'Wonderful World.' The Perry Como song is the first song on disc #2. Puzzled, I let it play thru the song, turned off the player, and then restarted it. This time the song, 'Wonderful World' came on. I turned to the cell phone and asked, 'Honey, did you do this?' Right then, the lights flashed at 9:13 a.m. Dearest Jan, I will go home with you for the Forgey family reunion in Deadwood come July."

<u>May 21, 2011</u>
"Came home after the movie. My stomach still playing a bum game with me. Very irritating. So I got into bed, clicked on the CD player. What came on wasn't, 'Wonderful World,' it was Perry Como, 'And I Love You So.' I turned and looked at the player; it indicated disc #1 – 101. It was Jan again. I restarted the player, this time, 'Wonderful World' came on, and the lights flashed at 4:01 p.m. during, 'Bridge Over Troubled Waters.' My Jan, my bridge over troubled waters. The lights flashed again on, 'Unchained Melody' at 4:09 p.m. Yes Jan, 'I'll be coming home, wait for me.'"

Yes, Jan, you are truly amazing. All we ask is that you keep the messages coming.

Before moving on, I would now like you to seriously consider all that you have read up to this point. Did you recognize any of the signs that have been mentioned so far? Have any struck a nerve? Perhaps a smell, sound, dead air phone call, random thought, particular animal or plant, shape, unusual ache or pain, colors, or even electronic fluke could be an indicator of your loved one's continued presence. Just like Liong, sometimes it takes reflection before one is able to identify specific signs that indicate a presence. Take some time now to reflect back on how many of these same signs you may have brushed off as mere coincidence.

Now is the time for you to open your mind. Hopefully some of the incidents that I have related have caused you to reflect on an event that you may have deemed as odd or unusual at the time and never thought to connect with your departed loved one. Take a moment to consider ways they may communicate with you and talk to him or her. Ask them to show you a sign. Do not expect some grandiose display; rather if it comes, it will probably be something small and subtle, something that only you can recognize. You have to keep your eyes, ears, nose, and inner eye open to everything around you. Like I said before, it takes patience and a mind at peace. Just keep looking.

CHAPTER 13

Unexpected Messenger

As is our nightly ritual, Liong and I watch a movie together before retiring. At the time that this incident below took place, Jan had been gone for almost nine months and I knew that Liong was still grieving deeply for his other half. He was reading a lot of books, ranging from psychics, religion, psychiatrists, and everything in between, to try and get a handle on where his angel might be. He wanted to know if she was alright and trying to communicate with him.

One day it came to me that perhaps there was a movie that might give Liong a different insight to the afterlife. The movie I was thinking of is seen from the soul's point of view after a spouse has died, leaving its soul mate behind. I had seen this film before, prior to moving in with Jan and Liong. In this particular case, it is the husband watching his wife grieve for him and their two children who had died a few years before, leaving her alone to face the world. If you have not guessed already, the film is called *What Dreams May Come*, starring Robin Williams and Annabella Sciorra

I faced one very large obstacle: Liong is not a big fan of Robin Williams. I knew I was taking a chance that he would refuse to watch the movie with me. So I did a lot of promoting of the film on the point that it was taken from the soul's point of view. I began talking about the movie to test the waters before I ordered it. When no negative response was forthcoming, I submitted my request and placed it at the top of my Netflix queue. Little did I know that one film would forever change the course of Liong's life in a very positive and profound way.

> March 1, 2009
>
> "Yesterday Susan put in a DVD she ordered on Netflix. She had told me about it that it was about the souls. Robin Williams starred in the movie. As we watched, I felt Jan's presence; the smell of bananas was so strong in the first half of the movie. It described what the soul experiences when the person passes away, like trying to communicate with his loved ones. The second half was about the soul of his wife being lost and suffering in the gateway to hell. It was a very sad state of existence. All throughout the second half, I didn't once feel Jan's presence. I asked Susan what prompted her to order this movie. For the last few weeks, I have been talking to Jan about going to see her when Lisa should find someone good to love and take care of her, and when Susan will be on her own. I guess Jan didn't agree with my notion of ending my life to be with her, and she was doing this to send me her message.
>
> As I repeatedly told her, if it is choosing between living without her and dying to be with her, I would choose to be with her without a second thought. Jan, know it that I love you and miss you every day. Sometimes it hurts so deeply that you are not with me physically. I know you are with me in spirit every time I'm missing you badly. I love you Jan.
>
> Did you ever miss your soul-mate so badly that you felt going to see her is better than being without her?"

First I have to tell you that I was completely unaware that Liong had even contemplated the idea of suicide. The very idea that someone so strong and successful would even consider such a drastic action was incomprehensible to me. My only thought at the time was simply to offer Liong a different perspective of the afterlife. I can remember that as we watched the movie, Liong remained unusually silent. Normally, we talk through movies, considering them mostly to be background noise. A couple of times he asked aloud, "What made you order this movie?" Why did I order this movie? At the time, it just popped into my head . . . mmm.

Why did this movie make such an impact on Liong? The reason centers upon Anabella Sciorra's character, Annie Nielsen. When Annie commits suicide to escape her grief at the recent loss of her husband, combined with the loss of both of their children a few years earlier, she ends up as a lost soul sitting in the doorway of hell—alone. There was no joyous reunion with the rest of her family in heaven.

As Liong's journal shows, Jan was with him all through the first half of the film but was noticeably absent during the second half of the film after Annie commits suicide. This event alone made it abundantly clear to Liong that if he took his own life, it was possible he would not be reunited with Jan in the afterlife. He could end up being alone for all eternity; a lost soul for all time.

Liong had never even considered this possibility before. The significance of this realization was huge. Liong has always been a risk-taker. I have no doubt at all that he has the courage to take his own life if he thought he would be reunited with Jan. His fearlessness made him successful, yet when confronted with the possibility that he might not end up with Jan in heaven, he turned away from suicide as an option instantly. Liong will do nothing that could possibly keep him from spending all eternity with his angel Jan. The stakes for this gamble were now far too high.

February 08, (2011) – Tuesday

"I have been inputting my handwritten diaries into the computer file. As I was typing, I can't help but be amused by how crude my English was – spelling mistakes, tense errors, bad English. At any rate, my intent was, and still is, to have an honest and truthful record of events. A true description of my inner feelings, and a refuge for me when I feel sad, lonely, or bored. There were no exaggerations or distortions, for such would be an insult to Jan's love for me."

June 5, (2011) – Sunday

"It was three years ago today when Jan went 'Home.' Since I was a child, it has been imbedded in my mind by my parents that we should hold our respect and esteem; I do not like the word mourning, for someone we hold dear for a period of three years. Although Jan left for 'Home' three years ago, she has been by my side all this time. She cares for me and takes care of me. Our love has grown over the last three years. Jan comes to my side whenever she feels that I need her. From here on, I will probably not record the flashes that are now an integral part of my life. Three years of seeing the flashes every day now, and on the notable events associated with the flashes, are enough to convince me that we, on this earth, in general, do not understand the permanent existence of souls. I am blessed to have a soul-mate in Jan."

Throughout the course of this book, the emphasis has been placed on Jan and her communications with Liong, family, and friends. However, the most significant aspect of this story is the one, single incident that centers on Liong. Out of the entire journal, this is the only entry that explores his innermost thoughts and actions. Little did I know that one apparently innocuous action on my part changed the course of Liong's life forever and proved to be my greatest role in this adventure. There was no spectacular feat that I performed. No, Jan kept it much simpler than that. I ordered a movie for Liong and me to watch. Do I believe that I was used by Jan to be her messenger to Liong? Absolutely!

I believe most writers of this kind of book have a sincere desire to improve, enlighten, and expand the perceptions of the lives of their readers. In that regard, I am no different from the rest. If this one chapter can change the course, for the better, of another human being's life like it did for Liong then I have truly succeeded.

CHAPTER 14

Love Letters

The one thing that has remained consistent throughout Jan and Liong's life and in this book is the depth of love shared between them. In some of the chapters, I have included love letters that they wrote to each other through the years. Take for example this love letter that was written by Liong on the occasion of Jan's birthday in 2000.

> "Dearest Jan,
>
> I bless this day of many years ago when John and Lucy brought you to this world.
>
> If I can put a value to the warm, sincere, and total love you have showered upon me all these years that I have known you, I would have owed you a debt un-repayable even for another lifetime to come.
>
> You know me to be a person short in expression of words when it comes to you. I simply try to convey such feeling by the many small things that I can do for you.

On this your Birthday, however, I will try to be very vocal by saying the eight letter words you have whispered to me countless of times –

I LOVE YOU

LIONG

Year 2000"

Even without Jan being in his physical life, Liong has found a way to continue writing his love letters to his beloved, in his journal. After all, if you think about it, is not this journal one long love letter to Jan? Here in its pages we have been allowed to listen in on Liong's continuous and intimate expressions of love for his lady. Each page shows us the depth of intimacy that he continues to share with his soul mate, and I have selected a few more entries for you to savor and enjoy the elegance of his prose.

<u>October 14, 2008</u>
"Dearest Jan,

It's been more than 4 months since you left. I miss you more than ever. At times I feel like sitting in this earthly prison waiting for my time to go and join you. I miss the laughter we shared every day. I miss seeing your angelic smile. If only you can come into my dreams, at least let me relive those moments with you. I know when you are around me, and I feel it when you were gone. Words cannot describe how it hurts when I am in the state of missing you, as I am at this moment of writing. I love you so much. Remember I used to tell you what Papa said about me? That I will die for the one I love. I would have died for you anytime. I also told you that I have lived a full life and that I could go without regrets. Now I have one regret that you left me here all alone. We will see each other again, that I am sure. Jan honey, it hurts so much. I miss you."

February 13, 2009

"While I was watching Glenn Beck on Fox News, he was talking about the wife whose husband perished in the 9/11 attack in New York. She was able to speak to him till the last moment when an explosion ended the conversation. She said, "Sometimes pain is a way of love." Yes, to feel pain is a proof of love. I never knew I loved Jan so much until she passed on. The pain that I felt and still feel is indescribable. It hurts so deeply. But again, it is how bad it hurts that makes me realize how deeply I love her, and how much I miss her.

Jan, my love, I now know why you told me many times months before you left, that we are so lucky to have found each other. Yes, honey, me from the Philippines, to Taiwan, to Wisconsin, then back to the Philippines, and back to Los Angeles; the fates had it that I got very lucky in business to afford me to come to Vegas countless of times to find you when you needed me most. You, from a small town in South Dakota, to Wyoming, then to Las Vegas, and the destined meeting of our eyes at the Golden Nugget.

Jan I have to tell you, the time when we went outside the side door at the Golden Nugget when we kissed; I can still feel the feeling now. It seemed that time had stood still. I felt like I was floating, swirling in space, so peaceful. I don't even know how long we were locked in an embrace and kissed. I only know I had never felt that way and I can still feel the feeling now every time I think about it. Jan, we found each other. You best wait for me and be there to meet me when I come to look for you. I told you in one of my letters that I will find you no matter where you may be, and I will."

<u>June 6, 2009</u>
"The pain of losing you, the hurt when I miss you, are as deep today as it was one year ago, and I know the pain and hurt will continue for the rest of my conscious life on earth. My only consolation and joy is that you have been showing me signs that you are still with me and watching over me. Please do not stop doing so because it is what keeps me going on with life. When the time comes, I know you will be there waiting for me. The other day, Monday, June 1st when Susan was wheeled into the surgery room, I sat down in the lobby. I shut my eyes and saw you at my left side right away. This time you were surrounded by a fog like mist, and I saw wings behind you. I asked you what are they, and you just smiled. Yes, my Jan is an angel, and because she is an angel, I know she will be waiting for me. I love you Jan."

<u>December 23, 2009</u>
"Only two more days will be Christmas. I miss you Jan, so much. Remembering the old days when you would be busy making decorated candles, Happi Hearts and gift baskets . . . all the happiness that you spread around to everybody. I was so blessed to have you in my life in this lifetime, and I want to be with you forever after this lifetime.

The fragrance comes regularly at times when I am in the casino playing slots, or watching TV, or just thinking about you. The cell phone green lights blink at times when I do not know what to do with my life. As I told you before, and you always agreed with me, that when you don't know what to do, don't do anything. So I shall rest my mind and wait for you to guide me along. Susan is a happy person now. So different from the girl you coined as "quirky" before. You told me before you left that Susan is a good girl. I think you are right. She turned out to be a very simple, kind hearted and warm person. Lisa is happily adjusting to her new job at the Aria; happy with her Dakota. The Forgeys are fine. Merry Xmas to you, Honey, I miss you so much."

<u>February 22, 2010 – Monday morning</u>

"Been feeling increasingly aimless in life. It is always Jan on my mind from the time I open my eyes in the morning looking at my Jan and it is still Jan on my mind when I shut my eyes to sleep. What Jan had asked me to do I think I have done. I have taken care of Lisa via taking care of Susan. In turn, this makes John and Lucy happy that Lisa has again turned the corner. I have said it countless of times to you, Jan, that I will come to see you with a wide smile on my face. Don't know when that will happen but I certainly am looking forward to it. You bring me tinges of happiness via the signals you send thru happenings and the green lights on the phone. I don't know what I would have done without those signals. At times I just feel very tired of living. I am having a good life – no financial problems. Lisa, Susan, the Forgey family, my sisters Lusing, Yong-Yong, Vic, and other friends who love me. Yet, without Jan, I just cannot feel the same happiness that we shared for those 18 previous years. I am trying to find some purpose for going on. Honey Jan, give me some guidance . . . . I love you.

These last few days when I closed my eyes, Jan came to me with a different look; a different hair style, lots of bright golden light engulfing her, and a different color outfit, sort of blue base with a golden design.

The green lights flashed at 8:45 p.m."

February 19, 2011
"Jan must know that I was feeling lonely. If I were a ship moribund on the open seas, I wish Jan could guide me to my eventual destination. A safe harbor where I could be with my Jan again. I miss Jan dearly tonight. The lights flashed at 12:00 midnight. Jan wanted me to rest my weary mind. Goodnight my love."

January 27, 2011
"I know people might say that the flashes are just flashes; maybe electronic or telecommunication glitches, etc. I have lived for these flashes the last 2 years and 7 months. They have become a big part of my life. There are the flashes that just occur regularly these days without my thoughts, actions, or words. I regard them as Jan's messages to me that she was here with me. Then there are the flashes that responded to my thoughts for her, and then the flashes that respond to my questions to Jan, and last but not least, the flashes that occur instantly to circumstances involving our past lives together. After the last 31 months, to me and others who love Jan, there are no more doubts that my Jan is with us and watching over us, more than she ever did before her passing."

CHAPTER 15

Afterthoughts

I realize that Liong said in his journal that he was going to stop writing at the end of the three years. However at this time, it is so much a way of life for him that he does, in fact, continue to document Jan's ongoing dialogue; he cannot help himself. By writing down the daily events, he keeps Jan close in his heart.

Since he finished the formal writing of his journal on June 5, 2011, more things have happened and he is always trying to further refine his communication skills and understanding. Now he only has to ask Jan to send hummingbirds and they appear. The cell phone continues to flash, and Jan still controls the CD player to do her bidding.

If you are wondering if it is the same few songs that cause the flashes to occur, I can assure you she continues flashing on her favorite songs and a couple of new additions. In early August 2011, Liong asked me to make him a new CD which included more songs. I played around with it and we came up with final list of about twenty-three songs which I burned to a disc for him. The new CD contains all seven of her favorite songs from the original disc along with sixteen brand new songs. Three of the new songs have now become very popular with Jan, and she flashes often during Donna Fargo's "I'm the Happiest Girl in the Whole USA," the Beach Boys' "I Can Hear

Music," and the Browns' "I'll Meet You in the Morning." What I find really amazing about the new disc is that even though we have mixed up the order of the songs from the original CD, she still manages to flash frequently on "What a Wonderful World," "The Best," and "The Power of Love."

While ripping songs from the Browns' disc, I included the song "I'll Meet You in the Morning." I could swear it was on Liong's list. However, he assured me he had never even considered it for the CD. Naturally, I just took it to mean Jan wanted it on the disc for a reason yet to be determined. In fact, this incident kind of reminds me of the time when Lisa threw away Lyn's bowl of freshly cleaned mushrooms on October 22, 2009.

> <u>August 10, 2011</u>
> "Went out at noon to buy a few things. Came home and was longing to see the lights flash. Turned on the player, saw the lights flash at 3:09 p.m. on the song, "I'll Meet You in the Morning," by The Browns.
>
> The lights had flashed on this same song last Friday. I decided to look up the lyrics of the song. As I read the song lyrics, tears gathered in my eyes. They were happy tears. I now know that it will be a wonderful reunion for us.

For Liong, the lyrics were like an announcement from Jan. They so perfectly defined his vision of the afterlife that he will spend with her, especially the third and fourth verses: "You'll know me in the morning by the smiles that I wear, when I meet you in the morning, in the city that is built four square. I'll meet you in the morning at the end of the day on the streets of that city of gold . . ."

Liong is now sure, more than ever, that Jan is an angel. Look how she is watching over her family and several close friends, guiding and healing them when necessary. There is no doubt in his mind that Jan will be waiting for him in that "city of gold."

Right at this moment, I feel compelled to weigh in with some personal opinions and thoughts about what I have witnessed over the last three years. I stated in the Introduction that I was not going to put any kind of biased spin or religious dogma in the book, which I believe I accomplished. The reader is free to interpret these events any way they wish.

But why, I ask myself, is Liong so receptive to Jan's messages? Surely there must be other soul mates out there who have seen signs or received some type of message from beyond the veil. Why does he receive so many, so consistently? What makes his story and his experience so unique that it affords him the privilege to receive so much? It was only recently that an answer presented itself for consideration. For that answer, we only have to go back to the very beginning.

> <u>June 5, 2008</u>
> "Jan finished her journey on Earth; she went HOME first. Now I travel my journey on Earth without her. That one fateful day when we found each other; we looked deep into each other's eyes and saw love. Right then our souls embraced and became one forever. I knew then that I will never travel alone. Jan will always be by my side."

The answer was right there in the very first paragraph of the journal. He knew from the moment that he met Jan that she would always be by his side. He believed in the eternal nature of their relationship right from the beginning. He never doubted it for a minute. I suggest it is that belief that has allowed Liong to see, understand, and interpret the signs that Jan has sent. Through his inner eye, his finely tuned soul, he has allowed the rest of us the privilege to share in his conversations with her.

Being raised in a Christian household, as I reflect back on all the things that have happened over these past three years and are continuing to happen today, I have to say, without hesitation, I now fervently believe that Jan is an angel and angels walk amongst us daily.

I have witnessed what she has done for Liong and her expressions of care and concern for her family and friends.

Writing this book really made me open my eyes to the wonders of the afterlife. I am not saying that I am anxious to get there and would do something to precipitate my arrival. It was that overwhelming fear of the unknown that had me so terrified at the thought of my own death, of not being here with my family and friends. After all, I wanted to see how it all turns out; I did not want to miss any of the action, just like any great movie thriller. All of that changed when Jan passed away. It just became so clear to me what a wonderful time she is having on the other side, and she is still present and participating in her own way.

If you think about it, this bears a remarkable resemblance to what God is asking of us: to accept him without question and then be provided with the signs and the miracles afterward. Just like Liong, knowing from the moment he met Jan, that they would be together forever. It was that unquestioning faith in their bond that has allowed all these miracles to be witnessed and written for others to experience.

Accept God as your soul mate and let the wonders, both big and small, appear in your life. Look for them daily, even if only in the smallest details. I feel that if angels like Jan can do all these things for Liong and family then just imagine what God can do for us, if only we take the time to receive and accept him in our hearts. God, along with each and every one of us, is on this journey toward forever, and I have found that when you travel together, especially as soul mates, it will be a much more wondrous and enjoyable trip. Like Liong says, "It is not the trip that is important; it is who you are traveling with that matters."

CHAPTER 16

Liong's Journal

The complete journal of Liong's communication with Jan has been included for those of you who wish to follow this amazing story from the beginning. Because it was important to me to maintain the integrity of the journal as much as possible, only limited editing has been done to correct spelling, grammar, and punctuation to make it easier to read. A few passages have been omitted because there was no activity that day, the entry did not pertain to Jan, or the passage contained personal information regarding members of our families.

If you go through the journal looking at each incident individually, you may conclude that all these events are nothing more than one gigantic set of coincidences. As I have said before, if you step back and look at the entire body of work as a whole, it becomes increasingly difficult to dismiss all these events in such an arbitrary manner. This is especially true when you take into consideration that the manifestations evolved in both frequency and precision. In 2008, for example, there are only a handful of random entries, whereas by 2010, the journal entries are almost daily with signs now occurring within seconds of a request, favorite song, event, or some significant activity.

The best part of this story is that unlike other books dealing with the afterlife, I leave the conclusions to you, the reader. My job was simply to present some of the events that have taken place in the last three years for your consideration. It is now time for you to decide what you believe. It is also my belief that you are already smart enough not to need someone else to interpret the signs for you and that your heart is open enough to hear what is true. My greater desire is that this book will give you affirmation, or at the very least offer different avenues for you to look for confirmation that your departed loved one is near you; even if it is only through a seemingly insignificant occurrence, like the flash of a cell phone, a dead air phone call, or a familiar smell. By that I mean to say, never take any sign for granted, no matter how seemingly insignificant.

As much as we wish those who have passed could actually talk to us, we all know it cannot be. In the Preface, I told you that you must learn a new language of the spirit. Listen to your heart. First impressions are often accurate messages your loved one is sending you. Do not assume a random thought that comes into your head is just some weird coincidence; trust that it is your loved one letting you know they are there. If you think they are suggesting an idea to you, they probably are. Do not resist it. The more you accept on faith that your loved one is communicating with you, the longer, fuller, and more varying your messages will be.

Enjoy reading Liong's love letters to Jan, and may you too find continuing peace and happiness conversing with your loved one.

YEAR 2008

June 5 – 2008

Jan finished her journey on Earth; she went HOME first. Now I travel my journey on Earth without her. That one fateful day when we found each other; we looked deep into each other's eyes and saw love. Right then our souls embraced and became one forever. I knew then that I will never travel alone. Jan will always be by my side.

June 9 – 2008

Dreamed about Jan in bed looking like old days; chubby and rosy cheeks. When I asked where is the doctor? Who is going to give you the shot? She said, "What doctor?"

I said, "Well, you are not well, honey!"

"I am okay." – Jan.

"But . . ." – Liong.

"It never happened; forget about it, it never happened."

June 10 – 2008

Early morning; I was still half asleep, felt a warm glow next to my face. The image of Jan appeared vividly in my dreamlike state. Smiling, just like before, dressed in a lace gown; face glowing with an aura. I said, "Thank you honey." She shook her head with her contented smile then slowly faded away.

My legs have been hurting since her passing. Every morning the calves felt painful to walk on. This morning I got down from bed, I felt no pain in my legs at all.

June 11 – 2008

I went to Gold Coast. My cell phone showed two missed calls. I got out of the Gold Coast. I called Lisa to see if she did call. Lisa didn't. I called Susan, she didn't call. So I decided to go to the Orleans for lunch. Arriving at the 3rd floor parking garage, got down from the truck, my cell started buzzing. I looked at the display. To my surprise, the name Jan appeared with her cell number. I answered. Only heard a loud booming voice, but made no sense what it was. My first thought was that I must have lost Jan's cell and someone is using it. But I remembered well that her cell phone was on the table at home. I went home to find the phone on the table. I checked her phone; there was no record of a call being made. I listened to my message. It said the voice mail was received at 12:37 p.m.

Susan got home after work. I told her what happened. She didn't believe it. So I pressed my cell phone for the record of the call from Jan's cell. Susan saw it. It said call was made at 12:36 p.m. I called back at 12:37 p.m. How did it happen? I don't know. Maybe it's Jan's way of letting me know she is okay and happy.

June 14 – 2008

Susan and I drove to the Indio Wyndham Resort. I just wanted to get away. That night the room lights turned on and off by itself 3 times. I just said, "Jan I know you are here. Come sit down and watch TV with me." While leaving the room for dinner, Susan noticed the light in the kitchen turned on again. I guess Jan is playful with me like the old days.

June 27 – 2008

Susan came home. I was thinking about the song Jan and I had listened to years ago while going to Solvang. My mind has been quite forgetful after her passing. The air conditioner suddenly started fanning out warm air, not cool air. I got up to check it. It was putting out warm air. I had adjusted the thermostat to 76° F. It was working prior to this. Susan complained about the house being hot. The house temperature was at 82° F. I waited for an hour, still no cool air. So I decided to call an air conditioner repair service. Susan suggested a company; she said her company used their service. I called, went thru the whole procedure of listening to what the company does, what charges are depending on 1-hour, 2-hour and 4-hour windows. Then answering questions as to what is wrong with the air system. I told her a 2-hour window would be okay. After a few more questions, she put me on hold to contact their service guy for an appointment for tomorrow.

Just when I was holding, I told myself, the song is "I Will Miss You When You Go," by George Hamilton IV. It was the song that I told her years ago in the car that I hope this is one song we never have to play for each other. I started to look for the CD. At this point I felt the air turning cool. I got up and true enough the air has turned cool after almost one and a half hours of running without coolness. The air system has never done this since we serviced it couple of years ago. The girl came back on the phone. I cancelled the appointment. The air has been working till today.

June 29 – 2008

Susan had left last night to see her parents in Florida. I got up at 5:30 a.m., went to see Jan. I said maybe you want to be in the bedroom this morning. I took her urn and placed it on the bed dresser. I lit a tea candle for her. Jan loved tea candles. I went back to the kitchen. When I got back to the bedroom, the candle light has died. I lit it again. It died again the next time I went to the bedroom. I said, "Okay Jan, maybe you don't want to be in the bedroom. It is morning and you always were in the study doing your Happi Hearts." I put the urn back in the study. Without disturbing the tea candle, I lit it again, placed it where it had been all this time. The candle continued to burn until the candle was burned out.

Feeling very lonely and painful, I decided to go to the Suncoast Casino. Jan and I were given a comp room when it opened years ago. That night I ate at the Oyster Bar. Got very sick and we left for home before 1 am. I went to the registration, asked if I can get a room using my casino points for Coast Casino. The clerk checked with the host of Orleans and happily told me, yes, we can give you a comp room. You said you stayed here when we first opened. Let me checked your record. "Okay Mr. Tee, you are in luck, the room you stayed at is available. I will put you in the same room." After taking a shower, the time was past midnight, I started to feel sick. Maybe partly because of the thought that I left Jan alone at home, but I was really feeling sick, so without hesitation I gathered my things and headed down to registration to check out. Got home before 1 a.m. Told my Jan I am home and went to bed.

July 12 – 2008

Early this week, I told Susan and Lisa that I dreamt about Jan playing video poker and that she lost $500. On the morning of Thursday, her candle kept dying out several times after I lit it again and again. So I said, "Ok Jan I will take you to the Orleans for a walk." Well I played the video poker machines as if I was compelled to do so. By the time I left, I realized that I had lost $500, something that I never did when she was with me. I was always in control and never lost more than $250 before calling it quits. Was she telling me that she is fine and still likes to play video poker?

Again, this week I had told Lisa that I had a dream and I was holding up a baby. I didn't tell her that the baby had dark colored skin. Could it be that Jan was telling me that Kim's daughter is pregnant with a black baby? We'll wait to see if this is true!

July 15 – 2008

After going to the dentist at noon and getting a root-canal, came home, took a painkiller, Loritab, and got so sick; vomited badly twice. I cannot recall vomiting that way since childhood memory. About 9:30 p.m., while dozing off watching TV in Susan's room, a vision of a very dirty countertop in the kitchen came to me, and then I saw a bright light emitting from the wall in the living room from the place where I hang the picture of an angel sleeping among the flowers and birds. The frame and mat are now used for Jan's picture to be taken home next week.

Then I felt the left side of me brightening up with light. Not the left forward side which would be from the TV. The light disappeared shortly and I got up to talk to Susan who was working on the DVD. Before I turned into the living room, I had to rush to my bathroom. Did I vomit! I didn't think there would be anymore to vomit after the two previous times I vomited. I didn't eat anything. But so much dirty stuff came out.

After this, I felt so much better. Took a hot bath and Susan showed me her first draft of the DVD then I bid her goodnight and went to my bed. This morning I woke up, the bad feeling in my chest and stomach which I have felt every morning since Jan left me, had disappeared. I felt good; my left upper teeth which were hurting so much yesterday had subsided. I didn't tell the dentist about the upper tooth because I felt it was an infection. The dentist did say there is an infection on the one below which he found a large cavity, the root-canal inside. As of this writing, the pain on the upper teeth is now minimal. I couldn't eat on it yesterday.

Jan, whatever happened last night I know that you came to take care of me. You always insisted that I go to the dentist if my tooth ached. In fact, I was resisting going before I called the dental office until something compelled me to do so at the time. The receptionist Kathy told me if I can come over right away, the dentist will take care of me. I went over and the waiting room was full of patients. Jan, I know you did it for me. You cleansed my body of my aches and pains the way you did it on June 10 when you came to me in my dream to take away my pain in my legs.

I love you Jan, and I miss you so much. I will finish what you wished for me to do on earth. I know you will be waiting for me.

July 21 – 2008

I came home from the dentist at 12:30. There is a message from Sav-On to pick up a prescription drug. Went over to Sav-On. The nurse said there is no drug for Tee. I thought the dentist had called in the other day for my painkiller. The other nurse recognized me and said it must be for Jan. I looked at her and said, "Jan? Who called in?"

She looked at the bottle of cough medicine and said, "Doctor Davidson."

Well Jan hadn't seen her since January. What made her call in for Jan? Jan, are you kidding around with me?

Talked to Lisa about this – Lisa said remember every time she was going home, she always ordered some cough syrup to bring home to Dad and Mom. So, she did it again. But how did she make her doctor call in for the cough syrup? How did she send the prescription on the pharmacy's computer?

Rosie the cocktail waitress visited Jan at the rehab center 4 days before Jan passed away. Rosie met Lisa at the Mirage. She asked Lisa how Jan is doing, not knowing that Jan had passed away. Upon learning that, Rosie cried. Lisa comforted her by showing where Jan is now resting comfortably at home with Liong in her study room. Lisa showed her the picture of Jan's urn. Lisa had taken the picture off her cell phone. After parting with Rosie, Lisa heard her cell phone beep. When she looked at her cell phone, the picture of Jan's urn came on the cell phone again. Jan, are you telling Lisa that you were there when the picture was shown to Rosie?

July 22 – 2008

I have just finished binding the copies of Jan's star certification. Tamara, Lisa's friend, had registered to name a star after Jan in her memory. The song that I dedicated to Jan, "I will Miss You When You Go," has a lyric about Jan in the song that says, "I was born a silver star to shine brightly where you are . . . ." Coincidence? Tamara did this without knowing that I have always dreamed of Jan as a silver star in the sky.

I have kept the tea candle, Jan's favorite candle, lit every day.

Last week when Susan was finishing up the DVD, she was typing a quote on the "Sister" drawing, one of Jan's favorites, I told her that Jan is very particular about this drawing and the quote she chose for it. Susan said its okay; she had to finish the DVD. While she was typing a quote of her choosing, I was standing behind her, I turned my head and saw the tea candle light had died.

With that I told Susan, "I think Jan doesn't want another quote on her Happi Hearts." I went into the room and looked thru the Happi Hearts, found the Happi Heart with the sister drawing; gave the quote to Susan. I re-lit the candle. It burned the whole evening without dying again.

August 3 – 2008

These are events told to me while I was in South Dakota:

Dale mentioned one day he felt the presence of Jan at his house. He was alone and he definitely felt Jan was there with him.

Lyn said one night while she was still awake, she felt someone had blown air against her lips. There was no air movement in the room, but she was positive someone blew air on her lips, much like Jan would always do to play tricks on her.

Kathy, sister of Clarice, Neil's wife, told of a dream in which she saw Jan telling stories in front of some children in heaven.

August 4 – 2008

Last night while dozing off to sleep, I felt a motion liked someone had sat on the mattress. I thought maybe Susan had come into the room. I turned and no one was there.

I've had a nose bleed for the last two days, something that I very seldom had. Jan had some bad nose bleeds in the hospital her last week. I never had that in my life. The other day I had the same happen to me. Blood came out of my right nostril when I blew out the nostril. I had been having difficulty with my right nostril for a while. Was Jan trying to cleanse me of this problem?

I felt she was here again, because when Susan was preparing the DVD for her memorial service, she claimed that her program froze up three times at exactly the same photo when she was typing in the message where Aunt Jan gave Skylar her ring on her birthday, which is also the same day as Jan's. Susan never had mentioned about all the other gifts that were given to her other nieces, totaling 9 of them. So maybe Jan didn't want Skylar to be mentioned in particular. I told Susan to change the message. Last night she was working on the DVD and she did not tell me of any problems with her work. I have to find out whether she had changed her message.

Just called Susan, she said she did change the message and the program went on without a problem. The only thing is that a lot of the messages on the program had switched places on different photos; seems like Jan was playing tricks with Susan. Susan said this never happened to her in her computer work.

Sept 22 – 2008

Today Lisa told me that she had forgotten to tell me that her brother had told her a couple of weeks ago that Kaleen, the granddaughter of Lenora, is pregnant with a black baby from her black boyfriend. I went back to check in this little notebook, on July 12, I had told Lisa and Susan of my dream about holding a black baby. I guess Jan was really telling me about it back on 7/12. Jan, I know you are still with me and taking care of me and the people you loved. I miss you so much.

Sept 27 – 2008

Dreamt about Elinor early this morning; Elinor was very nice to Jan during her illness. I decided to give her a call. Did not get to talk to her. Hope everything is okay with her.

Oct 9 – 2008

Got home this morning. While talking to Jan, a thought came into mind that Jan wants to give her ankle bracelet to Lisa for Dakota, Lisa's new doggie, to wear. The ankle bracelet was all tangled up. I have tried very hard several times to untangle it but just can't do it. I got the bracelet, looked at it, and asked Jan if I will be able to untangle it this time. I sat down, looked at it, and said to myself, why don't you try it this way. I tried it, and it untangled easily. I told Jan, it is now ready for Dakota. I took it over for Lisa. Told Lisa what happened and we both knew Jan wanted it to happen.

Oct 14 – 2008

Dearest Jan,

It's been more than 4 months since you left. I miss you more than ever. At times I feel like sitting in this earthly prison waiting for my time to go and join you. I miss the laughter we shared every day. I miss seeing your angelic smile. If only you can come into my dreams, at least let me relive those moments with you. I know when you are around me, and I feel it when you were gone. Words cannot describe how it hurts when I am in the state of missing you, as I am at this moment of writing. I love you so much. Remember I used to tell you what Papa said about me? That I will die for the one I love. I would have died for you anytime. I also told you that I have lived a full life and that I could go without regrets. Now I have one regret that you left me here all alone. We will see each other again, that I am sure. Jan honey, it hurts so much. I miss you.

Oct 30 – 2008

I went to Anthem at around 1 p.m. to change the burned-out light bulb at Stephen's house. Knowing that it works on a light sensor, but not remembering that it was high up where I could not reach. Also, if I climbed up, stepping on the pipes to cover the light sensor, I won't be able to see the lights if they come on or not, to find out which one needed to be replaced. I hung the blanket over the sensor; jumped down and walked over to the corner to the garage. The lights were not on. While thinking that I may have to give up and come back at night, I turned and saw the lights come on. The left garage light was out. Then they all went out again. I walked to the side of the garage and saw the blanket lying on the ground. I backed up the truck, changed the light bulb then climbed up again to put the blanket over the sensor again to check if the replaced bulb was working. Well, the lights never came back again. I waited for a while to see if there was a time delay for the sensor. Nothing happened. Just then the cell phone rang and a (506) area code number came up. Three different 506 numbers have come up in the last two months. I went to Susan's office and asked her to dial the numbers. They said the numbers did not exist???

Honey Jan, did you make the lights come on so that I could know which bulb was out? Are the 506 numbers your way of letting me know you are with me? Oh, and I received a text message last month, saying, "Hey baby." The other one, the last couple of days when Lisa and I were on the way to Casper, Wyoming, read, "Sun to shine, thank God for Jesus," from Cynthia. I knew it cannot be from Cynthia, Susan's friend, because she doesn't believe in Jesus; she is a Jew. Too bad I had Lisa erase the text message because I would like to know who sent it. Jan???

Nov 4 – 2008

Called Danny tonight to congratulate him on his being elected to County Commissioner of Tripp County, S. Dakota. He said when it was announced that he had won the seat, his phone rang, no number, just one ring and nobody was there. He said he knew it was Jan's call to let him know how happy she was. Danny had kidded her about being his campaign manager. I can hear her saying to Danny, "Way to go!"

Nov 13 – 2008

Dearest Jan,

It's been 5 months and 8 days since you left this earthly world. Life has been increasingly aimless for me. I miss you so much. I would like to think that you are still with me. There are times that I am so sure that you are with me. I just wish that I can see you again, hold hands with you, laugh, joke . . . .

Since you left this world, things have changed so much. America has become a land of sadness. So much gloom and doom. Las Vegas is suffering. The Mirage is facing a real hard time. Workers are in fear of layoffs. Work hours have been cut. Lisa made the right choice when she switched to graveyard as a good gesture towards Hilda. Her hours have been cut but only 10%, compared to swing of 30%. All the stores that carried your Happi Hearts have closed. In a way, I am glad that you are not here to witness these downturns. You would have been so sad. I just wish that you can tell me that you are happy and feeling great. All I ever wanted to do is to see you happy and healthy. I love you so ever more.

Dec 6 – 2008

Lisa and Susan gave me a Xmas gift – a ticket to John Edward at the Flamingo. I was both anxious and nervous to go. The night before, I was asking Jan to be there to talk to me. I guess there are so many people in the showroom, not everyone can have the opportunity to be communicated thru John Edward. But the readings by John Edward and the questions by the audience did give me a lot of comfort. Based on the quick pace of readings by John Edward, and seeing the expressions of the people being contacted on the video screen, I cannot help but be more convinced now that when a person crosses over, he or she is rid of physical pain and they exist as an energy form. I guess honey Jan, you have been in touch with me in so many ways and occasions that you again did not want to take away the chance of other people who so desired to find out about their loved ones. It's just you, Jan, the ever loving and considerate person that you were.

The most important thing that I picked up from this occasion:

1. That you, Jan, are still with us on some occasions, like when we are together going out (Lisa, Susan and Jean) or eating together. Jan, you should know that we know because we always gave you your share of food, right?

2. That you communicate with us most readily through energy sources such as electricity or battery powered gadgets. This explains your presence by buzzing my cell phone, turning the lights on and off at the Indio Resort. Putting the light out on the candle. Sending me text messages twice, turning the air conditioner on and off on 6/27, and sending a doctor's order for cough syrup with codeine to the Pharmacy's computer, etc.

3. That senses like smell, light etc. indicate your presence. I could tell that you were at the show with me because I could smell the smell of bananas halfway thru the show.

4. Most people who came thru John Edward today were trying to convey love and care to someone (wife, daughter, Mother, . . .) that they thought they were lacking in life. I guess you never have to do that with me because we both know how much we loved each other.

5. I am more relaxed now, more convinced that you, Jan, are now happy and without pain. As John Edward said, don't look at someone's passing as losing a battle to cancer. Think of it as her winning the battle over the disease that overcame the physical part of her soul, because now she is well and living in another form.

6. I am now more convinced that we will see each other again when my time comes to pass over to your side. I love you; I miss you, and wait for me. I am going to see you, and we will be "together forever."

Dec 7 – 2008

I have to write this down early in the morning before I forget. Last night I took my usual half a pill of Tylenol P.M. to sleep. Jan took half a pill for a long time. It was 12:00 midnight. My mind just wouldn't rest, thinking mainly about Jan; about what was said and asked in the John Edward show. Next thing I know, looking up at the clock, it was already 2:15 a.m. So I decided to take another half of the P.M. pill. I turned on the dresser light, cut a pill in half, put back the scissors and turned off the light. I reached on the left side of the dresser where the water bottle is; the cell phone was next to the water bottle. I was leaning up a bit to grab the water when the cell phone in front of the water bottle lit up with only half of the crescent moon shaped green lights. Then the light went off. I knew I wasn't seeing things because any light in the dark appears to be very noticeable, and it was color green, not red.

I thought that it might be because there is a message from Lisa or Susan. I checked and there were none. I told myself there was no way the light could have come on. Even if the charger was on, it should be two of them, not just one. So I plugged in the charger, the two red lights came on and stayed on for a while charging, then turned green. Two of them, not just one, and at that time, I smelled the smell of bananas again. I knew then it was Jan letting me know she had pulled one on me again. I love you Jan.

I put on Jan's favorite Xmas songs by Johnny Mathis for her. I went into the room to watch football. When I came out, the music had stopped. I was surprised because it wasn't that long that I was in the room. I looked at the player; the disc had stopped at no. 6, which never happened before. I looked at no. 6 then at no. 5. The last song that was played was, "I'll Be Home for Xmas." Somehow Jan had stopped the player after no. 5. I remember what she told me days before she passed at the hospital when I showed her the Silent Night Happi Heart, one of her favorites. I started singing "Silent Night" and Jan sang with me. Then she said to me, "I'll be there this Xmas." Jan, maybe you are reaffirming your promise to be here on Xmas. I love you Jan.

Jan also used to tell me to stop the music when she wanted some quiet. So maybe tonight she wanted some quiet also; so what better way to send me a message than that? I guess like John Edward said, you come through as an energy source, with anything that uses energy. Keep coming to me with your messages, Jan, it makes life more bearable.

Dec 9 – 2008 (Tuesday)

After the cell phone's green lights coming on Saturday and the CD player stopped after no. 5, "I'll be Home for Xmas" on Sunday, I had a dream early Monday morning that we were going to get married, and Jan cannot be found. John, Lucy and I went to a house; a strange one and I saw Jan dressed in a white lace gown. I almost always see her in a white gown, looking like the first year that I met her. She waved at me. I rushed up some stairways to her, when I got to the balcony where I saw her, I couldn't find her. Instead there were some children there. I asked them where Jan went. They just giggled, and one girl said she now has magical powers; she can be anywhere she wants to be. I then saw John and I asked somebody else, I can't remember seeing anybody I was asking, "Did she go to see Danny?"

"Could be," was the answer I got.

I said, "Jan, I am going to find you, otherwise, what am I going to tell Yong-Yong?" I woke up. I told Lisa briefly of the dream.

Monday night around ten o'clock I was already in bed. I don't know why the thought of looking up the book mentioned by a lady at the John Edward show made me get up and turn on the computer. I logged on to Amazon.com. I didn't like the book review of Sarah Young's, "Many Lives" after reading the reader's comments. Instead, something kept me looking and I finally settled on Michael Newton's book, "Journey of Souls." I decided not to order it on Amazon.com. This morning I made it a "must" to go to Borders Bookstore. I wasn't able to locate the book. Just when I was going to give up, a girl walked up who worked there and I asked her help. She led me to the book right away. I bought two books; the second book is, "Destiny of Souls."

I started reading Journey of Souls. Interesting but did not stir much emotion in me. 10:30 p.m., I decided to open Destiny of Souls; I only got to page 44 of Journey. After reading up to page 22, I said to myself, "Jan, did you make me look up this book?" Many things written in these 22 pages explained a lot of things that had happened to me since Jan left on June 5.

Jan, I now know you were really with me many times, and as I am writing this moment, I can smell the banana smell. I know you are watching me right now. Well, I am going to turn my head to the left side of the bed where you slept before and tell you, "I miss you and love you more than ever, and I now am sure we will see each other again."

Dec 10 – 2008

As I was reading in bed and watching the Lakers play the Suns at 9 p.m., right now I smell banana again, Jan is here with me. A surging thought rolled into my mind. I remember shortly after meeting Jan, I told her that many years ago when I was still in the Philippines, must be in the late 70's or early 80's, I had dreamt about being in a faraway place and I saw a chubby girl dressed in black. I walked towards her and she looked at me and smiled. I told Jan that she looked just like that girl. Chubby, same smile; a smile that I haven't seen on any other human being I've set eyes on. I told her it must be destiny that we meet.

Tonight while reading, these things just rolled into my mind as if telling me, "Liong, yes, we have seen each other long ago. It was me that you saw."

I guess all these years we were so happy that that incident escaped our memories. Tonight, Jan, you are validating that incident. It may have been a dream at the time, but it was real in the sense that we have known each other long before this lifetime. I came back to America and I settled in Los Angeles. Miraculously created a situation where I was able to travel frequently to Las Vegas to meet you. You needed me at the time to lift you up and I was able to do so. You became the person you really were supposed to be – happy, caring, positive, and giving. Then when I needed you, we became one. You gave me back much more than I ever did for you. You gave me 18 years of happiness. You created heaven on earth for me. Whatever purpose there is for me staying behind, I know you will let me know time after time. Love you and miss you.

I know you are with me when I think about you, when I shut my eyes and you appear in my mind dressed in a white lace gown. Smiling, glowing in a pleasant aura. It was only after Lisa and I came back from South Dakota the last time that you started appearing in my mind with that glowing aura. You appeared in different faces at times. Sometimes you looked like when I first met you, sometimes the chubby cute face of the in between years and a few times as a younger version in your college years. There was only one time you appeared in a different outfit, something like the uniform you were wearing while working at Pizza Hut (from the photo you had taken at Pizza Hut. Well whatever face you appeared to me, it was still you Jan, the cute loving face I can never forget.

Jan (on left) in her Pizza Hut uniform

Dec 19 – 2008

When I went to the Court Interpreter Workshop in July 2008, I was told that there would be an exam given in Jan 2009. I was, therefore, naïve in thinking that I would receive a notice of exam date for January. Something told me to call the administrator the other day. However, it was always her recorded message for any caller to leave a message. On 12/18 evening, I was going thru the folder of the workshop, I just told Susan to go to the webpage of the Nevada Supreme Court to find out if there is an exam date. She printed out everything and told me she couldn't find any notification of the court interpreter exam. I thought well maybe I should just call again, but I was compelled to read what Susan had printed for me. It said there will be a workshop in January, a 3-day, and at the end of the workshop there will be an exam! I said to myself, yes, Jan is telling me to look it up. Moreover, it said the deadline for registration is 12/19, today.

Again, if I did not look at it, I could have missed it as the exam is held only once a year! And if John and Lucy were not leaving early morning of 12/19, I would not have bothered to take care of it. A message from Jan? I went to the courthouse this morning and was fortunate to see Andrea, the administrator. She said she just came back today from Carson City; snowed in by the biggest snowfall since 1979. She had to take a plane from Carson City to San Jose then Las Vegas. As it turns out, I would not have been able to see Andrea the last few days because she was in Carson City, and she was nice enough to allow me to register to be in the workshop. Another Jan arrangement?

Coming home from the courthouse, I met with Lisa. She asked me if I had telephoned Kristine in July. I said I couldn't have telephoned her because I do not even know her last name to find her number from Jan's phone book. I had wanted to give her the Akita notebook Jan had made for her years ago and didn't even follow up on it. Lisa said Kristine wants to know because Jan's phone number appeared on her cell last July. I know I did not call her. If this is so, then Jan must have done it, just like her number appearing on my cell phone last June.

Jan, I really believe now that you are with me; not all the time, but when I yearn for you, you always appear right away in my mind. These days you are usually enveloped by an aura. You look so warm and happy, just like before; a smile only God could create.

Dec 24 – 2008

Dearest Jan, I know you are home. I have been smelling the usual banana smell since yesterday. It was particularly strong last night.

I left the computer on the picture of you looking at me with so much love and joy. I tried to turn off the computer many, many times and it wouldn't turn off. I left it there for half an hour. I tried to turn it off again and still wouldn't turn off after many tries. I know you are home. You won't let it turn off until I am sure you are home. Honey, I miss you so deeply. It still hurts very much when I miss you.

Lisa, Susan and I had a Christmas meal at 3:00 p.m. Jan, of course, had her share of good food with us. We decided to turn off the power at 4:15 p.m. I left and came home at 6:30 p.m. Susan turned on the computer, this time the computer behaved like usual. No more not turning off on the photo of Jan & I.

Lisa called Susan and me shortly after she went home at 4:00 after the Xmas meal. She said she turned on her computer, and the same thing happened to her computer; the computer wouldn't turn off. Jan was with her also.

Dec 25 – 2008 (Christmas Day)

I woke up this Christmas morning with my Jan on my mind. Last thing I remembered of my dream last night was 5 aces appearing on a slot machine.

I turned on the computer and it was functioning properly. I turned it off and it did without any problem. What happened yesterday on my computer and Lisa's computer only tells us that my Jan kept her promise – she was here with us for Christmas.

Dec 30 – 2008

12:14 a.m. about 10 to 15 minutes ago, I came into my bedroom. My cell phone was, as usual, on my dresser to my right. The room was dark. I pressed the TV remote control to turn on the TV. Before the TV lit up, I was reaching for my cell phone to check if there were any messages. The green lights on cell phone, both crescent lights, lit up briefly then shut off. The cell phone was not being charged. I checked the phone for messages and there were none. I asked Susan when the green lights should come on. She thought that when there was a call to the phone, the green lights would come on. I told Susan to call my phone from her cell. The red lights came on, not the green. I know if I plug in the charger, the red lights come on during charging. When it is fully charged the green lights will come on until the charger is unplugged, then the green lights would go off. Is Jan letting me know that she is home? If so, the only things that happened today related to her are:

1. Last night during our traditional year-end dinner (Lisa, Susan, and Jean), Lisa and Susan were talking about making a "Jan's Sugar Cookies" cookbook. They were wondering where Jan kept her sugar cookie recipes. Tonight as I walked into the study room, after Susan came home, she had turned on the computer and left it on; the display on the computer screen was a sugar cookie recipe made by Jan. I told Susan about it. I thought Jan might have been reminding me of the cookbook idea, or that she thinks it is a good idea, or a message to Susan that the sugar cookie recipes can be found in the computer.

2. I received a card, a Xmas card made by Jan last Xmas, from John. It was a very touching card in that John wrote to thank me for giving Jan 18 years of happiness and that he misses Jan so very much. He thanked me for taking care of Lisa and Susan. I didn't tell John about Jan asking me to stay behind after she passed to take care of Lisa and Susan. She told me that roughly before she had to stay at Lisa's place because she could no longer climb the stairs; maybe two months before she passed away.

Is Jan telling me to acknowledge John? Does she want me to let John know that she knows she is missed very much? I will write John tomorrow.

Dec 31 – 2008

9:30 a.m. after Susan left for work this morning around 8:15, I sat down and started to think what I should write John in reply to his letter. A good 10-15 minutes passed and I still didn't write one word. A thought came into my mind; maybe I don't have to write John because I don't know what to write. After many more minutes of procrastination, I finally wrote a full page letter. I got up and then I noticed the candle which I have lit for Jan every morning had died out – 1st time since last July. I guess Jan was not too happy that I was thinking of not writing. I took another new candle and lit it. Then I told myself, try and light the one that died out. I got it out of the waste basket. Lit it and it has been 40 minutes and it is still burning. I got your message, honey.

YEAR 2009

Jan 22 – 2009

Last Sunday 1/18, the candle that I lit in the early morning died out. The last time it died was 12/31. I misread the sign as being wrong with my betting the Cardinals would beat the Eagles. I went to the Orleans and changed my bet to the Eagles. Well, the Eagles got beat by the Cardinals. I was thinking, my Jan was wrong this time. The candle has been burning out prematurely for at least five more times since that day of 1/18. I have been asking Jan repeatedly since 1/18 why she has not given me anymore signs that she is here with me. This early morning, my right foot hurt so intensely that I woke up. It hurt badly when I tried to bend my right foot and toes. I tried to do my push-ups and it was difficult because my right foot could hardly support the push-ups.

This afternoon, a notion suddenly came into my mind, "You silly, Jan has been trying to tell you she is here since 1/18. She has been giving me the signs by the candles burning out prematurely, like the first few months. I have been so sad missing her that I did not notice that those were the signs she gave me. Well, the foot hurting acted like a switch. I went to Jan and told her that I now realize that she is now here all this time since 1/18. After that my right foot stopped hurting. It was her right leg that went away from her in her last days.

Tonight as I was taking a shower, another thought entered my mind, "You silly, Jan is here because 1/28 is the birthday of Susan and 1/26 is Chinese New Year; an important day for Jan and I in past years. Also, John and Lucy are coming to Vegas around 2/3; all the reasons that Jan wants to be with me here.

This afternoon as Susan and I were walking towards Lisa's house, Lisa came around the corner with Dakota. Lisa said Dakota was running in circles so fast today, in the living room. The morning when John and Lucy left for the airport on their last visit, Dakota went on a running rampage in the yard outside of Lisa's house. He was running so fast that John and I couldn't catch him. I thought that it was Jan playing with Dakota. Today when Lisa told me that Dakota was running like crazy (Lisa didn't see Dakota run the last time because she was at work), I just looked at Susan and said, "See, Jan was here this last week."

Tonight I told Susan that one of the reasons Jan is here is because of her birthday. Susan was visibly moved by that notion.

Feb 12 – 2009

John & Lucy came to Vegas on 2/3. I brought Jan to Lisa's house so she can be with John and Lucy.

John and Lucy left early this morning at 3:15. Yesterday morning I told Jan that I will be bringing her home tonight. After saying that, my cell phone's green lights flashed briefly in front of my eyes. I guess Jan is happy to be home. I recall a month or so before Jan left, she had asked me if we should sell off the condo and buy a downstairs unit since she cannot climb the stairs anymore. My reply to her was, "Honey, this is our home." She looked at me and said, "Yes honey, this is our home." Yes, this is our happy nest. In this home, our souls became one; one home. She is happy to be home.

Feb 13 – 2009

While I was watching Glenn Beck on Fox News, he was talking about the wife whose husband perished in the 9/11 attack in New York. She was able to speak to him till the last moment when an explosion ended the conversation. She said, "Sometimes pain is a way of love." Yes, to feel pain is a proof of love. I never knew I loved Jan so much until she passed on. The pain that I felt and still feel is indescribable. It hurts so deeply. But again, it is how bad it hurts that makes me realize how deeply I love her, and how much I miss her.

Jan, my love, I now know why you told me many times months before you left, that we are so lucky to have found each other. Yes, honey, me from the Philippines, to Taiwan, to Wisconsin, then back to the Philippines, and back to Los Angeles; the fates had it that I got very lucky in business to afford me to come to Vegas countless of times to find you when you needed me most. You, from a small town in South Dakota, to Wyoming, then to Las Vegas, and the destined meeting of our eyes at the Golden Nugget.

Jan I have to tell you, the time when we went outside the side door at the Golden Nugget when we kissed; I can still feel the feeling now. It seemed that time had stood still. I felt like I was floating, swirling in space, so peaceful. I don't even know how long we were locked in an embrace and kissed. I only know I had never felt that way and I can still feel the feeling now every time I think about it. Jan, we found each other. You best wait for me and be there to meet me when I come to look for you. I told you in one of my letters that I will find you no matter where you may be, and I will.

Feb 15 – 2009

While at the Silverton Casino, I noticed a voice mail at approx. 3 p.m. It was Stephen's message saying he was returning my call to him at 2:30 p.m. I was very sure that I did not call him at 2:30 since I was having lunch with Lisa and Susan at Johnny Rocket's at 1 p.m. Then I proceeded to play video poker. I checked my phone to see if I had called him and not remembered. There was only one call when I called him to tell him about my car license numbers for registering with Anthem. I talked to him. So there can be no mix-up of any sort. I didn't call and there was no record of a call on my cell.

At about 3:30 p.m., I had an urge to take out my cell phone from my jacket. As I held my cell phone, the green lights flashed in front of me, but only the upper half light. Thinking about it afterwards, I guess Jan must be telling me it was she who left the phone number on Stephen's cell phone. The green light was to let me know that she was there with me and that she did it.

I later told Susan that every time I feel her presence so close and strong that I feel like my energy had been extracted from me. I always feel so tired. Maybe her energy was so dense that it sapped my lesser energy towards her, sort of like the black hole theory. Jan, I know you were there with me. Love you.

Feb 17 – 2009

Stephen called me yesterday morning before they left Las Vegas. I told him I had tried several times to call him yesterday and that I did not call him at 2:30 p.m. yesterday. He said his cell phone had shown that I called at 2:30 p.m. He also said that his cell phone was not working properly all afternoon soon after that.

"Strange." he said.

Well, Lisa then told me that yesterday when she called John and Lucy. John said to Lucy, "It's Liong, let me answer the phone." His caller ID showed my number.

Lucy then asked Lisa, "Why are you using Liong's phone?"

Lisa said, "I am using my own, Liong is not even here . . ???"

I guess my Jan was having fun that day with everybody: Stephen, John, us . . .

"Way to go, baby!" as Jan always said. Love you, baby.

March 1 – 2009

Yesterday Susan put in a DVD she ordered on Netflix. She had told me about it that it was about the souls. Robin Williams starred in the movie. As we watched, I felt Jan's presence; the smell of bananas was so strong in the first half of the movie. It described what the soul experiences when the person passes away, like trying to communicate with his loved ones. The second half was about the soul of his wife being lost and suffering in the gateway to hell. It was a very sad state of existence. All throughout the second half, I didn't once feel Jan's presence. I asked Susan what prompted her to order this movie. For the last few weeks, I have been talking to Jan about going to see her when Lisa should find someone good to love and take care of her, and when Susan will be on her own. I guess Jan didn't agree with my notion of ending my life to be with her, and she was doing this to send me her message.

As I repeatedly told her, if it is choosing between living without her and dying to be with her, I would choose to be with her without a second thought. Jan, know it that I love you and miss you every day. Sometimes it hurts so deeply that you are not with me physically. I know you are with me in spirit every time I'm missing you badly. I love you Jan.

Did you ever miss your soul mate so badly that you felt going to see her is better than being without her?

March 12 – 2009

Yesterday 3/11 Susan called at approx. 3 p.m. telling me that she has an early out from the office. As Lisa had agreed to go with us to the 24 HR Fitness after Susan got off work, I called Lisa right away to see if she wanted to go earlier. Lisa said yes. So I told Susan to come home and we will go together. We got to the gym at around 3:40. I left my cell phone at home.

I have been feeling weak the whole day; kind of without energy. This happens every time I feel Jan's presence strongly. Especially when I can shut my eyes and she would immediately appear in my mind; then she would come so close as to give me a kiss. I remember yesterday she appeared to me looking the way she was when she went to Hawaii. She was probably at her heaviest.

I remember that because I had meant to tell Lisa about her look yesterday. I usually tell Lisa how Jan looks, like that day when I saw her upon shutting my eyes.

When we came home after having something to eat at El Pollo Loco, I checked my cell phone and it said I have a missed call. The number was 510-4816, while Lisa's is 610-4816. It was made at 3:28 p.m. I took a picture of my cell phone showing the call. Lisa never made the call. The strange thing is the number 510, not 610.

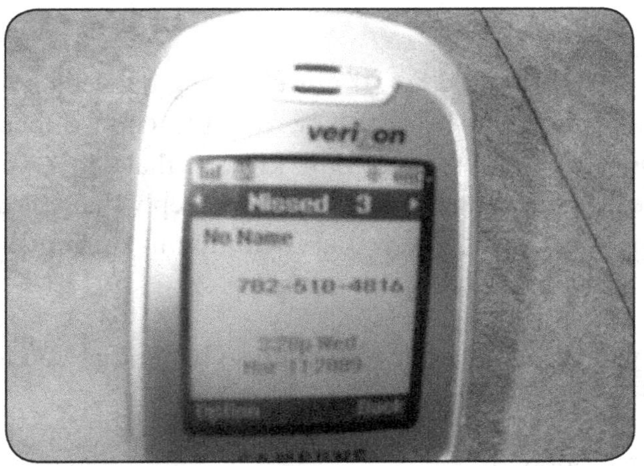

Three calls from a number almost identical to Lisa's

I guess my dear Jan just wanted to let me know, "Yes, I was with you and I kissed you." She used 510 because it would be different than Lisa's number. Just the way she sent her text message to my cell while Lisa and I were driving to Casper, Wyoming. The text read, "Sun to shine, thank God for Jesus – Cynthia." The only Cynthia I know would never have sent that message. Cynthia is Jewish and she doesn't acknowledge Jesus. So, my Jan did the same thing again. This happened 10/30/08 – I checked my notes.

It is 5:00 p.m., Susan just came home. While we were talking about the 510 number on my cell phone, she said this noon while at The Orleans; her cell phone rang with the tune of my cell. She has a different ring for Lisa and me. She thought it was me calling her, but it turned out to be Lisa calling. She can't figure out why it was the tune indicating it was me calling. Jan, you did it again today?

Know it when your soul mate is with you.

March 27 – 2009

It has been a while since I had the feeling that you want me to get rid of your diaries that you kept since knowing me. My feeling was that you want our lives to be kept private in our memories and no one should know about it. The other day I started cutting up the diaries. This morning at 7:53 a.m., as I was reaching for my cell phone, the two green lights flashed once in front of my eyes. I took it as your acknowledgement and approval for my cutting up the diaries. I finished cutting up the diaries this morning. Now it will forever belong to us in our hearts and minds.

I received a call from Lusing at 1 p.m. informing me that Chai had called Seng that Mama is not doing well. If Mama has to go honey, take care of her. You know how much Mama loves you. She did not know that you had left early and will be waiting to see her. Take care of her honey. I know you will.

April 6 – 2009

Honey Jan, it's been 10 months since you left. I miss you more than ever. Things have been happening the way I thought it to be. Sometimes ideas just pop into my mind, and I know it was your wish. I followed every idea that came into my mind. It seems you have a hand in all the good things that had happened to your loved ones. I try to take good care of them as you asked me to. Today I smell it so strongly. When I saw the bouquet of pink roses and small pink carnations, I just had to get it for you. At this writing, the smell I have been used to is coming on so strong. Honey, I know you are with me right now. I love you.

April 21 – 2009

When I went to South Dakota with Lisa last October 2008, John, Lucy, Lisa and I went to Allen Monument in Colome to inquire about a headstone for Jan and I. After getting quotes and brochure, I came back to Las Vegas, eventually coming up with a drawing for the headstone on 11/2008. I sent the drawing to the sales agent in Colome, and asked for a confirmation on the order. He emailed me and said he would get back to me. He said his wife was having surgery. Days went by and I never heard back from him. So I decided to just put the matter to rest and will ask Lisa to go to Allen Monument in Ainsworth, Nebraska to personally place the order when she goes back for the Forgey Family Reunion in July. Two weeks ago I sat down and started thinking about redesigning the headstone to order. But after sitting down and going thru the brochure, nothing concrete came into my mind. Then the notion came in, why waste time redesigning. The one that I had was what Jan wanted. So I told Jan, all right, the original design will be it. I placed the drawing at the home I created for Jan.

Yesterday afternoon, John called and informed me that he had gone to Ainsworth with Lucy to order their headstone. They had talked to the owner, Mr. Allen himself, and that the design I wanted would cost more than what Jerry had quoted me. Maybe that is why he never contacted me. John asked me if I still wanted the headstone. I said of course, whatever it cost, this would be our traceable love for each other in this lifetime. I called Tony Allen, no answer. At about 5 p.m., I received a call from Nebraska. At first I disregarded the call. The same call came again in an hour and I decided to answer it. It was Tony Allen, the owner. We discussed the matter and I am going to send the drawing to him. He will send me a confirmation and this matter will be settled.

Again, the timely manner that all these important matters in my life got done after June 5, 2008 convinces me that my Jan is taking care of things the way she wants it. I just have to be patient and she will send me the message.

Just when I think Jan has not sent me a message or sign for some time, at 6:25 p.m. when I went into Susan's room to pick up my cell phone, the two green lights blinked once just like the other times. I am thinking what made her show her presence today:

1. Lisa cooked my favorite chicken noodle soup and was home for dinner.

2. I have been going through all her photographs boxes to sort out an album of Jan for my keeping.

3. Susan's offer for the new house was submitted to the bank.

4. I have been worried about something that was on my mind for quite a while. The thought of going to the internet for answers came up this afternoon. I found the answer to my worry. I guess Jan wanted me to not worry so she directed me to look for the answer on the internet. I love you Jan.

I guess I missed out on the most important reason why Jan is here and seems to be happy. I have settled the issue of our headstone yesterday with the owner of the monument company in Ainsworth, Nebraska. Yes Jan, we will be, "Two Happi Hearts Together Forever."

May 14 – 2009

I came back to Las Vegas from the Philippines on 5/12. On the morning of 5/12, when I went in to see Mama before leaving, Mama looked at me, and to the surprise of Lusing, who was in the room, Mama said to me, "You are leaving today. You are alone now, take care of yourself. Call me when you get home, but call me when there is no one around. I will go to see you . . . ."

Mama has lost her hearing for many years. Nobody told her (how?) that I was leaving. Nobody told her about Jan's passing last June. Did she really know that Jan had passed by using the word "now?" How did she know that I was leaving that day? She did not acknowledge Seng or Lusing the days when we were all there. The maid taking care of her even said she was speaking in English some time the second day I was there. The only person she would speak to in English was Jan???

When I was in Honolulu on May 6, I truly felt Jan's presence with me. When I shut my eyes, she would appear to me looking like the way she looked in 2002, when she took Lucy to Honolulu as Employee of the Month at the Mirage. She was at her heaviest at the time, so that should explain how she appeared to me. My brothers do not believe in my communication with Jan. They think it is just me missing her. I guess if I believe in Jan, that is enough for me, for I truly miss her so much – day and night.

June 6, 2009

One year ago, God extended his hands to Jan. "Come home now, my angel." Jan took his hand and she had no more pain or suffering.

Jan had told her brother Danny before her passing, to not grieve for her, for her life was full now. Thank you, Jan, for feeling that way; because my life was also full after 18 years of being with you.

The pain of losing you, the hurt when I miss you, are as deep today as it was one year ago, and I know the pain and hurt will continue for the rest of my conscious life on earth. My only consolation and joy is that you have been showing me signs that you are still with me and watching over me. Please do not stop doing so because it is what keeps me going on with life. When the time comes, I know you will be there waiting for me. The other day, Monday, June 1st when Susan was wheeled into the surgery room, I sat down in the lobby. I shut my eyes and saw you at my left side right away. This time you were surrounded by a fog like mist, and I saw wings behind you. I asked you what are they, and you just smiled. Yes, my Jan is an angel, and because she is an angel, I know she will be waiting for me. I love you Jan.

July 13 – 2009

Stephen called me yesterday as he and family are coming to Vegas this week. He told me that he dreamed about being here at the condo and seeing Jan fixing breakfast. Then Jan talked to him about the Strip and that she doesn't need to go with them since he knows Vegas very well now. She also said to him, "I am no longer working." Stephen said the dream was so vivid. I told him Jan was always appreciative of his help since she was first diagnosed with the tumor back in 2002 or 2003. Jan is a person who appreciated every little love and care given to her.

After the phone call, I told Jan, "You must be home now from your Forgey Reunion." I took her urn to my bedroom last night to be with me. At 12:58 as I got up to go to the bathroom, something made me glance at the cell phone next to me. I always place the cell phone on the dresser to the right side of me. The two green lights on the cell phone blinked once. I said, "Thank you Jan, you are home." This happened on 2/15 when Stephen was here in Vegas. The last time the green lights blinked was 4/21. Thank you Jan for letting me know you are with me.

August 22 – 2009

I stood in the backyard of the new house thinking about Jan. How happy she would have been here in this house that she had chosen. Just two days ago Lisa commented about having to tell the hummingbirds that used to visit Jan outside of the condo's windows that Jan had changed addresses. Just when I entered the house and was closing the screen door, out of nowhere, a hummingbird appeared in front of my eyesight outside the screen door. The little bird just stayed there for maybe 5-10 seconds staring at me, then flew away. We have been here for almost two weeks and never saw a hummingbird. Was it Jan's wish? Did she send the little bird here?

Sept 1 – 2009

Sometime last week, I woke up with the thought that when I will be reuniting with my Jan, that I want to be cremated. However, Jan and I want our ashes to be scattered on places where Jan spent her growing up years, on and around the ranch in Colome. Our urns will be buried in the plot next to John and Lucy, so that we will be free to roam around together on the land that she loved so much. I did not write this down, but the thought just keeps coming to me regularly. I guess I should write it down and sometime later relay our wishes to Susan and Lisa. There, my dearest Jan, I wrote it down, and I will tell Susan and Lisa about it, or I will leave our wish on paper for them. Miss you so much.

Sept 4 – 2009 (around 10 a.m.)

This morning while standing in front of front door watching Jim painting the house, I suddenly noticed the string from the venetian blind on the front door started swinging. There is no air duct in the doorway. The fan in the living room was not even on. There was no air movement whatsoever; but the string just kept swinging back and forth. I finally gave up on trying to figure why the string can swing. I shut my eyes and asked aloud, "Jan, are you here?" The vision of Jan came into my mind right away. Her arm appeared to be causing the string to swing.

Sept 28 – 2009

The headstone was finished as of today. I received a Polaroid picture from Tony Allen; the headstone was laid down in the Colome cemetery.

Jan and Liong's headstone

October 12 – 2009

At 5:03 p.m., while I sat down in front of the computer, the cell phone was on my right side of the desk. For some reason I turned my head to look at the phone, and I saw the two green lights on the cell phone blink. Jan, you haven't done this for some time. You are here tonight. I love you. I came into the bedroom to light incense. I love you Jan, thank you for doing this again. But honey I am changing cell phones, but I will keep the old one with me, and I will keep it charged. Maybe you will now do something with my new cell phone? We shall be going home to Colome this weekend to see our headstone. I know you are thrilled and happy that we will be going home to see John and Lucy. Danny, Lyn, Skylar, Dawn and baby Elise will be there also.

October 14 – 2009

This afternoon at about 2:00, I came home after having lunch with Barbara, while sitting next to Lisa in the computer room Lisa got up and walked out. The familiar smell of bananas came to me so strongly. I told Lisa about Jan being home right now. Lisa left for Wal-Mart. I was feeling sick to my stomach, so I had the heating pad on my stomach and I lied down on the couch watching TV. I laid the two cell phones next to me. Three times when I looked down at the old cell phone, a blinking light occurred where the two lights are; not green, not red, but a bright yellowish light. It blinked brightly and shortly. Jan, you are home. You did it twice yesterday, now you did it three times. Love you. We are going home to see John and Lucy. Right after the last blink, John called me for his Saturday college football bets.

6:35 p.m., right after I wrote the last page, while walking out of the bedroom, I looked at the two cell phones on the right side of the bed dresser, the two green lights on the old cell phone blinked right in front of my eyes. Oh, Jan my love, you are still as playful as before. I love you so dearly.

October 17 – 2009 (Saturday)

9:37 p.m. at Steve's home in Casper, WY, can't sleep. Got up, turned on the light; looked at Jan's urn. Decided to turn off the light and try to sleep. After turning off the light, the cell phone's green lights blinked twice in the dark so brightly. It's Jan telling me that she is here with me on this trip. I had laid the cell phone on the night table of Steve's bedroom before going to bed in the hope of seeing Jan's message. Jan didn't disappoint me; she connected!

I lit a candle in front of her urn. 10:44 p.m., turned off the light, stared at the cell phone for maybe 5 seconds, the green lights blinked again! My dearest Jan, I love you!!

10:47 p.m. turned off the light. Stared at the cell phone and, yes, in maybe 5 seconds, the green lights blinked again. Honey Jan, you are the best!!

At 10:51, I kissed my Jan's urn. Asked my Jan if I should go to sleep now, or is she going to show me again. She did, the green lights blinked again.

10:54 the green lights blinked again. Honey, are you going to keep me up all night?

October 18 – 2009 (Sunday)

Arrived in Colome. Visited the cemetery. The headstone looks beautiful. The thought of losing Jan brought tears into my eyes for a while. Behind the tears, there was also a sense of happiness, that my Jan is free from all earthly problems, and that she is just as happy and playful like before based on what she showed me last night.

Tonight I sat alone in the living room; everyone else has gone to bed. I had the cell phone to the left of me on the couch. I asked Jan to show me a sign that she is home with me. At 8:20 p.m. the green lights on the cell phone blinked once. Jan, I love you. You are home with everybody.

October 19 – 2009 (Monday)

5:11 (7:11 a.m. Colome time), the cell phone blinked as if to tell me she is ready for the day – a day of fun with her family.

6:40 (8:40 Colome) – Cell phone blinked.

7:50 (9:50 p.m. Colome time) – Asked her to give me a sign, shut my eyes; saw her watching John and Lisa playing cribbage. She turned and said, “I am busy.” As soon as Lisa and John finished, I said, “Honey, they are finished playing.” No sooner than a few minutes, the green lights blinked twice in succession.

October 20 – 2009 (Tuesday)

This morning while standing in front of the refrigerator talking to Lucy, I felt somebody touching my arm from behind. Nobody was there.

I was driving John’s pickup following John’s tractor this morning. A thought popped into my mind that Jan wants me to get Lucy a new washing machine. Her old one conked out. After getting home, I called Lisa and asked how much it is going to cost to repair the old washer. Lisa said that she and Susan had just decided to chip in half of the cost of a new washer half an hour ago; just about the time the thought from Jan came to me. So I told Lisa about Jan's wish, and I put up the balance of the washer as a gift to John and Lucy.

12:20 p.m. (2:20 Colome time) – The washing machine was being delivered. I placed my cell phone on top of Jan's urn on the cabinet. I said, "Jan, they are delivering your washing machine for Lucy. Are you happy?" In about 1 minute, the green lights blinked twice in succession. Jan acknowledged me, she is happy!

4:00 p.m. (6 p.m. Colome) – Told Jan we were all going to Winner for Chinese buffet. The cell phone blinked as if saying, "Yes!"

October 21 – 2009 (Wednesday)

7:40 a.m. (9:40 a.m. Colome) – Asked Jan if she is going to have some fun today – cell phone blinked – yes!

1:50 p.m. (3:50 p.m. Colome). Feeling so lonely, missing my Jan. Alone in my room, the cell phone blinked in my hand. Jan, thank you.

Trip to Rosebud Casino: Went to Rosebud with friends of John and Lucy, 4 couples. We arrived at Rosebud Casino around 5:30 p.m. I went to the Bingo Hall and took out the cell phone. Told Jan that this is the place where we last had hot dogs, the green lights started blinking every 5 seconds or less. I showed it to Lisa, Susan, John, Lucy and Connie. Jan must be happy and excited for the blinking didn't stop until we left the casino. The Verizon wireless service had been disconnected by 10/19.

When I first arrived at Rosebud Casino, while walking through the main casino with Susan, I heard a voice calling "Liong." I turned and nobody was around. A few seconds later I saw Lucy walking away around 15 ft. away. I walked over and asked Lucy if she had called me, Lucy said no. Well, did I hear Jan? Because after that is when I went to the Bingo Hall and the green lights started blinking.

October 22 – 2009 (Thursday)

I was hoping to see the cell phone blink the whole day. It didn't. At any rate, I rested the whole day and it was uneventful. I had nothing in mind that I wanted to talk to her about. Tonight Lisa and Lyn were preparing dinner; Lisa unconsciously threw away a bowl of mushrooms cut by Lyn. They were all laughing and Lisa said she didn't even know that she had dumped it into the garbage. I was watching TV in the living room. Well, I shut my eyes and Jan appeared. She was laughing like her usual happy self and told me that she made Lisa do it.

Later after dinner, Susan, Lisa, and Lucy were playing cards in the dining room. I was watching football, Florida State at UNC, I told Jan that I wished she could blink me, although I said that I knew she was watching them play cards. I then told her that maybe I am now getting spoiled by her in expecting a response every time I ask her. Within minutes, the cell phone blinked once. It made me felt so warm inside; that was around 7:10 p.m. At around 12 midnight, everybody else had gone to bed except Susan. We sat in the living room talking about all these happenings. I told Susan that I had asked Jan if it is okay for Susan to put together all these happenings in a book; that it may bring comfort to many people who have lost loved ones and wish to be able to experience what I have experienced. We then talked about cancer. I voiced my opinion about what cancer is. At that moment, the green lights blinked. I asked Susan if she saw it. She looked at the phone, after which it blinked another three times in succession. We talked some more before saying good night at 12:15.

After talking to Susan, I went to bed and turned off the light. The fragrant smell came strongly before I went to sleep.

October 23 – 2009 (Friday)

9:50 a.m. will be taking Jan to the ranch to revisit the little cabin where she spent her childhood days; the smell of fragrance came to me so strong and has been with me for at least 5 minutes. I am alone at the house waiting for Susan and Lisa.

We went to Jan's beloved Colome High School across the street to watch Donkey Basketball, a fundraiser for the school. I took out the cell phone a couple of times at the game. I suppose Jan was having a good time watching all her folks and friends, no response.

I came home early and sat down with John watching TV. Approx. 8:40 p.m., the cell phone blinked. I told John that Jan is now home, the game must be ending. I raised the cell phone so that it faced John, the phone blinked five times and John seemed to have tears in his eyes. I thank Jan for showing her Dad the comfort he needs. Jan loved her Dad immensely. Her words when diagnosed with the cancer in 2003 were, "Daddy will be so sad, I don't want to die!"

October 24 – 2009 (Saturday)

Day to leave Colome and head back home to Las Vegas. At 7:00 a.m., I heard Dakota barking. While still lazily lying in bed; the room was dark; I saw the green lights blink. The cell phone was on night table next to bed and it kept on blinking at least six times. I said, "Ok Jan, I am getting up. I know it's time to get up." The blinking stopped. This is just like the old days when we traveled or came home.

7:20 a.m. I came out to the dining room. Lisa and John were playing cribbage just like the old days when Jan came home. She and John would always play cribbage before going home. I told them that Jan woke me up. I came back into the bedroom; the green lights started blinking again. It went on for at least six or seven times. I said, "Jan, I think you must be either excited to go home or you are getting sentimental. Maybe in time I can get to know what you want to tell me."

Arrived in Casper around 5:00 p.m. I went into Steve's house and forgot to bring Jan in; I simply forgot, don't know why. Got into the room, put down the cell phone, and it blinked four times. I was excited to be talking to everybody. Yet, this time, the cell phone stopped blinking in front of other people. It was only after we got back from dinner when Susan said, "You are bringing Jan into the house, aren't you?" that I realized my mistake. I took Jan into the room, lit the candle, told her I was sorry for leaving her in the car and don't be angry. The cell phone blinked and blinked. I asked Neil to come in the room. It blinked in front of Neil. I think she was happy again.

October 25 – 2009

On way back to Las Vegas, while driving thru Wyoming, Lisa said she had to pee, couldn't wait any longer. When she came back to the car, we were all laughing and Lisa told Toni that the last time they were coming back to Las Vegas, Jan did the same thing by the car. I held up the cell phone and the green lights blinked. I guess Jan was laughing with us.

11:43 – Settled Jan down in our bedroom, told Jan that I loved her and thanked her for a fun trip home. I lay the cell phone next to my pillow, the green light blinked to acknowledge me. I love you Jan and goodnight.

October 26 – 2009

Home. At 5:58 a.m., lying lazily in bed. Said the usual thing, "Good morning my baby." I turned on the TV and the green lights blinked. "Yes, baby, I know it's time to get up!"

October 29 – 2009

I must have caught a bad cold the last few days; feeling very low every day. I guess part of it was missing you badly. The last time I saw your presence on the cell phone was Monday 10/26, day after we came back from South Dakota. I know I am getting too spoiled by the idea that you can come to me readily thru the phone. My baby angel must have a lot of things to do over there in spreading happiness. I, however, did smell the fragrance this morning at 8:25 a.m. while in the computer room. I know I should start doing something or this loneliness is going to devour me. I love you honey. Give me the strength to go on without you beside me.

At 11:30 my cell phone blinked. Also at 12:09 it blinked again. I guess my Jan knew that I was feeling low and needed to hear from her.

November 3 – 2009

In another two days, Jan will have been away from me for 17 months. I decided to have a new notebook to record our connections. This morning's email from Melissa, Jan's niece in Casper, was both comforting and heart-warming. To know that Jan has visited little Vincent and played with him. To know that a two year old boy would not know how to make up a story; and also that Vincent never intellectually was able to know Jan when Jan held him in her arms in October 2007, opened the door to a whole new way of looking at departure from life, from his/her earthly physical body. I now firmly believe that my Jan is happy, playful, loving as she was on earth, and that we will eventually be together again. She has not left the family she loved, and she has not left me.

Read email from Melissa. Lifted the spirits of everybody in the family who knew about this. Jan was in Casper October 2007; Vincent was only a baby in her arms. Jan loved to see Vincent's photo on the internet, up to the moment of her passing. She called Vincent her little "Viking." Jan's favorite football team in life was the Minnesota Vikings. Vincent is only beginning to talk recently. How amazing. How heartwarming. My Jan is making the rounds to everybody she loved.

This photo was sent to me on August 21st, 2008 when Vincent was 1 yr. old. He is now 2 yrs. and 2 months old. The back of the photo says, "To great Uncle Liong, Go Vikings."

Attached are Emails:

1. I sent photos of the Headstone at Colome cemetery to family members on 11/1.

2. Melissa returned an email to me on 11/3 regarding little Vincent and Jan.

3. Teneil email to me on 11/3 regarding Melissa's email. Amazing? Miraculous? Comforting? Believable? – Yes!!!

4. Picture of me and headstone in Colome.

Emails from Liong Tee to Steve & Shirley on 11/l, Melissa to Liong Tee on 11/3, and Teneil to Liong Tee on 11/3 said it all!

p.s. Is this the baby, Vincent, that I dreamed about some time ago; that Jan was telling me she was playing with baby Vincent?

November 4 – 2009

Yesterday was filled with comfort and happiness because of what Melissa said about little Vincent's reaction to seeing the photo of our headstone in Colome.

Last night before I slept, I told Jan I now know that she goes around visiting her loved ones, and that I cannot be too selfish to expect her here all the time. I did ask her to let me know when she is home with me. I turned off the light. I have set the old cell phone next to me where I can see it every night. After saying goodnight to Jan, in probably less than 30 seconds, the green lights blinked in the pitch darkness. I went to sleep feeling very happy.

In the early morning hours, (I was supposed to wake Susan up at 5:30 a.m., she has a doctor's apt today), at approx. 5:00 a.m., the new cell phone, which was lying on my left side dresser, made a buzzing, vibrating on wood sound. It was short, but it also happened the night or early morning before. I checked the phone. It was not set on vibrating. Is Jan having fun with me on a new toy? I don't know. But from the blinking on the old cell phone, I knew that she was here.

This morning as I was in the computer room, about 8:20 a.m., the fragrance came on so strong that I decided to sit down and write this down for today.

Took Susan to Summerlin Hospital at 11:00 a.m. Coming home, Lisa was preparing lunch. She had a text message from Toni, Jan's cousin who drove us to South Dakota on the last trip. Toni said that last night she was alone with her grandfather, who is sick; she heard Jan's voice calling her name, then the usual "giggle." Toni was working at Spring Valley Hospital when Jan had her first surgery in 2003. It was then that Toni met Jan after losing touch with the Forgey family for a long time.

November 5 – 2009 (Thursday)

Last night at about 6:10 p.m., Jan gave me a thought that she wanted to use our old white comforter for winter. I changed the pink one her grandma quilted to this one for her. At 7:50, I glanced at the cell phone and the green lights blinked at me as if Jan was saying, "Thanks."

November 6 – 2009 (Friday)

Yesterday was a very happy day. Lisa got a call from City Center to go over for employment processing. I know it was what Lisa had been looking forward to. All these past months she had been keeping a happy posture about not getting the call but Susan and I knew deep inside she was very disappointed. She had given up any hope of going to City Center as she was just given a new position to train to be a Scheduler. Imagine the thrill when the call came. What was more interesting was when she found out that it was Brian who asked for her. Brian was the person in charge at the Mirage. He was promoted to be in charge at the City Center. Brian loved Jan immensely. He was at the Hospital visiting Jan twice with his daughter.

Last night I told Jan I suspect she must have influenced Brain to call for Lisa. I told her that Lisa was very happy. At 12:40, with the cell phone next to my right side, I awakened, don't know why, and within a few seconds, saw the flashing of the lights from the cell phone in the pitch darkness!

This morning at 6:45 a.m., with Dakota under the comforter, I held the cell phone in my hand towards Jan's photo. I said, "Jan, as you always wished, all is well with the Forgeys, and I love you." The cell phone blinked right after that. My Jan, I love you.

Nov 7 – 2009 (Saturday)

The whole day I was feeling sick; maybe because of the frozen pasta I ate the night before. Feeling sick made me miss Jan even more. I couldn't seem to connect with her the whole day. At 5:03 p.m. I came into my room, looked at the cell phone on my dresser, and asked Jan if she is home. The green lights blinked within 5 seconds. That made me feel a lot better. I had a good night's sleep. Feel a lot better today.

Nov 9 – 2009 (Monday)

Can't seem to see Jan when I shut my eyes. The whole day I seemed unable to feel her presence.

Received a voice mail from my brother, Chai, that Mama was rushed to the hospital with pneumonia. I asked Jan to please take care of Mama. Maybe she was there because I can't seem to get in touch with her. At around 8 p.m., I received an email from Sherwin saying that Mama's pneumonia seemed to have gone away. At 2:03 a.m., Yong-Yong called to inform me that Mama had passed away at around 9:00 p.m. Vegas time. I immediately went to search for a ticket to go home to Manila. At around 4:20 a.m., I walked into my room, the cell phone's green lights flashed. Must be Jan coming home.

Lisa received a text message from Toni that she saw Jan last night, early this morning, at around 1 a.m. Jan must have been in Lake Havasu to see her before coming home.

Nov 12 – 2009 (Thursday / Manila)

Took my cell phone with me. Couldn't contact Jan since I last got a phone call from sister Yong-Yong about Mama's passing on 11/10 in Manila. Rushed back to Manila on the first available flight via Asiana Airline. All along the journey I glanced at the cell phone periodically without any message from Jan.

Arrived in Manila at 12:15 p.m. While waiting in line at Immigration, I had the urge to take the cell phone from my pocket; the green lights blinked immediately. It kept blinking and I finally timed the intervals of blinking at approximately 5 seconds apart. Yong-Yong and family took me to lunch. Finally arrived at the mortuary, Arlington Memorial Crematory, at 3:30 p.m. I checked my cell phone; it was still blinking at the same pace, much like the time at South Dakota at Rosebud Casino. Shut my eyes; saw Jan, same appearance as when Mama was with us in Las Vegas in 1999 or 1998? Mama was with her, so was Papa. They were all smiling at me. As much as I was sadden by Mama's passing, I am comforted by their union and they all seemed happy together.

It is now 7:00 p.m. I am home at Yong-Yong's to take a shower; the phone hasn't stopped blinking since 12:15 p.m.

Nov 13 – 2009 (Friday)

The cell phone kept on blinking the whole night. I knew it because I placed it beside my bed. I got up two times in the night and saw it blinking brightly. I then placed it on the pillow right next to my eye. I could sense it blinking until I fell asleep. When I got up at 7 a.m. this morning, it was still blinking and kept on until I got back to the mortuary. The only time it stopped was when I went over to the SM Shopping Mall to buy a pair of white shoes for Sunday's funeral. I took out the phone and it had stopped blinking. However, when I got back to the mortuary, right in front of Mama, it started blinking again. It is now 4 p.m. and it is still blinking. I told Jan that her energy level must be at a high because the green light was brilliant.

The blinking stopped at 10:20 p.m. when I came home to Yong-Yong's house to take a shower and rest for the night.

Nov 14 – 2009 (Saturday)

The cell did not stop blinking the whole time. I decided last night to let it keep blinking and see what will happen when the battery is depleted. I got up at around 2 a.m.; the cell was still blinking regularly at approx. 5 second intervals. I checked the battery indicator; it only had one bar left; so I left it and went to sleep. At 6:00 I woke up. The cell was still blinking. I opened up to look at the battery indicator. I couldn't believe my eyes; it showed two bars. I rubbed my eyes a couple of times to make sure I was seeing two bars, instead of one. It was two bars – how can this happen? Without me charging the battery, the battery charged up by itself? By that time, I turned over and looked at the cell phone; I noticed the lights were not green anymore, but rather an intense bright white-yellowish light with a slight tint of green. The blinking intervals seemed to vary also. At times it would blink twice in succession, then in three second intervals. It would stop for 5 to 10 minutes, and then blink again in 4 second intervals, then 5 seconds. I don't know what those messages are, but like Susan said, "Why ask why? Have faith that it is Jan's communicating."

Nov 17 – 2009 (Tuesday)

Mama was cremated on Sunday 11/15 at 1 p.m. I was the one designated by the family to bring the urn to the Buddhist temple for Mama to be eternally with Papa. This marks the end of a most important chapter of my life. I have lost Papa, Jan, and now Mama. Right now I am on a plane going back to Los Angeles. I feel very tired. The cell phone stopped blinking while I was in the waiting area waiting to board the plane from Manila to Seoul. Although I have seen Jan with Mama and Papa during the wake at the Arlington Memorial, the sense of physical loss of Mama is still overwhelming. I saw Jan looking the way she was with Mama when Mama was living with us in Las Vegas. Mama appeared the way she was when she was with me in Los Angeles in the late 80's and Papa also. A new chapter is opening up for me and I do not have any idea how it will be written. Maybe Jan will be writing the script for me.

Nov 18 – 2009 (Wednesday)

Jet lag is not an easy thing to shake. Tired, but still missed Jan a lot. The loss of Mama, although long expected, is still very heavy to bear.

Now 19 – 2009 (Thursday)

Last night before retiring, told Jan that I missed her and loved her, and asked her if she had come home to be with me. At 11:11 p.m., shortly after I asked her aloud, she blinked the green lights.

Still unable to sleep, I asked her if she is with Mama now, and if she has now met Papa. Shortly after that, she blinked me at 11:44 p.m.

Nov 27 – 2009 (Friday after Thanksgiving)

Yesterday was Thanksgiving. Knowing how much Jan loved her parents, I know she must be home in Colome with them. Dale and the kids, Danny, Lyn, etc. are going to be at home. So I didn't expect Jan to be here with us; though the hope of seeing something from her was so strong. I guess I must be getting spoiled by her, thinking that she will respond to my wishes all the time. Feeling very sad today. Lie down to watch football.

Sometime around 10 a.m., my right leg began hurting for no reason. I didn't do any physical work lately. The thought that Jan must be with me made me go into the bedroom. I have always tried to maintain a lit candle all the time for Jan. Entering the room I noticed the candle had split into unusual shapes; a bigger heart shape had been formed with a bright color forming the heart and at the back side, two little hearts were formed. The inside of these three hearts was black in color. I called for Lisa and Susan to come quick and see it. They came into the room, looked at it, and rushed out to grab their cameras. Some pictures were taken. It was quite a sight. Attached is my drawing of the configuration of the hearts. After that, I came back into the bedroom and told Jan, "Thank you for the message of love to me, Lisa and Susan." Suddenly the three hearts burst into a bright glow and were gone after the glow. I took a picture of the candle after that burst, which shows the candle now burning normally with the wick in the center of the flame.

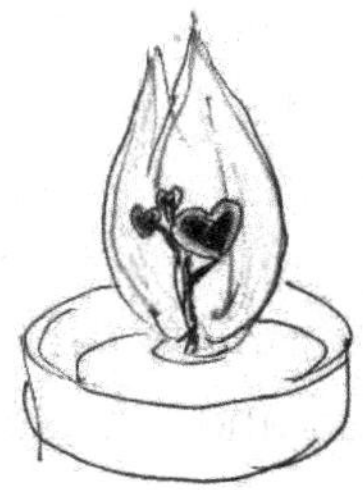

Liong's sketch of the three-heart burning candle

I told myself, you have been lining up the cell phone in my line of vision while watching TV every night for the last so many nights hoping the catch the green lights blinking. It didn't blink since 11/19. Tonight I said to myself, Jan will blink me. She is home with my right leg hurting for a while, then the candle hearts. I again lined up the cell phone on the pillow in my line of vision while watching TV. Well, at 12:24 a.m., the top half crescent of the green lights blinked. Then the lower half blinked at 12:49 a.m. – Saturday 11/28.

Jan, you are just like before, always trying something new and fresh. I remember the time you started making your original Happi Hearts. Every morning I would be awakened by your punching of card stock into hearts and other shapes. We had many laughs about that all through the years as your Happi Hearts became more and more beautiful and were loved by so many.

Nov 30 – 2009 (Monday past midnight)

12:11 a.m., before going to bed, I told Jan that Lisa is leaving this morning for Colome, and that I won't mind her going home with her to see John and Lucy, & Danny, Lyn, Skylar et al. She blinked the phone after 10 to 15 minutes of my talking to her. I watched TV for another 40 to 60 minutes then signed off to sleep.

Drove Lisa to the airport at 9:30 a.m.

Dec 6 – 2009 (Sunday)

8:45 a.m., while watching the video, "Who Was Jesus," on NBC news on the computer, the smell of bananas hit me so strongly. The video was incomplete. I wasn't able to watch the whole story. The smell persisted quite long. I am still smelling it right now at 9:20 a.m. Honey Jan, you are home! You must have had a nice visit with Lisa in Colome. I saw the photo of our headstone decorated with snowmen and Christmas. Lyn and Lisa did the décor. You must have had a good time with them. Happy for you. Welcome home, honey.

Dec 7 – 2009 (Monday)

Picked up Lisa from the airport at 3:25 p.m.; it was raining hard.

Had a bad nosebleed this morning. While watching the movie, "Beowulf" after midnight, the cell phone blinked at 12:01 a.m. and 12:49 a.m. Honey Jan, you are home with me.

Lisa showed me some photos of the Xmas décor on our headstone in Colome. The arrangement of the candy canes looked like one of Jan's Xmas Happi Hearts; will look it up to see.

Dec 12 – 2009

Saturday early morning at 12:36 a.m., while I was watching, "Trouble at Little Tokyo," you blinked the cell phone to let me know you had come to see me. Honey, thank you for giving me the comfort and warmth and that you took time to visit me. Love you always.

Dec 15 – 2009 (Tuesday early morning)

At 1:15 a.m. after I went to the bathroom and came back to bed, before I shut my eyes, the green lights on the cell phone blinked so brightly in front of me. I had asked Susan to print copies of the photo where Lisa and Lyn had decorated our headstone in Colome with candy canes, a wreath, and little figurine. I placed the copies in front of Jan before going to bed at 11:45. I guess Jan is happy and was acknowledging me. Love you Honey!

Dec 23 – 2009

Only two more days will be Christmas. I miss you Jan, so much. Remembering the old days when you would be busy making decorated candles, Happi Hearts and gift baskets . . . all the happiness that you spread around to everybody. I was so blessed to have you in my life in this lifetime, and I want to be with you forever after this lifetime.

The fragrance comes regularly at times when I am in the casino playing slots, or watching TV, or just thinking about you. The cell phone green lights blink at times when I do not know what to do with my life. As I told you before, and you always agreed with me, that when you don't know what to do, don't do anything. So I shall rest my mind and wait for you to guide me along. Susan is a happy person now. So different from the girl you coined as "quirky" before. You told me before you left that Susan is a good girl. I think you are right. She turned out to be a very simple, kind hearted and warm person. Lisa is happily adjusting to her new job at the Aria; happy with her Dakota. The Forgeys are fine. Merry Xmas to you, Honey, I miss you so much.

Dec 24 – 2009 (Xmas Eve)

Honey Jan, you promised before you left us, that you would be home last Xmas, and you did show us signs that you were here with us.

Tonight I asked that you spoil me by coming home again, and you did. While I was watching the Hawaii Bowl football game between SMU and Nevada, I held the phone in my hand and it blinked the green lights at 7:42 p.m. Thank you – you made me felt so peaceful.

Dec 25 – 2009

2:40 p.m., while watching NBA game between the Lakers and Cavaliers, the banana fragrance came on so strong while I was in the computer room. I came in to write it down. All the time I was writing in our bedroom, the fragrance stayed strong. It's been 10 minutes and the smell is still so strong. I should tell Lisa and Susan that Jan is visiting with us.

The first quarter of the Lakers/Cavs game is over; it is 3:50 p.m. and the fragrance is still hanging in the air in the bedroom.

4:26 p.m., the green lights on the cell blinked. I know Jan is here to have Xmas dinner with Lisa, Susan, Jean and I, just like last year!

Dec 27 – 2009

10 a.m. I was feeling very low yesterday. Last night I felt sick, no energy whatsoever. Took a dose of Theraflu and went to bed early. This morning while sitting in the computer room, the fragrance came strongly. I know you are here to take care of me. Honey Jan, I love you dearly. I will be okay, honey.

While watching Chris Wallace on Fox News at 11:50 p.m., the green lights on the cell phone flashed.

Dec 28 – 2009

While watching the Monday Night Football with Susan, it was the Minnesota Vikings vs. Chicago Bears. The Vikings had been Jan's lifelong favorite team but was the team that had every one, including family and friends tease her about. The Vikings never won a Super Bowl but she was just loyal to the team. Of course, it later became the symbol or joke whenever she said, "You know, they are the Vikings!" It was in OT; Chicago Bears were about to kick a field goal at the 25 yard line. I suddenly smelled the banana fragrance so strongly. I asked Susan, "Did you smell anything?" Susan looked at me and said, "No, why?" I said the smell was so strong. It is still hanging around. Susan laughed, "Jan is here watching the game!" Well, the Bears missed the field goal. But they did win the game after A. Petersen fumbled later. I guess Jan would say, "You know, they are the Vikings!"

Dec 29 – 2009 (Tuesday)

Today is the 49th day after Mama passed away last Nov 10. In the Chinese culture, we celebrate her passing over and settling down in the other world. I had been feeling a little unsettled the whole morning.

The last words from Mama when I was last with her the previous trip before she passed was, "I will go to see you." She repeated it twice. Lusing, my sister was present. Lusing cried.

I tried not to write this incident that occurred a couple of weeks ago, but today, I just have the strong urge to let go of a couple of things in the notebook.

First, a couple of weeks ago, after I shut off the TV set and was ready to go to sleep, I heard the clear sound of something falling. A popping sound followed by the sound of an object falling and hitting something. I thought I had knocked over something on the dresser, over my head, when I reached up to pull a pillow from under my head to place down at my feet inside my blanket; a ritual. I ran my hand over the spaces around me and didn't touch anything. I disregarded it and went to sleep. The room was dark as I had turned off the battery operated candles by Jan and her tea candle lights had been blown out. I had placed a tea candle light in a glass holder on top of the plastic casing that made up Papa and Mama's altar earlier, and had lit a candle. That candle had burned out long before I went to bed.

The next morning while I was lighting the candle for Jan and turning on the little night light for Jan, while getting the incense from next to Papa and Mama, I suddenly noticed some splintered glass on the cabinet. I looked and the glass tea candle holder had actually split in half with the burned out tea candle base still sitting in the half broken holder. The other half had fallen off the plastic casing of Papa and Mama. The splintered glass was on the cabinet and on the floor. I had used that glass candle holder for Jan since Jan passed. I had taken it from the condo to the house. I just couldn't explain how it could split up in half when the candle wasn't even burning? I told Susan and Lisa about it. Was it Mama, or Mama and Jan, or Papa, or Mama and Jan that caused it to split?

The second thing I had to write was when Jan was transferred from the Rehab Center back to Summerlin Hospital for her pericardiocentesis; drawing off her fluid buildup inside her upper body. While being taken by the ambulance that was there to pick her up, Jan told Lisa, "No more."

While waiting in the ER at Summerlin Hospital, Jan repeatedly told me, "Don't let me suffer, don't let me suffer." I looked at her and promised her I wouldn't. On June 4th, Jan was not communicating. I had instructed the Doctor to give her morphine, a pain killer, continuously. She was having a hard time breathing. On the morning of June 5th, Jan's blood pressure started dropping slowly but steadily. I had told her the night before, upon seeing her breathing difficulty, that it was, "Okay for her to go now and be without pain. Be at peace, everything will be taken care of." Jan's breathing became increasingly difficult as the morning went on. Her blood pressure kept going down.

Everybody, Lucy and the others went down to the cafeteria. Lisa was sitting by herself in the lobby. John was dozing off in the chair next to Jan. Jan opened her eyes. I shouted to John, "Quick, John, Jan wants to see you!" I reached for her eyeglasses because I knew Jan couldn't see far without her glasses. I put on her eye glasses. I dialed Lisa to come quick. With her eyeglasses on, Jan looked at me and at John, and tears started coming down from the side of her eyes. I wiped off the tears. Jan tried to talk, but her throat was bubbling with fluid. Tears came down again. Jan shut her eyes.

Lisa came running in. At this time, Jan opened her eyes again, looked at Lisa, John, and me. Tears came down again, and then she shut her eyes and left us to be with God. In the 18 years that we shared, the only times that I saw Jan shedding tears were times when she was happy or touched by kindness. I had never seen her cry because of pain or sadness.

Right after writing the above, I dressed up and was prepared to go have a haircut. Then a thought came in my mind, I went over to take Jan's urn in my arm. I kissed the urn, went over to the CD player and as usual tried to play the CD Susan made with all of Jan's favorite songs. Especially Louis Armstrong's "Wonderful World," the song Jan was listening to when I called her the first time. That CD was in holder #1. I have played it so many times for her. Well, the CD player would not play. I tried it four or five times. Checked the CD if it is in #1. It was, but still wouldn't play. I was still holding the urn. I said, "Jan, are you doing this?" I started the player again, this time it started playing. The only thing is that while the display said it was on disc #1, the song that came out was that of disc #2, The Browns – "The Three Bells!" I said, "Ok Jan, I am putting you back." I placed Jan's urn back in her place. Went back and played the CD again. This time, it showed #1, and was playing "Wonderful World." Cannot explain why, but like Susan said, "Why ask why?" It was Jan.

Dec 30 – 2009

Put a bet on Nebraska football against Arizona for John. Nebraska won handily. I asked Jan if she is happy that John is happy. Jan blinked the green lights at 11:55 p.m.

Dec 31 – 2009 (Thursday)

Last day of 2009 I woke up, lit the candle, turned on the lamp light and asked Jan if she would be here to see me before the New Years. At 9:42 a.m., after I made the bed, the cell phone's green lights lit up. Jan is with me.

YEAR 2010

Jan 2 – Saturday (2010)

Before going to sleep, I told Jan that I went to watch the "Elvis" show at Aria, the newest Casino in Vegas. While there, I saw Elinor, a dealer friend of Jan's at Mirage. Talked to Elinor. Within a minute of me telling Jan about Elinor (Elinor visited Jan several times before her passing), the green lights flashed. I went to sleep feeling happy. It was 11:46 when the lights flashed.

Jan 3 – Early after Midnight

Went to the bathroom, came back into the dark bedroom. Looked at the cell phone. I told Jan I might be getting too spoiled by hoping that she comes to me every time I want to see the green lights flash. But it does give me a lot of comfort every time I see the green lights blink at me. I asked her if it takes a lot of energy for her to do that, find other ways to show me her presence. The green lights flashed in the darkness. It was 12:14 after midnight.

At 8:30, while sitting in front of the computer reading the newspaper, the fragrance of banana came on strong. I went out to Arizona Charlie's; the fragrance came on again while I was driving. I just love you so much Jan and I miss you very, very much.

Jan 3 – Sunday 10:40 p.m.

I was missing Jan so badly, in the dim candle light, I took the urn from her place, cuddled it, kissed it repeatedly and told her how much I missed holding her. I drifted into memories, after maybe 15 minutes; I saw the green lights flash on the phone.

Jan 5 – Tuesday (Early morning after midnight)

I had taken the urn and cuddled it while watching TV. After a while, (I always tell Jan how much I love and miss her), I put the urn back in the cabinet and the green lights flashed at 12:20 a.m.

Today her niece, Kelsey, is coming thru Las Vegas on her way to California to study. The last time Kelsey came here was years ago and Jan was always fond of her nieces and nephews. I gave her a room at Arizona Charlie's. After turning off the TV, as I turned sideways towards the edge of the bed, I felt the bed move as if someone just got into the bed. This is the second time I have felt this motion in this bedroom. I turned to see if I could see or feel anything. Just like the last time, I saw nothing and felt nothing. But it was comforting to think that maybe Jan had found a way to let me know that she is with me.

Jan 6 – Wednesday 11:30 a.m.

Wanted to play, "Wonderful World" for Jan. Turned on the CD player just like countless of times. The disc showed #1. Again, the song that came on was from disc #2, "The Three Bells" by The Browns. This happened on 12/29, I checked the journal. I remember "The Three Bells" was Jan's friend, Sherry Sheema's all-time favorite. We even cut a CD of The Browns for her. Sheema talked to Jan almost every day for years during Jan's fight with cancer. Maybe Jan was and is telling me that she is with Sherry. Jan and Sherry worked together at the Mirage Casino; Sherry was her supervisor. They were liked very much by many clients who frequented the Mirage. They called themselves the "Jan and Sherry Show." Their table would always have the most tips among all the table games.

Sherry passed away before Jan after suffering a stroke. Jan was grief stricken by Sherry's passing. Although in much pain, Jan asked me to bring her to the hospital to see Sherry for the last time. Sherry was in a coma and never woke up. We were in the hospital room at the same time the pastor came for Sherry's last sacrament. Thereafter they pulled her life support. Honey Jan, I am glad you are reunited with Sherry again. Both of you must be having fun just like the old days. Happy for you!

Jan 6 – Wednesday

Green lights flashed at 11:35 p.m. Nothing important. Jan just want me to know that she is here.

Jan 7 – Thursday

I took the urn and cuddled it while watching TV. 10 minutes after I placed it back, the green lights flashed at 10:45 p.m.

I jokingly asked Jan if it would be too much for me to ask her to flash me one more time; Jan did it again at 11:05 p.m. I said, "Jan, will you do it again?" She flashed me again at 11:25 p.m. While switching channels, I came across a channel showing the place of the Nativity in Israel. The narrator was in Israel showing the sites where Jesus was born. I said, "Jan, you are an angel. I suppose you have been to these places. I am so lucky to have found you and share 18 years of my life with you. Thank you for making my life full." The time it was about 11:40 and Jan flashed me again at 11:47 p.m. I said, "Thank you, Jan. Goodnight."

Jan 11 – Monday early morning (after midnight)

Have been feeling low for a few days with pain in my left shoulder; the sprain suffered on the last trip to Manila in Nov '09. Hope to hear from Jan. At 12:48 and 1:08 a.m., Jan flashed me on the cell phone.

Woke up this morning feeling much better. Thank you Jan honey.

Jan 13 – past midnight – 12:08 a.m.

I cuddled Jan at 11:30 p.m. Told Jan that I finally felt strong enough to discard her old tax returns and I also went through some of her few remaining files on her family. Jan acknowledged me by flashing the green lights at 12:08 a.m. Jan flashed me a 12:28 a.m., and again at 12:48 a.m. At 1:15 a.m. I bid her goodnight and turned off the TV.

Jan 14 – Thursday early morning

Cuddled Jan at 12:05 a.m., past midnight and told her I love her. Meditated a while; I have been cuddling Jan's urn and meditating since 1/5; I checked my writing. I turned on the TV to watch, "Once Upon a Time in America," Jan flashed the green lights at 1:09 a.m. I had thought after one hour, that Jan is not going to be here tonight.

Jan 15 – Friday early morning past midnight

Came to the room at 12:30 past midnight. Lisa had called to say that her boyfriend Dale had surprised her by coming to see her without telling her ahead of time. I did that so many times when I was coming from LA to Vegas to see Jan. Lisa said she was ecstatic and happy. I cuddled Jan and told her to guide Lisa with the hope that Lisa has finally found a good man to love her. I placed the urn back at 12:40 a.m. Jan flashed the green lights at 12:48 a.m. I went to sleep at 1:30 a.m.

Jan 15 – Jan 16 Friday late night / Saturday early past midnight

Took Jan into my embrace at 11:30 p.m. and meditated as I have done since I started cuddling her before I sleep. Talked to her about how happy Lisa appeared to be with her new boyfriend Dale. I asked Lisa today, "Do you feel what Jan felt when I surprised her with my visits from Los Angeles?" Lisa beamed, "Oh yes!" I put Jan back at 11:38 p.m.

Jan flashed the green lights at 11:58 p.m., then again at 12:19 a.m. I went to sleep at 1:20 a.m. after the movie, "Never Back Down." Goodnight my Jan.

Jan 17 – Sunday

Last night I did the same meditation with Jan in my embrace. The whole time before I went to sleep at 1:30 a.m., Jan did not flash me. I thought maybe I am really getting spoiled since she has always comes to see me after I meditated, since 1/5. This morning when I came back from Arizona Charlie's at 10 a.m.,

Susan informed me that Uncle Jim, Jan's uncle, brother of John, had passed away early last night. Maybe Jan was there to greet Uncle Jim. Maybe that's why she didn't come to see me last night. As Susan said, "Who else better than Jan to be there to greet Uncle Jim?" We had visited Uncle Jim last October when we went home to Colome to view the headstone. I remembered Uncle Jim was very moved when Toni was saying goodbye to him; Toni is Uncle Jim's granddaughter. We all sensed that Uncle Jim knew that it would be the last goodbye with Toni.

12 noon – while watching the Vikings/Dallas football game, the banana fragrance came on so strong. Jan is here and she is letting me know.

Tonight I cuddled Jan and meditated for her to acknowledge me. I waited the night until I went to sleep. Jan didn't flash the green lights.

Jan 18 – Monday

Came home at 1 p.m. Lisa told me that Jan's old friend, Ruth, at worked passed away yesterday – a stroke. Ruth is in her seventies. Jan must be waiting for her. No wonder she didn't flash me last night.

2:10 p.m. – I've always left the cell phone on in the hope of seeing those comforting green lights flash. While waiting last night for the green lights that didn't come, I don't know why something told me to open the cell phone. The phone was off. I didn't turn it off at any time yesterday or the day before. So I turned it back on. I am not going to try to contemplate why it was off. I am just glad I found out. Maybe now I will be able to experience the joy of seeing my Jan flash me the green lights.

Jan 19 – Tuesday

Lisa gave me a CD of Susan Boyle. She said she sang "Silent Night." I put on the CD. When the CD got to "Silent Night," I held up the cell phone in view of Jan's picture and her urn. My emotions were running freely to her, tears were in my eyes. When the song was replayed, the green lights flashed at 3:27 p.m. My heart was pounding; Jan, I love you. I went and told Lisa. Lisa smiled. "It's Jan." she said.

Jan 21 – Thursday

It has been raining heavily for the past two days. Gloomy days never made me feel happy as it makes me miss my Jan even more. Yesterday was the funeral for Uncle Jim. I came home yesterday to see a new quilt on our bed. It was the quilt Lisa had made with many of my Happi Hearts drawings for Jan. Lisa said it was Jan who made her put it on. The quilt had been hanging in Lisa's room as decoration all these years. She said Jan loved it and that she just got the feeling that Jan wanted it to be on our bed. I took some pictures of it.

This morning while lying in bed watching TV (it is raining hard outside), the green lights flashed at 9:57 a.m.

A rainy day. I decided to go to Arizona Charlie's and pass my time. Before I left, a notion to bring the cell phone with me came to mind. So I said to Jan, "Let's go to Charlie's and mess around a bit?" Jan's favorite statement to me when she wanted to go to the casino and play the video poker machines. Got to Charlie's, pulled out the cell phone and laid it on the slot machine and the green lights flashed. My Jan was having a nice time. The smell of the fragrance came many times which I was playing video poker.

Tonight I told Jan, I am going to pull the Happi Hearts quilt over me. Isn't it pretty? I raised the cell phone towards her, the green lights flashed! It was 6:25 p.m.

Jan 22 – Friday

Toni came back from Winner, S.D. from Uncle Jim's funeral. Staying here tonight and will leave for Lake Havasu tomorrow. Had a nice chat with Toni. Told her many things about Jan and I – the love we shared. Went to bed after midnight. Meditated with Jan at 12:40 a.m., and she flashed me at 12:54 a.m. before I went to sleep.

Jan 24 – Sunday

Today the Vikings are playing New Orleans for the NFC championship. "Jan will be watching," I teased Lisa. The Vikings played liked the Vikings, losing a game they should have won. I was tired after the game; unusually tired, so I retired to the bedroom at 9:59 p.m. Meditated with Jan in my embrace. While watching, "Spartacus: Blood and Sand," the green lights flashed at 10:27 p.m. I went to sleep shortly after that.

Jan 25 – Monday

Went to the library. The librarian, Jennifer, wasn't there. I had seen her last Friday – an unusual feeling to see her as she had told me couple of weeks ago that her husband wasn't feeling well. One doctor suspected cancer; another doctor said it is not. Medication will have to be taken for life. Friday Jennifer told me that her husband is not well, that his legs are swollen and he can't walk. She was going to take him to the doctor that day. I gave her a hug and wished her well. She asked for my phone number and gave me hers. I called her from the library. She told me that her husband had passed away on Saturday. She was crying. I felt so sad because I know how she is feeling.

Honey Jan, it's been more than 19 months. I miss you dearly.

Dear Jan, you must know that I am feeling sad today because of Jennifer's husband passing. You flashed the green lights at 4:22 p.m. when I was in bed watching Syracuse-Georgetown basketball.

Tonight Lisa prepared waffles and sausage, some of Jan's favorite food. Lisa said we must give Jan her share of waffles and sausage. I prepared a small plate of it, placed it before Jan's urn, lit incense and told Jan to enjoy the waffles and sausage. I left the room to eat with Lisa and Susan. Must be less than 10 minutes before I came back to the room, the green lights flashed at 6:51 p.m.

Jan flashed the green lights again at 7:50 p.m. then again at 8:11 p.m. Jan must be happy today and staying home longer. Jan flashed the green lights again at 11:47 p.m. after I asked her if she will bid me goodnight.

Forgot to mention that right after Jennifer informed me of her husband's passing, I went to Arizona Charlie's and was playing video poker to pass the time. The fragrance came for a long time and was very, very strong.

Jan 26 – Tuesday 7:10 p.m.

Susan gives Dakota a walk around the neighborhood every night after dinner. Susan walked into the bedroom with Dakota on the leash and said, "Ok, Dakota is taking me for my walk!" The green lights flashed right at that moment. Same Jan, she was laughing!

Jan 27 – Wednesday

Told Jan I am taking her to Oceanside for Susan's birthday. I took out her pink luggage and her traveling kit. Jan loved the ocean. She cried the first time I took her on a surprise cruise from San Diego to Ensenada, Mexico. She flashed the green lights at 4:22 p.m. Then she flashed again at 6:45 p.m. She must be looking forward to the trip.

Jan 28 – Thursday

Susan's B-day. Packed up my Jan in her pink luggage. Brought along my cell phone for her to contact me. We headed out to

Oceanside, Calif. Yesterday was rainy. Today the sun is shining; a very good day.

When we stopped at Victorville for gas, I got the urge to take out the cell phone, and asked Jan if she is happy. The cell phone flashed the green lights within twenty seconds of my asking. Jan is with me and Susan. She is happy to be at the sea side.

Jan 29 – Friday

Drove to SeaWorld this morning. At the parking lot, I asked, "Honey, we are at SeaWorld. We were here many years ago; are you happy to come here again?" The green lights flashed twice.

At 12:50 p.m., while we were in the Arctic World, while Susan was watching the white whale and polar bear, I asked, "Jan, are you with us?" The room was dark; I was standing behind people in front of the glass window with the cell phone in my hand in the dark, and the green lights flashed almost immediately. Glad you were with me, honey Jan.

Feb 1 – Monday

Jan honey, after the last time you flashed the green lights, Friday 12:50 p.m., I wasn't able to sense any contact with you. Saturday Lisa phoned to inform me that John & Lucy had decided to leave Colome and head to Las Vegas that Friday afternoon, and should be in Las Vegas on Sunday. I now understand why my Jan wasn't in touch since Friday afternoon; she was with John and Lucy.

Susan and I rushed home to Vegas on Sunday. John and Lucy were already home. Last night at 10:03, Jan flashed the green lights, and she flashed it again at 10:30 p.m. when everybody had retired to bed.

Feb 2 – Tuesday

The "Home of the Happi Hearts" was filled with laughter. John, Lucy, Lisa, and Susan were playing cards all night. We had a nice dinner at home. While they were having fun playing cards, I went to the bedroom. Meditated a while, thanked Jan for making the happiness impact John, Lucy, Lisa, and Susan. I meditated at 6:30 p.m.; Jan flashed the green lights at 6:36 p.m.

John and Lisa finished their cribbage game. John went to bed and the green lights flashed after that at 7:34 p.m.

Jan flashed the green lights six more times (eight in all) at 8:03, 8:36, 8:59, 10:31, 10:51, and finally at 11:16 p.m. The banana fragrance came on strong before the last time she flashed the green lights. Goodnight my Jan.

Feb 3 – Wednesday

Last night I came into the bedroom and meditated at 9:06 p.m. Susan and Lucy were playing cards. John just went into his bedroom. I guess Jan was with Lucy and Susan. She flashed the green lights only after Susan and Lucy finished their card game and Lucy retired into her bedroom. She flashed it at 9:56 p.m., again at 10:19, and then 11:21 p.m. After that I went to sleep.

Vic, Jan's partner in card games and my brother-in-law, and Lusing, my sister, are coming in from Dallas to visit for the Super Bowl weekend. This must thrill Jan because she always had fun with Vic when they visited us before.

Feb 4 – Thursday

Spent the day with Vic & Lusing. Took them to Aria last night. Came home late. Went to bed at 10:00 p.m. Meditated. Talked to Jan at 11:18 p.m. I was getting sleepy, so I told Jan maybe I won't hear from her tonight, but I still am saying goodnight. Right then, the green lights blinked; it was 11:19 p.m. Jan said, "Goodnight."

Feb 5 – Friday (Thursday events)

Received an email from Judy Hales, Jan's only female cousin from her Mother's side was in Vegas for a convention. Judy was Jan's favorite cousin, only girl cousin and she prepared Jan's tax returns for Jan. We met with Judy at the Mirage for dinner, then headed for Aria to see Lisa. I happened to bring my cell phone with me. While at the Mirage, I looked at the cell phone various times and saw no flashes. However when we were at the Aria, I took out the cell phone and it flashed at 9:55 p.m. I guess most of Jan's friends are now gone from the Mirage and are now at the Aria. She is more at home at the Aria now; Lisa is there.

Feb 6 – Saturday

Yesterday, Friday morning, when I got up to go to the bathroom at 6:46 a.m., the green lights blinked. I came back to bed thinking that I can get some more sleep as I had a long day of walking on Thursday. No sooner had I laid in bed when the green lights flashed again at 7:15 a.m. I said, "Okay, honey, I am getting up." Just like old days when John and Lucy were visiting. Spent the day with Vic, Lusing, and John. Went to see Red Rock Canyon. At 11:11 p.m., before I went to sleep, Jan flashed the green lights. I said goodnight to my baby.

Feb 9 – Tuesday

John and Lucy left Las Vegas early this morning at 4:30 a.m. I got up at 1:59 a.m. Didn't want to go back to sleep for fear of oversleeping and not be awake to see them off. I meditated and asked Jan to be with John and Lucy to make sure they have a safe trip home, and to come back after that. I will be fine. The cell phone flashed the green lights at 2:02 a.m., 3 minutes later. It flashed again at 2:23 and again at 2:48 a.m. It flashed the last time at 3:08 a.m. John and Lucy left at around 4:20 a.m.

Checked with Lucy at 5:10 p.m.; they were in Wyoming getting close to Casper – Steve's home. Jan flashed the green lights at 5:25

p.m. while I was resting. Jan flashed the lights again at 8:45, 9:44 and the last time at 10:17 p.m. I went to sleep at 12 midnight.

Feb 11 – Thursday

Found out last night around six that Jim Flakus, John's best friend had passed away. Jim was here with Connie and friends to visit us during Lisa's birthday. We had fun for a few days. Now he is gone. I know John and Lucy will be very sad. I told Jan to go and take care of John. He needs a lot of comforting. I think Jan did just that because I could not make contact with her last night.

Feb 12 – Friday

Couldn't feel Jan's presence since learning of Jim's passing in Colome. Missed her badly. Woke up early, past 5 in the morning. Thought I heard Lisa coming home from work. Turned out it was not. Cannot go back to sleep. Meditated for Jan in the darkness. I asked her if she is home now to show me a sign. In a short time, the green lights flashed in the dark vividly at 5:28 a.m. Love you honey.

Feb 13 – Saturday

Jan and I had made it a tradition to go out to a Chinese restaurant before Chinese New Year to have a dish of whole fish. It is a Chinese saying that you will have a year of abundance; of surplus. I invited Jean, Susan and Lisa to go to Kan's Kitchen for dinner. We had a nice dinner with a fried flounder, a whole fish. Coming home, I settled down to watch the basketball game between Pittsburgh and West Virginia. During the game, I asked Jan if she had been with us at the dinner. She flashed the green lights, it was 7:16 p.m. Told her I really missed her on days like this. She flashed the green lights again at 7:42 p.m. God, I really miss my Jan.

Feb 15 – Monday

Yesterday 2/14 was Valentine's Day; it was also Chinese New Year. I went out early to get roses for my Jan. Vic had already left her chocolate. I got her a box of chocolate the other day. Came home and the green lights flashed at 10:42 a.m. The thought came in that I want to take my Jan for a ride in Susan's new car. So I took her to the Suncoast Casino. Stayed a while; reminisced old times with her there.

Went to the movie, "From Paris with Love," with Susan. Came home, entered the room. Said to Jan, "Honey, I am home." The green lights flashed instantly.

Feb 16 – Tuesday

Been watching the series, "Henry VIII." Came in the bedroom past midnight last night. Wanted badly to hear from Jan; so I meditated to hear from her at 12:23 a.m. Jan flashed the green lights at 12:44 a.m.

Got up this morning at 2 something to go to the bathroom. When I got back into the room, the green lights flashed so brightly in the dark. It was 2:31 a.m. I think I should enjoy a good day today. Sun is shining. Jan is with me.

Feb 17 – Wednesday

The last time Jan flashed the green lights was Monday early morning 2:31. I missed her so much that I tried hard to meditate to get a message from her. Tuesday morning till today, I was not able to feel her. Feeling a bit low. Then this afternoon Lisa told me that Danny had a good sale of his cattle at the auction in South Dakota. So did John. Lisa also said that Danny mentioned to her that after he made the sale, his cell phone rang. It said, "Restricted No," and nobody was at the other end. Danny felt that it was Jan. This also happened the night Danny got elected as County Commissioner of Tripp County. I told myself no wonder Jan was not here. She was busy in Winner with Danny and John.

Tonight, while watching NCAA basketball, Duke versus Miami, the green lights flashed at 6:12 p.m. Jan is home. The green lights flashed again at 11:40 p.m. after I gave her some bananas.

Feb 18 – Thursday

The green lights flashed today at 5:17 p.m., then at 5:58 p.m. – after I started researching for a generator for John. John was looking to buy a generator when he was in Vegas a few weeks ago. I will have to find out more from Lyn or Danny what John is really looking for.

Feb 20 – Saturday

Cannot sleep, watched movie, "Prom Night," at 1:10 a.m. the green lights flashed. Time to sleep.

Feb 21 – Sunday

Picked up Vic at airport; Vic is here for a meeting, staying at the Paris. Reminded me of the time Jan and Mama went there when the Paris first opened. The green lights flashed at 6:10, and then at 6:30 p.m.

Feb 22 – Monday morning

Been feeling increasingly aimless in life. It is always Jan on my mind from the time I open my eyes in the morning looking at my Jan and it is still Jan on my mind when I shut my eyes to sleep. What Jan had asked me to do I think I have done. I have taken care of Lisa via taking care of Susan. In turn, this makes John and Lucy happy that Lisa has again turned the corner. I have said it countless of times to you, Jan, that I will come to see you with a wide smile on my face. Don't know when that will happen but I certainly am looking forward to it. You bring me tinges of happiness via the signals you send thru happenings and the green lights on the phone. I don't know what I would have done without those signals. At times I just feel very tired of living. I am having a good life – no financial problems. Lisa, Susan, the Forgey family, my sisters Lusing, Yong-Yong, Vic, and other friends who love me. Yet, without Jan, I just cannot feel the same happiness that we shared for those 18 previous years. I am trying to find some purpose for going on. Honey Jan, give me some guidance . . . . I love you.

These last few days when I closed my eyes, Jan came to me with a different look; a different hair style, lots of bright golden light engulfing her, and a different color outfit, sort of blue base with a golden design.

The green lights flashed at 8:45 p.m.

Feb 23 – Tuesday

Green lights flashed at 6:52 p.m.

Feb 24 – Wednesday

My shoulder hurts more today. The green lights flashed at 4:56 p.m. while I was resting in my room. I talked to Jan about my worry of Lisa's recent behavior, about her different appearance, about the outfit she wore which I seem to remember seeing sometime before. My memory says it was associated with Mama.

The green lights flashed at 5:05, then 5:14, 5:49, and then 5:51 p.m. At 5:52 it flashed twice consecutively. This hasn't happened since we were in South Dakota to view our Headstone.

It flashed twice consecutively again at 5:54 p.m., then 6:01. It last flashed once at 6:06 p.m. The green lights flashed at 11:42 p.m. before I went to sleep.

Feb 25 – Thursday

Feeling very tired, without any energy. I guess every time I feel the strong presence of Jan near me; the energy gets zapped out of me. Yesterday the flourish burst of flashes on the cell phone did indicate the strong presence of Jan.

Feb 28 – Sunday

I suggested going to a movies, like old times. We went to see, "Avatar" at The Orleans; had popcorn then dinner at TGI Fridays before coming home. The green lights flashed at 7:58 p.m. The smell of bananas came at 8:22 p.m. Then the green lights flashed again at 11:12 p.m. I dozed off to sleep.

March 1 – Monday

At about 1:30 p.m. while reading, "The Survival Files" by M.E. Allen, just after Lisa came into the room to tell me she is going to the grocery, I felt a slight pull of the bed spread to the left side waist position. I thought it was Dakota who came up on the bed. I turned and it wasn't. Guess Jan was telling me that Lisa is coming along fine.

March 2 – Tuesday

While reading in bed, the banana smell came on strong at 12:33 noon. At 4:46 p.m. the green lights flashed; the last coming at 11:23 p.m.

March 3 – Wednesday

1:41 p.m., missing her badly. Asked Jan if she knew how badly I wanted to communicate with her, then the green lights flashed.

March 4 – Thursday

Early morning, I was awakened by Dakota barking. I thought at first the dog was having a bad dream. Yet he kept barking. I looked at the clock; it shows 3:15 a.m. I went out to see if something was wrong. Lisa gets off work at 4 a.m. She doesn't normally get home until 4:30 a.m. There was nothing noticeable. I came back into the pitch dark bedroom. Asked Jan if she is here, the green lights flashed brightly at 3:34 a.m. I laid in bed till 4:05 when I told Jan goodnight, the green lights flashed. I went to sleep.

March 5 – Friday

12:31 a.m. – green lights flashed. The green lights flashed again at 5:40 and 6:52 p.m. while watching NBA Cleveland/Detroit.

March 7 – Sunday

The green lights flashed at 12:50 p.m. I stayed at home watching NBA games and college games the whole time. The green lights flashed 8 times starting at 5:35 p.m. It flashed at: 5:35, 6:44, 7:10, 7:30, 8:11, 9:07, 9:32, and 9:54 p.m. Lisa was home, talking and laughing with Susan just like before. Jan must be happy tonight.

March 8 – Monday

Decide to put the phone in front of the computer. I check the news, emails, and stock market every morning. Today I just decide to take it easy, and sat down in front of Jan's computer reading the, "Survival Files." Jan sat in front of her computer every morning. She stopped only after she moved in with Lisa weeks before her passing because she was no longer able to climb the stairs. As I read the book, the cell phone, which was situated next to the book's line of vision, flashed at 9:28 a.m. Oh! I did have a good night's sleep – no dreams; a peaceful feeling.

Lisa seems to have come to her good self. She cooked tonight, spaghetti and fruit salad. Jan of course got her share of the cooking. The green lights flashed at 5:36 p.m. watching NCAA basketball WM/ODU; then at 6:02, 6:22 (watching NBA), 6:56, 7:16, 7:37, and 7:57 p.m. Watched a movie with Susan. Came back into bedroom at 11:20 p.m. Talked to Jan about Lisa. Lay down in bed at 11:23, the green lights flashed at 11:25 p.m. and then at 11:54 p.m. I went to sleep.

March 9 – Tuesday

Feeling lazy this morning. Turned on TV and laid in bed. The green lights flashed at 6:39 a.m. and 7:06 a.m. Guess she was saying, "Get up! The sun is shining on your butt!" This was Papa's statement when we were young and didn't get up on time.

There were many times when I asked myself, what if the green lights just flash because of another circuit phenomenon, or I just happened to see it by chance? Last 9 months of events tell me that it is my Jan connecting with me; the buzzing of my cell phone, then Jan's call on my cell etc., the nonstop flashing in South Dakota, and the continuous flashing during my stay in Manila for Mama's cremation. Most importantly, when I had left the cell phone out of my sight for a long period, the cell battery didn't seem to be using energy. It is only when I saw it flashing many times for days that I notice the cell battery indicator getting low.

I am an engineer; my educational background dictates the searching for plausible explanations. In my case with Jan, too many occurrences have no explanation. So I have since accepted that my Jan is with me when she chooses to be. Where is she? How does she make the green lights flash? The many times random thoughts coming to me without any outside influences. Just like Susan says repeatedly, "Why ask why?" Jan is an angel, she always has been. She will always find a way to let me know of her presence.

While watching NCAA basketball UConn/St. John, green lights flashed at 11:33 noon. Then when Lisa left the room saying she is taking Dakota for a daily walk, green lights flashed at 12:15 noon. Green lights last flashed at 6:15 p.m.

March 10 – Wednesday

An unusual day. Today is Romie Semenza's birthday. Romie loved Jan's Happi Hearts so much. She asked to meet Jan after seeing Jan's Happi Hearts at the Country Touch store. Thus began a friendship between us and Romie and Larry. Larry is a lawyer. He helped so much in preparing the required documents for Jan and I at the last days of Jan. We will forever be grateful to them for that.

The unusual thing today was that Jan flashed the green lights so many times (46 times) starting at 4:36 till 7:55 p.m.; a span of 3 hours and 19 minutes. The times were: 4:36, 4:40, 4:43, 4:44 (twice), 4:51, 5:06, 5:08 (twice), 5:14, 5:19, 5:22 (twice), 5:23, 5:24, 5:30, 5:31 (twice), 5:32, 5:36 (3 times), 5:38, 5:41, 5:48, 5:50, 5:51 (twice), 5:59, 6:02, 6:04, 6:08, 6:09, 6:10, 6:54, 7:05 (3 times), 7:06, 7:13, 7:20, 7:24, 7:30, 7:35 and 7:55 p.m.

At 7:05 p.m. I asked Jan is there something she wants to tell me, why is her energy level so high tonight. This occurred only when we made the trip to S. Dakota to view the headstone, at Steve's home, at Rosebud Casino, at John and Lucy's home, on the way back to Vegas, and then at Mama's cremation. The last was 2/24 when Lisa was thinking about quitting her new job and moving out of Vegas. I asked her if it is very good news. The green lights flashed three times consecutively after I asked. I told her I will find out soon.

March 11 – Thursday

At 6:45 a.m. the green lights flashed. I didn't get out of bed – lazy. The green lights flashed again at 7:06. I got up, went through the daily love routine of greeting my Jan good morning; lighting a candle for her, turning on the two lamp lights for her; and then went to the computer room. The TV news had reported the stock market to be down and the gold price was also down. But when the screen appeared on Susan's investment account, it had spiked up for both office and home to a record high. Maybe this is why Jan was so happy. When I told Susan, she promptly went to Jan, burned incense and thanked her for the blessing.

The green lights didn't flash again until 5:08 p.m. Then it flashed again at 8:11, 8:31 and 9:10 p.m.

March 12 – Friday

After the last few days of a strong presence of Jan, I feel very weak. The green lights last flashed at 12:13 early morning (past midnight). It didn't flash anymore the whole day.

March 13 – Saturday

Stayed in bed, the green lights flashed at 11:53 noon; then no more.

March 14 – Sunday

Toni came at noon for her birthday. Susan was giving her a birthday party. Susan's nephew, Grant, is visiting Las Vegas. He was at the party, as were Jean and Rachel. It was a very happy get together. I am sure Jan was with us. The green lights, after staying dim since 11:53 noon yesterday, finally flashed again at 6:49, and 7:13 p.m. The banana smell came on strong at 7:17 p.m. Then it flashed again at: 7:40, 8:00, 8:42, 10:09, 10:45, then last at 12:26 past midnight. I was already feeling a lot better after the party. Maybe Jan stayed away from me to let me recover?

March 15 – Monday

Removed weeds in the front yard this morning. Lay in bed. The green lights flashed at 10:52, 11:16 a.m., and then at 3:33, 4:52 and 5:36 p.m.

Around six o'clock, Lisa and Susan were laughing loudly in the kitchen. I looked at Jan and said, "Honey, do you hear the laughter of the two girls? You brought this laughter to them." Then right away, the song, "And I Love You So" came into my mind. I started singing it. The green lights flashed right away.

I put a Perry Como CD in the player. When it played the song, "Only One," the green lights flashed again at 6:28 p.m.

The lights flashed again at 6:53 and 7:47 p.m. I wrote down the lyrics of "And I Love You So." The song said it all – how I feel.

"And I Love You So"
– This verse is dedicated to the love of my life – my Jan

I guess I understand; how lonely life has been, but life began again; the day you took my hand.
And yes, I know how lonely life can be; the shadows follow me; and the nights wouldn't set me free.
But I don't let the evenings get me down; now that you are around me . . .

March 16 – Tuesday

Missing Jan badly today. Decided to stay in bed to be with my Jan. The green lights flashed at 1:20, 2:02, 2:42, 3:13 and 6:50 p.m. Jan was happy to be with me.

March 17 – Wednesday

The green lights flashed early morning past midnight at 12:24 and 12:49 a.m. I was still awake watching TV.

Watched basketball on TV starting at 4 p.m. The green lights flashed at 5:24, 6:25, 7:50 and 8:17 p.m.

March 18 – Thursday

March Madness was one of Jan's favorite weekends. She was always happy because it brought people to Vegas. She enjoyed the NCAA pool tournament at work; the energy, the laughter. I watched the first game. The green lights flashed at 4:59 p.m.

March 19 – Friday

March Madness is in full swing. The green lights flashed at 3:49 p.m. Then the fragrance filled my senses strongly at 8:20 p.m.

March 20 – Saturday

Waited the whole of last evening since 3:49 p.m. and all of today to see the flash of the green lights. Jan didn't flash the green lights until 4:20 p.m. Then it flashed again past midnight. I watched the series, "Breaking Bad," and didn't come into the bedroom until

12:02 a.m. The green lights flashed at 12:08, 12:11 (twice), 12:12, and then 12:20 a.m. After that I said goodnight to Jan.

March 22 – Monday

Nothing happened on Sunday.

Today we are preparing king crab for dinner, one of Jan's favorite dishes. The green lights flashed at 4:38 while I watched NIT Virginia Tech vs. UConn. At 6:20 p.m., brought Jan's share of crab legs into the bedroom for her. The green lights flashed at 7:28 p.m.

Earlier, Lisa found a bottle of dog shampoo, said she is going to give Dakota a shampoo. At 7:28 p.m., Lisa said we are ready to give Dakota a bath, the green lights flashed shortly after Lisa said it. The shampooing started and the green lights flashed at 7:34, 7:35, then 7:42 p.m. amid the laughter of Lisa and Susan. Susan was taking pictures of a wet Dakota. The green lights flashed again at 7:44. Jan must really be having fun. The shampooing finished at 7:48, at which time the green lights flashed twice. The lights flashed again at 7:51. I said to Jan, "I am so happy that you are here having fun with Lisa and Dakota. Let me play your favorite song, "Wonderful World" for you. I put on the CD of Louis Armstrong. Louis Armstrong's voice came on and the green lights flashed right away.

Lisa and Susan came in the bedroom, said she and Susan are going to Wal-Mart and asked if there is anything I might need. I said get some of Jan's tea candles for me. The green lights flashed twice at 8:14 p.m. when Lisa left the room. It flashed again at 8:15, 8:17 and 8:38. At this time, my sentiments were all choked up by memories of our lives together. I asked Jan if she knows that I miss her so much that sometimes it hurts. I told her at times I felt like crying. But then I also said that my tears were already used up when Papa, my Jan, and Mama passed. I only want to reunite with my Jan come that time to be together forever. I said, "Jan, when that happens, let's not come back to earth, let's just roam everywhere together holding hands." The green lights flashed right after that. My heart wanted to sing and cry at the same time, it was 8:54. The lights flashed again at 9:23, 9:30, 9:41, and 10:04.

Do I believe my Jan was here with me? Absolutely! 21 months of coincidental occurrence? I don't think so.

March 23 – Tuesday

Green lights flashed at 4:37, 7:02, 7:08 and 7:42 p.m.

March 24 – Wednesday

Woke up feeling weak and lazy. While still in bed, the green lights flashed at 9:11 a.m. Went out for a while, felt very tired, teary eyed, no energy at all, decided to come home. Felt very ill, haven't felt that way for a long time. I told Jan I am very tired. Would be more than happy if it is time for me to be with her. The green lights flashed at 2:19 p.m. I don't know if Jan is responding to my mindset. I will leave it up to my Jan.

Sick, feeling bad, tired, the green lights flashed many times: 2:38, 3:00, 3:32, 3:59, 4:34, 5:36, and 6:21 p.m. Within 4 hours, the lights flashed 8 times.

Lisa came into the bedroom, told me that when she saw the three bananas on the dining table, she had the idea of making banana nut bread – Jan's pride. She had been making banana nut bread since she was a child for a 4-H contest, came into mind. Interestingly, Susan came home, looked at the bananas, and asked Lisa if she has Jan's banana nut bread recipe. Did Jan put that idea in their heads?

March 25 – Thursday

Woke up at 7:08 a.m., feeling much better today. While still in bed and turning the TV on, the green lights flashed three times consecutively, then it flashed again at 7:12 a.m. I got up to tidy up. At 10:04 while I was dressing up, the green lights flashed again.

Came home and lay in bed, the green lights flashed at 2:38 p.m. It didn't flash again until 7:27 p.m.

March 26 – Friday

The green lights flashed at 9:14 a.m. while I watched the morning news.

March 27 – Saturday

Came back to the bedroom at 12:15 noon. Turned on TV to watch NCAA March Madness, Kansas St/Butler. The green lights flashed at 12:34 p.m. The green lights flashed again at 2:41 and 3:06 p.m.

March 28 – Sunday

Prepared to spend the day watching March Madness; starting with Michigan St/Tenn. The green lights flashed at 11:57, 12:39, 3:27, 3:47 and 4:23. I went to do some work in the yard. Came back in at 5:39 p.m., the green lights flashed at 5:38 and 6:07 p.m.

Susan and Lisa wanted to go out for some fun, much like old times with Jan. We went to the Orleans for dinner at Don Miguel's. I shared a fajita dish with Lisa just like old times when I always shared a fajita with Jan; came home at 9:25 p.m. Walked into the room, said to Jan just like old days, "I am home, honey!" The green lights flashed right after I said it!

Got into bed, watched TV, felt a slight tug on my left arm T-shirt. I thought Dakota had come into the room and was tugging my T-shirt. I said, "Dakota," and turned my head, Dakota wasn't there! It was 10:25 p.m. I thought to myself, maybe Jan won't flash the green lights again tonight. The green lights flashed again right after that thought came into my mind. It flashed at

10:44, 12:04 past midnight, and then 12:26 a.m. I dozed off to sleep after that.

March 29 – Monday

Lazy day got into bed to watch TV at 2 p.m. The green lights flashed at 4:14 p.m.

March 30 – Tuesday

Didn't see the green lights until 2:56, 5:26 and 7:46 p.m.

March 31 – Wednesday

Bad day for allergies; wind blowing. Went to Arizona Charlie's shortly. Felt light headed, teary eyed; so came home to rest. The green lights flashed repeatedly at 12:22, 12:23, and 12:26 p.m. I guess Jan must be a bit worried about my allergies. The fragrance came on strong at 12:30, 1:21 and 2:45 p.m.

The green lights flashed at 4:07, 6:19, 7:24, 7:37 and 7:57 p.m. It didn't flash anymore tonight before I went to sleep past midnight.

April 1 – Thursday

It's my birthday. I have never paid too much attention to my birthday all my life. But how I wish my Jan was here with me today. I laid in bed thinking about Jan. At 10:02 a.m., the green lights flashed. Yes, my Jan is with me today.

I smell the strong fragrance at 2:39 p.m. The green lights flashed at 5:13, 5:55 and 6:15 p.m.

April 2 – Friday

It's Good Friday. The green lights flashed at 9:19 and again at 9:20 a.m. I didn't get up. The lights flashed again at 9:39 a.m., then 12:08, 12:09, 6:15 and 7:24 p.m. Before sleeping, a thought came into mind to take Jan's urn with me and revisit some of the places we used to go. Every time this happened, I knew it was Jan's wish. So I told Jan, we will go tomorrow morning. The green lights flashed after that at 12:26 past midnight. I switched off the TV and went to sleep.

April 3 – Saturday

I placed Jan's urn into her pink traveling bag. We left the house at 7:30 a.m. Went to McDonald's for breakfast on Spring Mountain Rd near the old condo complex. We drove by our old condo. Said hi to Jean and then drove to Desert Breeze Park. We then went to the Gold Coast, the Rio, and the Palms.

While watching NCAA March Madness, Duke/W. Virginia, the green lights flashed at 6:19 p.m.

Lisa came into the bedroom with a plate of tuna pasta for Jan. The green lights flashed after Lisa left the room at 6:48 and 7:46 p.m. The fragrance came on strong at 8:13 p.m., and the green lights flashed at 11:25 p.m. I was tired but didn't want to go to sleep, much like last night. The green lights flashed at 12:02 past midnight with the thought that Jan was telling me to go to sleep; same thought as last night.

April 4 – Sunday (Easter)

Feeling tired, allergies bothering me. Came into the bedroom at 11:00 a.m. Lying in bed, green lights flashed at 11:11 and 11:13 a.m.

Lisa and Susan wanted to go to the movie. I told Jan that we will be at the movie. The lights flashed at 12:29 p.m.

Came home from the movie. Placed some chocolate Easter eggs for Jan. The green lights flashed almost immediately twice at 7:15, 7:19, 7:35, twice at 8:05 and 11:07 p.m.

April 5 – Monday

Woke up feeling hot at 2:23 a.m. past midnight. Went to the bathroom. Came back and the green lights flashed at 2:46 a.m.

I have been resisting going to see an Acupuncturist since my shoulder started hurting. Today, something compelled me to go and see an acupuncturist. Waited at her office till 3:20 p.m.; first thing she checked was my blood pressure. All my life, my B-P has always been 110-120/70-80. The last time I checked it was before Jan passed away. The acupuncturist told me my B-P was at 171/101. I was surprised, because never in my life had I known my B-P to be over 120. With disbelief, I came home and checked it myself, it was even higher. The doctor had said it can happen because of stress, loss of sleep, and the pain. I looked at Jan, and told her that if this is a sign I am going to see her soon, so be it. I am not going to see a doctor, nor let Susan know about it. If my B-P goes down, good; if not, my Jan can take me anytime.

I looked at Susan and Lisa. In as much as I feel happy seeing Susan metamorph into the girl that I thought she should be, and I appreciate the love and care she shows me, I am sure she can now manage her life and safeguard the blessings Jan and I have given her. To be honest, the joy and happiness of our (Jan and I) togetherness was beyond any other happiness I have ever experienced in my life. I shall leave it up to my Jan.

April 6 – Tuesday

After writing yesterday's entry into this journal about my B-P being excessively high, and my desire to see her, I took a nap at 2:00 p.m. Woke up at 3:45 p.m.; turned on the TV, the green lights flashed in front of me instantly three times in a row at 3:46 p.m.! It then flashed twice at 3:51, 4:01, 4:08, 3 times at 4:14, 4:17, 4:22, 4:29, 4:31, 4:59, 5:10, two times at 5:11, 5:13, 5:17 and 5:18 p.m.

At 5:27 p.m. I received a call from Jean informing me of the passing of an old neighbor, and that another neighbor having a month's time left.

So, between 3:45 and 5:27 p.m., a span of l hour and 42 minutes, Jan has flashed the green lights 22 times. My Jan is obviously bothered by my wish and my B-P condition, also my pain in the shoulder (it has been almost 3 weeks since I can barely reached my hair with my left arm), and it was very depressing to learn about the passing of so many old neighbors, I count 3 already and 1 to happen.

The green lights continued to flash at 5:57, 6:38, 6:40, 7:57 and 8:29 p.m. I left the room to watched a movie with Susan, came back at 10:50 p.m., the green lights flashed at 11:02 p.m. Jan wanted me to go to sleep.

April 7 – Wednesday

I am writing this at 2:42 p.m. Wednesday. Woke up feeling the best in weeks; went out for a haircut. Came back, and while taking a shower, surprised to find that I can raise my left arm to shampoo my hair, first time since my left shoulder began to hurt! Why? I don't know, because I still couldn't raise it without pain last night. Jan? After the vomiting incident that took place after Jan's passing, I hardly took any pills these last 22 months after the incident. No pain from my life-long ulcer? Why? Like Susan said, why ask why?

After the flurry of flashes these last few weeks, I noticed the charge of the cell was down to a single bar, so I charged it between 6:30 and 9 p.m. After noticing the green lights on fully and permanently, indicating the battery was fully charged, disconnected the charger, the green lights went off as always. Came into the bedroom at 11:24 p.m. after watching an old time movie, "Rock Around the Clock," with Susan. Turned off the lights, turned on the TV, a mind full of my Jan; didn't want to go to sleep. The green lights flashed two times at 12:15 after midnight. I still didn't turn off the TV, the green lights flashed again at 12:19 a.m. I said, "Okay, Jan I am going to sleep."

April 8 – Thursday

Came home and lay down in bed for a rest at 2:35 p.m. The green lights flashed at 2:37 p.m. Then it flashed again at 4:15, 4:35, 5:44, 6:48, 8:31, 9:13 and 11:36 p.m. I didn't turn off the TV, so, the green lights flashed again at 11:56 p.m., at which time I said goodnight to Jan.

April 9 – Friday

Watching NBA Knicks/Magic, green flashed at 5:47, 5:58 and 8:05 p.m.

April 10 – Saturday

Susan came home with a bouquet of Roses for Jan. Susan left the room, the green flashed at 1:30 p.m. Lisa had asked Susan to bake a shepherd's pie today. Susan did make the pie. She forgot to give Jan a share of the pie. At 7:07 p.m., the green flashed, the thought came into mind Jan was asking, where is mine? The green flashed again at 7:08 and 7:10. I told Susan, Jan is asking for her pie. Susan right away prepared a little dish for Jan. I took a hot bath, came into the room, the green flashed at 7:44, 7:46, and 8:04. Susan came into the room with a heart-shaped shortcake for Jan. The green flashed at 8:22, 8:48, 8:50 (twice), 8:51 and 8:54. Jan must be happy.

April 11 – Sunday

Lisa came home late, she worked overtime. The fragrance came strong while I was in bed. Lisa came home; I put on the music "Unchained Melody." It was Jan's favorite song. The green flashed at 1:53 and 2:03 p.m. I took a nap. Woke up at 2:52, the green lights flashed at 2:53 p.m. I decided to take Dakota for a walk. Came home, the green flashed right away at 3:42 p.m. when I entered the room and said, "Honey I am home."

Watched the movie, "Talking to Heaven" late into the night. Came in the bedroom at 1:05 a.m., the green flashed at 1:08 a.m. I guess Jan wanted me to turn off the TV and go to sleep. I did.

April 12 – Monday

Dressed up to go to the library. The green flashed at 9:41 a.m. before I left the room.

Watching NBA, Clippers/Dallas, green lights flashed at 8:11, 8:31, 9:57, 10:19, 10:39, and at 11:41 p.m. I said goodnight to Jan.

April 13 – Tuesday

Came home at 3:10 p.m., turned on TV to watch the news and the green lights flashed at 3:12 p.m.

I watched the movie about Van Praagh, "Talking to Heaven." I have read two of his books. Felt a bit emotional since last night after watching the movie. The green lights flashed so many times today. It flashed at: 3:15, two times at 3:18, (2x) at 3:25, (2x) at 3:26, (2x) at 3:29, then 3:38 p.m. It flashed (4x) at 3:45, then 3:51, 4:28, (3x) at 4:29, 4:30, (2x) at 4:34, and 4:37 p.m. I went out for a while. Came back and the green lights continued to flash, at: 5:44, 6:04, then four times (4x) at 6:05, (2x) at 6:07, (2x) at 6:10, 6:11, 6:14, (2x) at 6:15, and 6:17 p.m. Had dinner, came back into the room, the lights flashed again (2x) at 7:01 and 8:30. It didn't flash anymore after that. Went to sleep.

April 14 – Wednesday

Got up to go to bathroom at 5:30 a.m., still dark, got back into bed. Thought about Jan. Asked Jan if she was here, the green lights flashed at 5:39 a.m. Cannot miss bright green lights flashing in the dark. I felt good and went back to sleep.

Came back at 1:47 p.m., got into the room, said the usual words, "Honey I am home," the lights flashed almost immediately at 1:48 p.m. I took a nap, opened my eyes at 2:14 p.m., the lights flashed at 2:15 p.m.

Lisa prepared homemade chicken noodle. I told Jan that she will get her chicken noodle, the lights flashed; it was 5:49 p.m. Susan came into the bedroom and told me that she had found a cheap ticket to go home to see her parents in June. The green lights flashed as Susan was standing by the bed, it was 6:22 p.m. Jan had always told Susan to love and honor her parents – unconditionally. Jan must have been happy to hear Susan is going home to Florida to visit her parents.

At 12:08 a.m. past midnight, the lights flashed, I said goodnight to Jan.

April 15 – Thursday

While dressing up to go out, the green lights flashed at 9:55 a.m. It flashed again at 5:17 p.m. just when I walked into the room saying "I am home, honey." The lights flashed at 12:03 a.m. when I was still watching TV. Turned off TV and said, "Goodnight, honey."

April 16 – Friday

Got up at 8:01 a.m., the lights flashed. The lights flashed at 11:58 noon when I walked into the room. Again it flashed at 1:06 and then at 8:02 p.m.

April 17 – Saturday

Woke up not feeling well. The lights flashed many times today: at 4:37, 4:59, 8:04, 8:26, 9:00, 9:20, 9:40, 10:20, 10:43 and 11:34 p.m.

April 19 – Monday

The lights flashed at 7:35 a.m. when I woke up. Went out to Realty School to get program for my real estate renewal. Came home, the lights flashed twice at 12:22 p.m. The lights flashed at 6:59 p.m. while I was watching NBA, Cavaliers/Bulls. It flashed again at 10:54 and 10:56 p.m.

April 21 – Wednesday

Found out today that there was a bad auto accident at Colome yesterday. A teacher at Colome High, a friend of Jan's, was involved in the accident. Her car was hit by another car whose driver was said to have suffered a heart attack. There were two kids from Colome High in the car, one child was killed. Jan had talked to the class on her last trip home to Colome before she passed away. I guess Jan must have been in Colome because of this.

I waited until 5:32 p.m. when the lights finally flashed again. It flashed again at 5:50 p.m.; then no more for the night.

April 22 – Thursday

After I dressed up to go out, said to Jan, "I'll be back, honey," the lights flashed.

My shoulder is still painful when I raised my arm in a horizontal position. So I decided to go to the Acupuncturist again. Got my treatment, my shoulder and arm looked like a bloody mess after the treatment; suction left the spots reddish. Staying in bed to rest, the lights started flashing at 6:03 p.m. and they continued the whole evening: 6:15, 6:16 (twice), 6:17, 6:18, 6:22, 6:24, 6:29 (twice), 6:49 (three times), 6:50, 6:52, and 6:53 p.m.

I lit a candle and told Jan not to be too worried, the lights flashed right away at 8:04, then 8:33 (three times), 8:39 (three times), 8:44 (5 times), 8:46 (twice), and 8:50 p.m. (twice).

After seeing the lights flash 32 times between 6:03 to 8:50 p.m. (2 hours 47 minutes), I said to Jan, "Since you are here with me, let's enjoy some of your favorite songs, ok?" I put on the CD made by Susan. The first song is, "Wonderful World." When the song ended, the lights flashed. The second song is, "I'll Never Find Another You." The lights flashed again after the second song. The first flashed at 8:54 and the second at 8:56 p.m. The CD kept playing. When it got to the middle of Tina Turner's, "You're Simply the Best," the lights flashed at 9:09 p.m. The lights flashed again at the end of, "Unchained Melody" by the

Righteous Brothers at 9:23 p.m. The lights flashed twice again tonight at 9:29 and 9:32.

I checked the journal; the last time the lights flashed in this manner was on April 6, the day after I went to have acupuncture. Guess my Jan was worried seeing my shoulder with all the blood red spots after the treatment.

April 23 – Friday

Allergies are bad, wind was blowing wild. Decided to take it easy in bed. Got the feeling Jan will be around me. The lights flashed at 11:52 a.m. and 12:12, 12:32, 4:28, 5:09 and 5:50 p.m.

April 24 – Saturday

Have a slight infection inside my mouth. Got up at 6:49 a.m. and went to the bathroom. Came back and lit a candle for Jan. "Good morning honey," and the lights flashed right after I got back into bed. The lights flashed so many times today: 7:56, 11:40 (3x), 11:44, 11:47, 11:48 and 11:58 a.m., and 12:01,12:03, 12:05, 12:06, 12:43, and 1:22 p.m. Susan served me and Jan her favorite broccoli soup. Shortly after that the lights flashed at 6:21 (three times), then again at 12:00 midnight.

April 25 – Sunday

Tested my blood pressure because I was feeling bad. After the lights flashed at midnight, I tested my B.P.; I was expecting it to be around 180/104. My last reading on 4/6. It came out 140/88. How did it go down that much? "Why ask why?" as Susan said.

The lights flashed at 12:26, 1:05, 2:36, 2:51 and 6:55 p.m.

April 26 – Monday

Went to Grandview for orientation, criss-crossed town to get my license from old broker to be transferred to Grandview. Went to the real estate Division for the transfer and came home tired. The lights flashed at: 5:54, 6:37, 7:13, 7:18 and 7:19 p.m. Felt Jan's presence so strongly; put on the CD. Right in the middle of, "I'll Never Find Another You," the lights flashed, then at 7:37, 7:40, 7:42, 7:44 (twice), 7:50, 7:53 (twice), and 8:00 p.m. (twice).

April 27 – Tuesday

First day at work. Lights didn't flash until 11:19 p.m. Said goodnight to Jan.

April 28 – Wednesday

Came back from work, rearranging some of our photos, the lights flashed – 4:50 p.m.

April 29 – Thursday

Came home from work. Missed my Jan. Thought how much I wish to see the lights flash. The lights flashed at the thought – 3:25 p.m. Thank you my Jan, I love you.

At 4:44 p.m., as I was sorting out some of her Happi Hearts which I was thinking of giving out to people I will be meeting at work, the lights flashed twice almost immediately at 4:44, 4:45 and 4:50 p.m. My Jan was always so proud of her Happi Hearts; her greatest joy in life was when people loved them, and they all did. The lights flashed again at 5:16, 5:37 and then 8:27 p.m.

May 1 – Saturday

The lights flashed at 7:27 and 7:51 p.m. I was at work today.

May 2 – Sunday

Rested at home, saw the lights flash at 2:53, then at 3:53 p.m. right when I got into the room after a tiring round of yard work on the front lawn. The lights flashed again at 5:31 and 6:04 p.m.

Met this woman at work, Sharon; Susan and Jean said she looks like Jan. I have to admit there are similar features in their faces, but I do not personally think she comes close to my Jan in radiant personality. My Jan has a smile that is so contagious – a heavenly smile. I was talking to Sharon on the phone tonight. She asked me, "Can I ask you a favor?" I said, "Okay." She said, "I have dreams, can you draw them for me?" At that moment, my mind flashed back to my Jan. Anybody who she talked to in her last 5-6 years, she always told people, "Liong draws what I dream." Right after Sharon said that, the green lights flashed! I was out of words. I didn't even ask Sharon what she dreamed. I told Susan and Lisa, they were both stunned. This was 8:42 p.m. The lights flashed again at 9:23. I watched the Robin Hood series and then came into the room at 12:15 a.m. past midnight. Asked Jan if she had talked to me thru Sharon, the lights flashed at 12:16 a.m.

May 4 – Tuesday

The lights flashed at 6:03 p.m. after I came back from work. Flashed again at 11:59 p.m. I asked Sharon today what was her dream. She said the dreams had been coming over some time. She said she had been waiting to know an artist who can draw them. The thought to ask me came when I showed her a few of my drawings with Jan's favorite quotes. "It just came into my mind to ask you." She then described the settings of her dreams. It appeared that she was describing a landscape of greens. She stopped before elaborating and switched to another topic.

May 7 – Friday

Susan was out walking Dakota – Lisa's dog. I laid myself in bed and told Jan I missed the flashing. I miss her so much. The lights flashed at the thought at 9:13 p.m. Then it flashed again three times at 9:18, 9:19, then two times at 9:20 p.m. I then asked Jan to let me know what she wants to do for John and Lucy on their birthdays in July. The lights flashed at 9:26 p.m. She will let me know in time.

May 8 – Saturday

Today is Taylor's graduation day in Nebraska. Taylor is one of Jan's favorite nieces. Jan had her nieces come one time, booked them into a suite at the Bellagio, and got them a Cabana at the pool. The room faced the dancing waters with music piped into the room. Taylor sat in front of the wall-to-wall window watching the dancing waters the whole evening. Lucy is going to attend Taylor's graduation. John couldn't go with her because there were hunters coming to hunt. I know Jan will be there with Lucy. The lights didn't flash until 7:53 p.m. Jan must have just come home.

May 9 – Sunday

Mowed the lawn and rearranged the garage. Felt tired, old age I guess. In bed to rest, lights flashed at 4:36 p.m.

May 10 – Monday

Resting, lights flashed at 1:59 and 2:35 p.m.

May 13 – Thursday

It's been more than two days without the lights flashing. Missing it very badly. I told Jan that I missed seeing the lights and at 7:23 p.m. the lights flashed and also at 8:17 p.m. – comforting. At 12:24 past midnight I bid Jan goodnight, the lights flashed at 12:24 a.m.

May 16 – Sunday

Missing Jan badly, the lights flashed at 9:13, 9:35 and 10:51 p.m.

May 17 – Monday

The notion came to mind that Jan wanted me to decorate her urn with Happi Hearts. I got the stickers, Jan has lots of them, and decorated the urn. The fragrance came on strong at 6:48 p.m. while I was with Susan. Susan said she didn't smell it. The lights flashed at 7:07 p.m.

May 18 – Tuesday

Came home from work, the lights flashed at 4:49 p.m.

May 19 – Wednesday

Meditated. Soon after, the lights flashed at 6:21, 6:59, 7:46 and 8:49 p.m.

May 21 – Friday

Lights flashed Thursday morning at 12:18 a.m. after saying goodnight to Jan.

May 22 – Saturday

Cuddled Jan's urn and talked with her. The lights flashed shortly after at 7:37 p.m., very comforting feeling.

Lisa said John wants to come to Vegas to visit. I told Lisa to find two tickets for them. I guess this is what Jan wants for their birthday gift.

May 23 – Sunday

The lights flashed at 11:14 a.m. and 12:33 p.m. I was going to stay at The Orleans tonight, but decided instead to come home. I really miss my Jan. After coming home, the lights flashed at 9:36 p.m. At 12:11 past midnight, I said goodnight and the lights flashed.

May 24 – Monday

The lights flashed at: 9:42, 10:05, 10:25 and 11:17 p.m.

May 25 – Tuesday

Lights flashed at 11:10 p.m.

May 27 – Thursday

Lights flashed at: 7:02, 8:28, 9:22 p.m. and 12:24 a.m. – said goodnight.

May 29 – Saturday

Lights flashed at 11:34 p.m. when I said goodnight to Jan.

May 30 – Sunday

Missing Jan a lot. I looked up at Jan's picture, told her how beautiful she is, the lights flashed at 10:43, then again at 11:55 a.m. when I came home from Michael's with a jar of lamp oil for Jan's lamps. The lights flashed regularly today while I rested the whole day: 12:27, 6:16, 6:36, 8:34, 8:54, and last at 11:35 p.m. when I said goodnight.

May 31 – Monday

I stopped working at Grandview. The atmosphere in the workplace was too depressing. Lights flashed at 3:35 p.m.

June 2 – Wednesday

Meditated with Jan after waking up. Lights flashed after meditation – 8:54 a.m., then again at 3:05, 3:35 p.m., and last at 12:40 a.m. when I said goodnight to Jan.

June 3 – Thursday

Many flashes from Jan today: 4:18, 4:39, 6:32, 7:15, 9:02 and 9:38 p.m. Last flash came at 12:32 a.m. after saying goodnight to Jan.

June 4 – Friday

Lights flashed after I woke up at 8:23 a.m.; last at 1:10 a.m. after saying goodnight to Jan.

June 5 – Saturday

It was 2 years ago today when Jan left this world. She must be busy with something today as the lights never flashed the whole day. I waited to see the flashes, but Jan didn't show.

June 6 – Sunday

John and Lucy are visiting Las Vegas today. I have sent two round-trip tickets to them as their birthday gifts. Jan wanted this for them. Woke up at 6:45 a.m., talked to Jan a while, the lights flashed at 6:50, then at 8:24 a.m. Jan is here waiting for John and Lucy! Lights flashed again at 12:58 and 1:52 p.m. Lisa fetched John and Lucy at the airport, arrived home at 3:15 p.m. Took John and Lucy to dinner at the Suncoast Casino. Came home, Lisa played cribbage with John. Everybody went to bed. I came into the room and the lights flashed 3 minutes later at 10:53 p.m. I said goodnight to Jan and lights flashed at midnight.

June 7 – Monday

Lights flashed at 10:04 a.m. John and Lucy spent the day at The Orleans. Jan would have been with them before. The fragrance came on strong to me in the living room and bedroom tonight. But none of them smelled anything.

June 8 – Tuesday

Jan flashed the lights at 6:25 a.m. early morning. I guess Jan was ready to spend a good day with John and Lucy.

June 9 – Wednesday

John went to bed early. Lights flashed at 9:52, then at 10:16 p.m.

June 10 – Thursday

9:32 a.m. the fragrance came to me strong. John and Lucy had left at 8:30 a.m.

June 11 – Friday

Measured my blood pressure this morning, it was 141/72, down from 190/105.

7:35 a.m. the lights flashed, felt very comforting. Waited the whole day to see the green lights; but they didn't flash.

I took Jan's urn into my embrace, talked to her, within minutes the lights flashed at 9:01 and then 10:16 and 10:43 p.m.

June 12 – Saturday

The lights flashed at 8:03 a.m. while I was still in bed. It flashed again at 1:19 p.m. while watching World Cup Soccer – England/ USA.

Checked my B-P again at 8:07 p.m., it was 131/73. Smelled the fragrance at 8:26 p.m.

June 13 – Sunday

The lights flashed at 8:19 a.m. Decided to get up and mow the lawn. Two hummingbirds appeared in front of me. Looked at me for a while then flew away. The last time I saw a hummingbird at home was last August when we first moved in. Jan loved the hummingbirds. She always watched them outside of our condo's windows.

12:14 a.m. past midnight, lights flashed goodnight.

June 14 – Monday

The lights flashed many times today. It has been a long time since it did this: 7:05, 8:27, 10:59 and 11:30 a.m., then at 1:22, 2:04, 2:36, 3:06, 3:53, 4:17, 4:46, 6:00, 6:27, 6:47, 10:38 and 11:11 p.m. –16 times.

June 16 – Wednesday

Lights flashed at 5:24 p.m. Waited for the next 3 hours to see another flash. It didn't occur. I took Jan's urn in my embrace, meditated to her. The lights flashed after half an hour at 9:59 then again at 10:31 and 11:02 p.m.

June 17 – Thursday

Woke up to a bad dream about Dakota having his leg broken by a Lion? Feeling strange why I had such a dream, the cell phone was right on my side and flashed in front of my eyes at 5:34 a.m. The lights flashed again at 6:08 am, then twice at 11:03 p.m.

June 18 – Friday

Lights flashed at 6:48 and 7:35 a.m. Went for job training at the Jockey Club. Lights flashed tonight at 8:06, 9:23 and 10:11 p.m.

June 19 – Saturday

While in bed feeling lazy, lights flashed at 7:38 a.m. I guess it is Jan's way of telling me to get up.

Susan is coming home today after visiting her parents in Florida. She called me from Dallas in transit. I was telling her that Jean appeared to be getting weaker and had called me at 6:30 p.m. to inform me that she was tired and going to bed (first time she did this), the lights flashed twice in front of me. I guess Jan is also worried about Jean. 12:58 a.m. past midnight, lights flashed after I said goodnight.

June 20 – Sunday

Lights flashed at 8:00, 9:00, 9:47, 11:16 and 11:39 p.m. Said goodnight to Jan, I have to go to work tomorrow.

June 22 – Tuesday

The lights flashed at 3:44 and 8:32 p.m.

June 23 – Wednesday

Lights flashed when I said goodnight at 11:13 p.m.

June 24 – Thursday

Said goodbye to Jan, going to work, lights flashed right away 8:41 a.m.

June 25 – Friday

6:45 a.m. lights flashed. Guess I better get up.

June 26 – Saturday

Dakota was barking at 6 a.m. Early for him to be barking. Checked it out, nothing in particular. Went back to bed. Mind full of Jan. Looked at cell, the lights flashed, it was 6:16 a.m. Stayed in bed, lights flashed again at 7:28 a.m. Got up.

Bought same Chinese pink lilies for Jan. Told Susan to come in and take a picture. Susan came in. As she was taking the picture, lights flashed – 4:44 p.m.

June 27 – Sunday

Feeling sick, came home early from work. Stayed in bed. Lights flashed at 7:10, 9:19, and 9:42 p.m.

June 28 – Monday

I am not happy going to work anymore. The lights flashed at 2:32 p.m. It flashed again at 11:46 p.m. and 12:50 past midnight.

June 29 – Tuesday

The lights flashed at 8:53 a.m., and 3:33 and 11:47 p.m. Miss my Jan's smiles so much.

July 1 – Thursday

The lights flashed at 9:06 a.m., then no more.

Found out later that Elexis has an eye problem. Doctors in Casper didn't want to do anything. Teneil had to take Elexis to Denver to see a specialist. The doctor said Elexis has a benign cancer behind her eye. Elexis is one of Jan's favorite grand-nieces. I think Jan must have been with them today. There were no flashes after 9:06 a.m. I am sending some Guyabano juice to Elexis.

July 2 – Friday

John and Lucy are in Casper, spending time with the kids. If so, I don't expect any flashes today. The lights flashed at 7:05 and 7:29 a.m., then no more.

July 3 – Saturday

The lights finally flashed at 12:28 p.m. (twice). I guess Jan came home to see me. John and Lucy are still in Casper. No flashes after 12:28 p.m.

July 4 – Sunday

Lights flashed at 8:46 a.m. Miss Jan so much. Cuddled her tonight and played her favorite songs and sang to her. The lights flashed after that at 11:03 p.m.

July 5 – Monday

A hot day, lazy in bed. Flashes at: 8:40 and 9:13 a.m. and 12:12 and 1:04 p.m.

July 6 – Tuesday

Went out to mow the front lawn at 9:15 a.m. A hummingbird flew and stopped in front of me, looked at me, then flew away. The last time a hummingbird came in front of me was last year when we moved in the house; I think I had written that down. My Jan came to see me.

July 7 – Wednesday

Still awake at past midnight, watching TV, the lights flashed at 1:10 a.m. Guess Jan wanted me to go to sleep.

July 8 – Thursday

Said goodnight to Jan at 12:46 past midnight; lights flashed at 12:48. Goodnight Jan. Knelt down in front of bed, talked to Jan, within seconds, the lights flashed – 7:17 p.m. Said goodnight to Jan at 11:55 p.m. and the lights flashed at 12:19 past midnight.

July 9 – Friday

Lucy's birthday. No flashes from Jan. Must be with John and Lucy.

July 10 – Saturday

John's birthday. Lights flashed at 8:30 a.m., then no more.

July 13 – Tuesday

Felt the same way right after Jan's passing two years ago – weak, no energy and sad. The lights finally flashed at 12:53 past midnight; 3 days since the last flash.

July 15 – Thursday

Dentist appointment at 12 noon to extract wisdom tooth.

7:36 a.m. lights flashed. 8:06 a.m. lights flashed. Came home after tooth pulled. 1:51 p.m. lights flashed while resting in bed. 12:28 past midnight, lights flashed after saying goodnight to Jan.

July 16 – Friday

No flashes in daytime. Said goodnight to Jan at 11:44 p.m. Lights flashed at 11:58 p.m. – goodnight Jan.

July 18 – Sunday

Tooth bothering me and slight fever. Lights flashed at 9:19, 9:39 and 10:46 p.m. I guess Jan is worried about me. Said goodnight and lights flashed 11:58 p.m.

July 19 – Monday

7:01 a.m. – lights flashed. 9:35 a.m. – lights flashed. Went to the dentist to get a prescription. Came home, napped, woke up and lights flashed at 2:27 p.m.

July 20 – Tuesday

9:26 a.m. – lights flashed.

July 21 – Wednesday

Went to library. Came home, lights flashed at 12:28 p.m.

July 22 – Thursday

8:28 a.m. – lights flashed.

July 24 – Saturday

Missing Jan badly the whole day, so I took Jan into my embrace and talked to her. Lights flashed after a short time at 12:34 past midnight.

July 25 – Sunday

Lights flashed at 10:14 p.m.

July 26 – Monday

Lights flashed 9:05, 9:43, 10:07 and 10:34 p.m. Said goodnight to Jan at 11:31 p.m., lights flashed at 11:33 p.m. Goodnight Jan.

July 27 – Tuesday

Woke up, had a notion Jan is going to flash me, opened my eyes, lights flashed instantly at 7:57 a.m.

Lights flashed tonight at 7:29 p.m.

July 28 – Wednesday

Birthday of my Jan!

Woke up at 5:22 a.m. and lit the lamp Lucy gave me. Sang happy birthday to Jan and meditated to her. Told her how much I love her and miss her. Cut a piece of her favorite red-cake. Lisa made it; Jan had asked me to have Lisa make it, and then served my Jan a cup of coffee. The lights flashed brilliantly in the darkness at 5:29, 5:55 and 6:24 a.m. The banana fragrance filled the air the whole morning and afternoon.

Had a bit of difficulty breathing. Took my blood pressure at 4:24 p.m. It was high – 151/91. My B-P has been running around 123/80 the last two months. Why this high today? Tested it again tonight; still the same.

Went to Ping-Pang-Pong, Jan's favorite restaurant with Jean, Susan and Lisa to celebrate Jan's B-day.

No flashes tonight, but the fragrance is still filling the room tonight.

July 29 – Thursday

Woke up at 6:45 a.m. Tested my B-P – 125/67. So what happened yesterday?

Fragrance still strong in the room this morning. Lisa talked to John. According to Lisa, John told her that he had forgotten about Jan's birthday. Well, Jan woke him up Tuesday and he suddenly remembered the next day, Wednesday, is Jan's birthday. Guess Jan didn't want her beloved Daddy to forget!

Lyn placed flowers on our headstone in Colome and sent over a photo; lovely and comforting.

July 30 – Friday
Lights flashed at 6:03 a.m.

Said goodnight to Jan at 12:28 a.m. and lights flashed at 12:33 a.m. Goodnight Jan.

July 31 – Saturday
Blood pressure taken at 11:00 a.m. – 126/75. Said goodnight to Jan at 1:04 a.m., flashed at 1:06 a.m.

August 1 – Sunday
Lights flashed at 8:51 a.m., time to get up said Jan.

August 2 – Monday
Went to see the dentist at noon. With mouth numb, slept and woke up at 3:21 p.m., lights flashed at 3:22 p.m., 3:55, 4:06 and 4:08 p.m. My Jan always cared about toothaches. She must be worried.

August 3 – Tuesday
Lights flashed at 9:02 a.m.

August 4 – Wednesday
Susan has started reading my journal. She wants to get a head start on her book about Jan. Surprisingly, Susan said that before Lisa left for work at 7:00 p.m. last night, Lisa had told her that Jan had been appearing to her in her dreams, talking to her. Telling her to cheer up and do something. Jan suggested to her to make

some handbags. Lisa had made some for Jan before, using Jan's Happi Hearts drawings.

Lisa woke up at 2:00 p.m. and starting cleaning the kitchen. Then she went out to the grocery. Told me she will be making homemade chicken noodle soup tomorrow. Jan had occasionally asked Lisa to make it for me since I love her chicken noodle soup. Lisa was kind of cheerful. Maybe Jan did talk to her!

Lights flashed at 8:10 p.m. Said goodnight to Jan at 12 midnight. Lights flashed at 12:15 a.m. – goodnight Jan. I didn't go to sleep right away, still watching TV, lights flashed again at 12:40 a.m. This time I went to sleep.

August 5 – Thursday

Lisa made chicken noodle soup. She was cheerful and talked a lot; thank you Jan. Lights flashed at 8:27 p.m.

August 6 – Friday

Lights flashed at 6:15 p.m. Lisa cooked dinner. Jan, you are truly a great sister.

August 7 – Saturday

Lights flashed at 8:04 a.m.; got up. Watched a WNBA game. Lights flashed at 1:47 and 2:05 p.m.

August 8 – Sunday

Today is the one year anniversary of our new home. We prepared some of our favorite food to share with Jan. The room filled with fragrance at 3:29 p.m. Then the lights flashed at 7:22 p.m.

I said goodnight to Jan at 11:22 p.m. The lights flashed at 12:47 a.m.

August 10 – Tuesday

7:21 a.m. lights flashed after I said good morning to Jan.

11:47 p.m. said goodnight to Jan. Lights flashed at 11:48 p.m. Goodnight.

August 11 – Wednesday

8:12 p.m. – missed Jan so much. Played her favorite CD. The CD starts with, "What a Wonderful World," and at 8:14 p.m., lights flashed before the song ended.

12:05 a.m. past midnight, fragrance filled the room. 12:43 a.m., lights flashed, goodnight Jan.

August 12 – Thursday

10:16 a.m. the fragrance filled the air. Talked to Jan last night before sleeping. Asked her why she hasn't come into my dreams for some time. Woke up this morning, remembered I dreamed about talking to Lucy. Lucy was asking, "Where is Jan?" I said Jan told me she was going somewhere there is water and a place with the word "creek." I told Lucy, "It is not as if I wouldn't let her go. I don't know why she didn't tell me." – Funny dream.

Went to The Orleans, while driving home on Decatur past Sahara Ave., out of the blue, the thought that Jan wants an apple pie from McDonald's came into mind. We used to go to McDonald's after her treatment at Steinberg Diagnostic. I told myself, it's been a long time, maybe McDonald's doesn't sell apple pies anymore. So I turned onto our street. Again, the thought that Jan wants a McDonald's apple pie came in. I didn't turn into the house but went straight to McDonald's on Charleston Blvd.

After parking the pickup in front of the drive-through, I looked at the menu, didn't see any apple pie. So I was going to get back into the car and a thought came in and said, "Go in the store and check it out!" I went into the store, stood and looked at the menu. Saw a sign for cherry pie. Told myself, "Okay, no apple pie." But on a second look, there was small print before the cherry pie. On a closer look it said apple pie. Okay, so I got in line. I ordered

#11, fish filet, Jan's favorite. The attendant said, "Want an apple pie? It's on sale right now, 2 for $1." Okay, I told myself, Jan you won. Came home with two apple pies and placed them in front of Jan. I guess she just wanted to see if I will do things for her. She knows I will do anything for her. Love you, honey!

11:40 p.m., as I was going through our photo album and the fragrance filled the room. 12:31 a.m. the lights flashed, time to sleep.

August 13 – Friday

Went to Smith's, saw a beautiful bouquet of daisies, etc. in a very cute Happy Face vase. Got it for Jan. As I was putting the flowers next to her urn, I could swear I heard a small voice say, "Honey." I turned to look. There was nobody at home at the time.

Lisa was in a very good mood. She went out to buy Jan's favorite Baja Fresh tacos for her.

August 14 – Saturday

Pre-season football starts today. Woke up at 7:45 a.m., the lights flashed.

At 3:50 p.m. I said, "Jan are you waiting for football to start?" at 4 p.m. Lights flashed at 3:57, then again at 5:13 p.m.

August 16 – Monday

Lights flashed at 9:09 a.m. and 11:50 p.m.

August 17 – Tuesday

Lights flashed at 5:20 p.m. Felt very sad the whole day, can't find a reason why. Told Susan I was just so sad.

August 18 – Wednesday

Woke up still feeling very sad. Went to the casino to pass my time.

6:25 p.m. got a call from Lusing. Informed me that sister Yong-Yong had a bad fall in Manila, and was hospitalized with a cracked vertebra. She was in awful pain the whole evening. Sister Yong-Yong is not someone who complains about pain. The pain must be severe. My heart aches so much. She loves me and Jan so much. I talked to Jan right away, to go and see Yong-Yong, to take care of her, to lessen her pain. Jan loved Yong-Yong very much.

August 19 – Thursday

Since 6:25 p.m. last night, after talking to Jan about Yong-Yong, the cell didn't flash the whole night. 8:15 a.m. received an email from Phillip that Chai visited Yong-Yong. She is now doing better and the damage is not as bad as first diagnosed. Thank you, Jan.

August 20 – Friday

Lights didn't flash Thursday and today. Jan must be with Yong-Yong.

Came into bedroom at 12:25 a.m. past midnight, asked Jan if she has come home, the lights flashed at 12:33 a.m. Jan is home, goodnight.

August 21 – Saturday

Said goodnight to Jan at 11:55 p.m., lights flashed at 12:08 a.m. Goodnight honey.

August 22 – Sunday

Had a birthday party for Lisa; invited Jean, our neighbors and Lisa's friends. Jan had her share of favorite cake and food. After Jean left, I came into the room, the lights flashed. It was 7:24 p.m. Jan was with everybody in the party. Lights flashed again at 11:41 p.m.

August 23 – Monday

Lights flashed at 8:45 a.m. – good morning Jan. Reading the book, "We Are Their Heaven" by Allison Dubois, lights flashed at 3:15 p.m.

Played the CD of Jan's favorite songs. Lights flashed on, "A Bridge Over Troubled Waters" at 8:06 p.m. I was Jan's bridge and she was mine in our lifetime. Said goodnight to Jan at 12:15 a.m., lights flashed at 12:46 a.m. Goodnight Jan.

August 24 – Tuesday

Today is Lisa's birthday. Lisa got up at 1:28 p.m., lights flashed at 1:29 p.m.; then again at 2:18, 2:45 and 7:48 p.m.

Said goodnight to Jan at 11:50 p.m., lights flashed at 12:01 a.m. Goodnight my love.

August 25 – Wednesday

6:11 a.m. lights flashed as I said good morning to Jan.

Lisa made an important decision. She will be going home to South Dakota come October 22. She said Jan had been appearing in her dreams lately and was always smiling at her. I checked back on the journal and saw that Lisa's demeanor had changed since August 4. She has been happy. I guess if Jan thinks that it is time for Lisa to go home to be with John and Lucy, she being the only daughter now, and if Lisa will be happy, then it is time for her to go home. I am very happy for her.

August 26 – Thursday

7:25 a.m. lights flashed good morning sunshine. Lusing called shortly informing me of Yong-Yong's situation.

Came into room at 12:20 a.m., fragrance was strong. Lights flashed at 12:47 a.m., goodnight love.

August 28 – Saturday

Dakota came into the room, jumped on the bed and lay down to sleep. The lights flashed 7:42 a.m. Felt like Jan was saying, "Hey, Dakota is sleeping on my place!" Miss her so much. Told her that I would give up anything to feel the same kind of happiness we shared together before. The lights flashed after I said it – 8:09 a.m.

Came into the room at 11:56 p.m. and said goodnight to Jan and the lights flashed at 12:15 a.m.

August 29 – Sunday

Woke up and was watching FIBA USA/Slovenia. Lights flashed at 7:18 a.m. Good morning Jan.

Went to the movie, "The Expendables," with Lisa and Susan. Enjoyed the same popcorn and hotdog. When Susan passed me the popcorn, Jan's favorite while watching movies, the fragrance filled my senses. Susan never smelled anything.

August 30 – Monday

6:00 a.m. – flashed. Good morning Jan. Stayed in bed; lazy. Lights flashed again at 7:33 a.m. I know Jan was saying get up.

August 31 – Tuesday

6:44 a.m. lights flashed – good morning Jan. 9:29 a.m. lights flashed when Dakota jumped into bed.

Sept 1 – Wednesday

Lights flashed at 10:36 a.m., twice in a row, after Lisa told me that John might have to have knee replacement in Sioux Falls next month. The lights flashed again at 3:48, 4:08, 4:09, 4:15, 4:16 and 11:05 p.m.

Toni, Jan's cousin, had come to stay overnight, leaving early next day for Memphis. She talked about dreaming of Jan. Lights flashed at 11:05 p.m.

Sept 2 – Thursday

Start of NCAA college football. It is John's favorite sports day. John always called in for me to place bets for him on games. So, I was expecting Jan to be happy today, and she was. The lights flashed at: 7:23 and 7:43 a.m., and 4:40, 5:21, 5:51, 7:29, 8:18, 8:47 and 11:52 p.m. – 9 times today!

Sept 3 – Friday

Lights flashed at 7:20 a.m., and then at 5:56 p.m.

Sept 4 – Saturday

College football on Saturday. Lights flashed at 9:45, 10:20 and 10:43 a.m., then at night 11:50 p.m. – goodnight Jan.

Sept 5 – Sunday

Lights did not flash the whole day. Felt a little empty. Came into the room at 12:20 a.m. past midnight; said goodnight to Jan and lights flashed at 12:25 a.m. Very comforting to me. Goodnight Jan.

Sept 6 – Monday

Labor Day. Watching football Boise State/Virg. Tech. Lights flashed at 7:32 and 8:19 p.m.

Sept 7 – Tuesday

Knelt down yesterday cutting the lawn and felt pain in my right knee. Didn't think I hurt it. It started hurting last night. It really hurts today. Cannot bend my knee and cannot walk without pain. The right leg is completely stiff. Dreamed about Jan last night. She looked just like old days. Lights flashed at 10:47 p.m.

Sept 8 – Wednesday

Very bad night sleeping. Couldn't find a comfortable position to sleep as leg hurts intensely. Came into room at 11:10 p.m. Said goodnight to Jan. Lights flashed at 11:15, then at 11:35 p.m.

Sept 9 – Thursday

Again a bad night sleeping, leg hurt badly. Morning news said that Dallas is experiencing heavy rains and flooding. Decided to call Vic and Lusing to find out if they are alright. As I dialed, the lights flashed at 6:25, 7:13and 7:33 a.m.

NFL football starts today with the Vikings, Jan's favorite team, playing New Orleans Saints. I expect Jan to be watching with me. The lights flashed at 5:24 p.m. as Susan came home with dinner. Then again at 7:40 and 8:20 p.m. The smell of fragrance filled the room at 11:51 p.m.

Sept 10 – Friday

Woke up and said good morning to Jan. Lights flashed almost immediately at 7:16 a.m. Then fragrance filled my senses at 7:26 a.m. The lights flashed again at 7:43and 9:05 a.m. My leg still hurts badly.

Sept 11 – Saturday

Nine years ago today was a day of intense anger for Jan. The New York Twin Towers World Trade Center was attacked. I expected Jan to be agitated today. The lights flashed at 9:25, then at 11:44 and 11:48 a.m.

Ohio State played in the afternoon. John and Lisa have a bet on Ohio State. Ohio State was also Jan's favorite team because of her teacher at her writing course she took with Susan years ago. So she must be watching with me. 3:00 p.m. – flashed when Ohio State scored a touchdown. 3:20 p.m. – flashed when Ohio State kicked a field goal. Lights flashed again at 4:06, 5:02, 6:15, 6:35 and 7:05 p.m.

Came into the room and put Jan's CD on. When it reached, "Unchained Melody," our song – as Jan always said, the lights flashed and fragrance filled the air at 9:30 p.m.

Sept 12 – Sunday

Watching football, resting my leg. Lights flashed at 10:52, 11:15 a.m., and then at 3:00 and 3:41 p.m.

Sept 14 – Tuesday

7:43 a.m. flashed, good morning Jan. 9:11 a.m. – flashed. Got up and decided to go see my Chinese doctor for some herbal medicine for my hurting knee.

2:18 p.m. flashed after I applied some medicine on the knee. Lights flashed again at 2:42, 3:42, 4:29 and 6:47 p.m.

Sept 15 – Wednesday

Slept a bit better last night. Woke up at 7:49 a.m., the lights flashed. Good morning Jan.

Lights flashed again at 2:12 p.m. Started reading Suzane Northrop's book, "Second Chance." Lights flashed at 4:07 p.m.

Susan came home, came in the room to ask how I felt; my leg. As Susan turned to go out, the lights flashed at 4:58 p.m. Jan was acknowledging Susan's concern for me.

The lights flashed again at 6:32 p.m. I took a hot bath and applied medicine to the knee. Miss Jan a lot. Put on the CD. When it reached the 2nd song, "I'll Never Find Another You," the lights flashed at 7:34 p.m. Said goodnight to Jan at 12:09 a.m. and the lights flashed again at 12:11 a.m.

Sept 16 – Thursday

Received an email from Dale, informing me of what Jan's niece and nephew are doing. Everyone is doing okay. So I lit a candle, told Jan about it, and when I lied down in bed, the lights flashed twice at 2:41 p.m. I think Jan is happy. I started reading the book, "Second Chance" by Suzane Northrop, the lights flashed at 2:55 p.m. At 6:06 p.m., the lights flashed while I was watching football, NC State/Cincinnati. 7:33 p.m. lights flashed again.

Sept 17 – Friday

2:52 p.m. lights flashed while I was reading. 3:24 p.m. Dakota jumped into bed, lights flashed three times. Came into the room at 12:47 a.m. and said goodnight to Jan. Lights flashed at 12:56 a.m.

Sept 18 – Saturday

11:10 a.m. lights flashed while I watched football. 12:59 p.m. John called. He is in a happy mood, the lights flashed while I was talking to John.

The lights flashed at: 1:07, 1:14 (2x), 1:36 after Nebraska scored a TD, then 1:55 p.m. Nebraska scored another TD, 2:28, 2:32, 2:33, 2:39, 3:04 and at 7:32 p.m. I was feeling very tired at this point. Measured my BP, was 136/87, later my BP was 167/93 at 11:25 p.m. This morning my BP was 130/76.

Sept 19 – Sunday

Woke up at 5:20 a.m., took my BP, it was 133/73, lot lower than last night. Jan didn't flash me since 3:04 p.m. yesterday.

Sept 20 – Monday

Woke up, said good morning to Jan. Lights flashed right away at 6:16 a.m. Lights flashed again at 8:18 p.m.

Susan and Lisa were going through some old stuff in the garage. They found a book with Jan's dedication to me. One of her lines said, "Are you really a spy?" That was one of our jokes; she always liked it because of the James Bond movie, "The Spy Who Loved Me." Susan and Lisa were asking me about another line Jan wrote, which they don't understand. I explained it to them.

Susan was not feeling well tonight, so we didn't watch a movie like we do regularly every night. So I came into the bedroom, switched on the TV. While going through the channels to find one that I might like to watch, right there on channel 344 was, "The

Spy Who Loved Me!" Coincidence or was it my Jan being playful again? 11:19 p.m. lights flashed; I guess it is goodnight Jan.

Sept 21 – Tuesday

Dozed off while reading Sylvia Browne's, "Soul's Perfection." Woke up, the lights flashed at 3:20 p.m. 4:16 p.m. I continued reading. When I was reading about soul mates, the lights flashed.

Sept 22 – Wednesday

Leg felt the best since Labor Day weekend. Lights flashed at 4:56 and 6:48 p.m. Came into the bedroom at 11:18 p.m. and said goodnight to Jan. Lights flashed at 11:22 p.m. Goodnight Jan.

Sept 23 – Thursday

Woke up at 5:32 a.m., went to the bathroom, came back to bed. Took the cell, the lights flashed brightly in the dark before daybreak. Good morning Jan.

Came into the bedroom at 10:58 p.m. Turned and said goodnight to Jan. The lights flashed at 11:05 p.m.

Sept 25 – Saturday

Football day. The cell flashed many times: 10:11 and 10:32 a.m., and then 7:38, 7:58, 8:18 and 11:59 p.m. – goodnight Jan.

Sept 26 – Sunday

Woke up with soreness in my right knee at 5:37 a.m. Reached for the cell and placed it on the pillow, the lights flashed brightly in the dark as I said good morning to Jan.

6:13 p.m. watching football between Miami/Jets. The lights flashed again at 8:06 p.m. At 8:33 p.m. the lights flashed because I was missing Jan so much and was talking to her.

Sept 28 – Tuesday

Waited the whole day; saw no flashes. The lights finally flashed at 7:23 p.m.

Sept 29 – Wednesday

It was a surprise when Lucy called me at 9:05 a.m. Haven't talked to Lucy for some time. We talked about Lisa going home. Everybody is happy she is going home of her own choosing. I know she is not happy and feeling lost without Jan. The lights flashed at 9:53 a.m. and then tonight at 11:42 p.m.

Sept 30 – Thursday

Lights flashed at 6:45 a.m., good morning Jan. They flashed again at 7:31 a.m. while I was still lazing in bed. Guess she wanted me to get up. Jean called and the lights flashed at 8:13 a.m. while I was talking to Jean. The lights flashed again at 10:25 a.m. I smelled the fragrance at 11:15 a.m., and then the lights flashed at 11:18 a.m.

Went out the front yard to mow the lawn. Get tired easy these days. Came back to take a shower, the lights flashed at 4:53 and then at 6:57 and 7:14 p.m. Relaxed in bed to watch a football game between Oklahoma State/Texas A&M. I had placed a bet on Oklahoma State. Jan must be watching the game with me, and just like old times, Jan reacts to the game. The lights flashed so many times, let's see: 7:16, 7:17 (5 times), 7:18 (two times), 7:19 (three times), 7:21, 7:24 (3 times) and 7:27 p.m. (two times). I called Susan to come into the room to tell her how the cell has been flashing. Susan came in and said, "Hi, Jan!" The lights flashed three times in front of her instantly. The lights continued to flash: 7:28, 7:33 (2 times), 7:35, 8:02 (3 times), 8:03 (7 times), 8:04 (2 times), 8:08 and 8:28 p.m. (2 times). I counted 37 flashes in 76 minutes! I felt both excited and tired. Measured my BP, it read 146/86. Measured my BP this morning, Friday, it read 126/74, down from last night. My right leg felt the best in a long time since Labor Day weekend.

Came into bedroom, said goodnight to Jan at 12:38 a.m. and the lights flashed at 12:39 a.m. Goodnight my Jan.

Oct 1 – Friday

Lisa and Susan were going through Jan's collections of old Happi Hearts. She wants to bring some home to give to friends as gifts this Xmas. I was happy and came into the bedroom. Looked at the cell, told Jan about Lisa, the lights flashed at 4:50 and then at 7:30 p.m. Came into bedroom at 11:35 p.m., said goodnight as usual. The lights flashed at 11:47 p.m. Good night my love.

Oct 2 – Saturday

Noticed a call from Stephen at 5:32 p.m. last night. Called Stephen. Stephen told me that Rollie and Joy are in Illinois visiting with them. Rollie was fixing his computer and Jan's picture appeared on the screen. Rollie didn't know why it came on. Jan loved my nephews. Stephen was very helpful to her during her ordeal. Jan must just want them to know that she remembers them and was saying hello.

The lights flashed at 11:30 and 11:32 a.m. Came into bedroom at 1:52 a.m. in the morning, and said goodnight to Jan. Lights flashed at 2:01 a.m. Goodnight my love.

Oct 3 – Sunday

10:10 a.m. lights flashed. Ready to watch pro-football. Lights flashed again at 10:32 a.m., 2:56 and 3:41 p.m.

Susan brought dinner for Jean. She called me from Jean's home. As Susan handed the phone to Jean, the lights flashed three times. I told Jean that Jan was saying hello to her.

Settled down to watch the 5:30 p.m. football game. Jan was watching the game with me. The lights flashed when good plays were made. I can picture her pumping her fist saying, "Yes!" The lights flashed 38 times between 6:00 and 8:24 p.m.: 6:04, 6:21,

6:22, 6:30, 6:31 (two times), 6:32, 6:34, 6:35 (2x), 6:36, 6:37 (2x), 6:45 (3x), 6:46 (5x), 7:14 (5x), 7:16 (3x), 7:20, 7:26 (2x), 7:56, 8:03 and 8:24 p.m.

We had a fun time together!

Oct 4 – Monday

Today is Papa's birthday. I told Jan, and I know she will be here with me to remember Papa. 8:55 a.m. the lights flashed. Good morning Jan.

Monday night football, the lights flashed at: 6:08, 6:23, 6:41(2x), 6:42 (3x), 6:50, 7:49 and 7:52 p.m. (2x). Game turned into a blowout by New England. I stopped watching. The lights didn't flash again until 10:50 p.m. I stayed up and continued watching TV, the lights flashed again at 11:18 and then 11:38 p.m. I told myself Jan really is telling me to go to sleep. Goodnight honey.

Oct 5 – Tuesday

Woke up at 5:28 a.m., the lights flashed at 5:30 a.m. Good morning Jan. Lights flashed again at 5:54 and 6:17 a.m. Lazy in bed. Guess I better get up.

Lights flashed today at: 3:48, 4:10, 6:01, 6:10 and 7:07 p.m.

Oct 6 – Wednesday

Jean is having her hip replacement surgery today, so I was expecting Jan to be home.

Came home at 1:46 p.m., lights flashed at 1:48, then 2 times at 1:51 p.m.

Jean's surgery started at 2 p.m. The lights flashed: 2:02, 2:04 (3x), 2:07 (3x), 2:08, 2:10, 2:11 (8x), 2:12 (3x), 2:13 (5x), 2:14 (2x), 2:15 (4x), 2:31, 3:31 (4x), 3:32 (6x), 3;34 (5x), 3:38, 3:41, 3:42 (3x), 3:44, 3:45 and 3:46 p.m.; 55 times between 2:02 – 3:46 p.m. Jan is really watching over her 82 yrs. old neighbor.

I came into the bedroom at 11:52 p.m., said goodnight and the lights flashed at 12:09 a.m. Goodnight honey.

Oct 7 – Thursday

Jean's call at 8:30 a.m. surprised me. Said she was feeling fine. 9:48 a.m. lights flashed good morning Jan. At 11:32 and 11:52 a.m. flashed again.

Got into bedroom at 12:02 a.m. said goodnight to Jan. Lights flashed at 12:17 a.m.

Last night I told Susan something I had kept to myself for the last 28 months since my Jan's passing. I told her that all throughout the five months of Jan's ordeal before she passed, I did not feel any sadness or sorrow. There was no notion that my Jan was leaving me. The hurt only came after her passing. This has been eating me up inside. Today, as I was reading Sylvia Browne's, "God, Creation, and Tools for Life," on page 102:

'We meet a soul, outwardly like any other, and get a feeling that this one has wound its way to find us. You know there was a preordained reason that you were to come together for that brief moment, or for whatever time you are together, and we have a sense that we are home. That is what going "Home" feels like – that fleeting euphoria . . . We will spend our time down here, see the sights, then go Home.'

Yes, I think those five months, we knew deep inside, that my Jan was going "Home."

Oct 8 – Friday

8:53 a.m. lights flashed. Good morning Jan.

Entered bedroom at 11:53 p.m., said goodnight to Jan.

Melissa, Jan's niece had a baby on Monday. It was an induced birth. Melissa told Lisa that prior to her going to the hospital; Jan had come to her assuring her that everything will be fine. Jan loves the family.

Oct 9 – Saturday

My day for NCAA football. Jan was watching football with me. The lights flashed at: 10:06, 10:15, 11:20 and 11:44 a.m.

In old days, when Jan watched football with me, she would shout, "Yes!" on exciting plays made by her favored team and today she was doing just that.

12:05 p.m. flashed on an exciting play. 12:07 p.m. flashed, Indiana pass incomplete, 16 seconds left for an Ohio State win. John has a bet on Ohio State. 12:08 p.m. flashed when Ohio State intercepted Indiana; game over. Ohio State covered. John won his bet. Jan was happy!

12:15 p.m. flashed, 12:19 p.m. flashed when Virginia Tech won and covered with a 24 point win. Jan always laughed at me for betting the Hokies of Virginia Tech.

This same thing went on for the Alabama game. Lights flashed at 12:35 and 12:37 p.m. Susan walked into the room at 12:42 p.m. I told her that Jan is watching football with me. Susan said, "Hi Jan." The lights flashed instantly four times in front of her.

The lights continued to flashed throughout the game: 1:30, 2:27, 2:41, 2:47, 2:48, 2:50, 3:02, 3:03 (twice), 3:07, 3:08, 3:12, 3:14 (4x) and 3:15 p.m. (4x).

Oct 10 – Sunday

A day for pro-football. Jan was again watching football with me. The lights flashed continuously throughout the day: 2:02, 2:43, 3:37, 4:04, 4:24, 5:53, 6:30, 7:39, 7:59, and 8:21 p.m.

Oct 11 – Monday

Woke up at 6:00 a.m., went to the bathroom. Came back into the room. Lit a candle for Jan. Turned on TV to watch market forecasts. Turned to say good morning to Jan. Fragrance filled my senses, the lights flashed at 6:24 a.m. Good morning my Love. The lights flashed again at 6:41 a.m., I was still in bed.

Oct 12 – Tuesday

Woke up missing Jan a lot. Told Jan that I missed her this morning. It was 8:55 a.m., the lights flashed at 8:56 a.m. and again at 9:44 a.m. the light flashed.

1:22 p.m. came home, turned on TV, it was showing the 9/11 event of ten years ago in NYC. Jan was very emotional that day. Thought about Jan. The lights flashed at my thought.

Mowed the lawn, got pretty tired out. Came back and took a shower. Slumped into bed. The lights flashed – 4:22 p.m., 6:06 p.m. – flashed.

Came into bedroom at 11:45 p.m. and said goodnight to Jan. Lights flashed at 11:47 p.m., goodnight Jan.

Oct 13 – Wednesday

10:19 a.m. lights flashed, still in bed. Good morning Jan.

Came into bedroom at 11:00 p.m. Said goodnight to Jan. Lights flashed at 11:11 p.m. I didn't turn off the lights to go to sleep. Lights flashed again at 11:31 p.m. Told myself Jan wanted me to go to sleep – goodnight honey.

Oct 14 – Thursday

8:52 a.m. lights flashed, good morning Jan.

4:20 p.m., lights flashed. I was in bed waiting for the 4:30 p.m. game between Kansas St and Kansas.

Came into room at 11:32 p.m. and said goodnight to Jan. Lights flashed at 11:42 p.m. two times – goodnight.

Oct 15 – Friday

7:26 a.m., lights flashed. Good morning and got out of bed.

Oct 16 – Saturday

Haven't seen any flashes since 7:26 yesterday morning.

It's 7 p.m. and just learned that many nieces and nephews were at John and Lucy's house. John is having knee surgery on Monday; Jan must be there with them.

Lisa told me that four of Jan's high school best friends were gathered at Casper for a reunion. All four expressed surprise that they could all find time to get together, and all had Jan in their mind. Jan must be with them having fun.

7:15 p.m. lights flashed, Jan came home to see me. 7:38 p.m. lights flashed. Came into bedroom at 11:31 p.m., said goodnight to Jan. Lights flashed at 11:50 p.m.

Oct 17 – Sunday

Day for NFL football.

Lights flashed regularly at 11:38 a.m., and 1:03, 1:42, 2:31 and 3:57 p.m. – the Vikings won the game against Dallas.

Colts/Redskins started, lights flashed at 6:49, 7:14 and 8:24 p.m.

Came into bedroom at 11:25 p.m., said goodnight to Jan. Lights flashed at 11:30 p.m. Goodnight honey.

Oct 18 – Monday

John having surgery at 5:00 a.m. Vegas time. Got up to go to the bathroom, came back to bed at 4:58 a.m., lights flashed brightly in the dark. 5:19 a.m. lights flashed again.

10:24 a.m. Lucy called to inform me that John's surgery went well. Lucy told me that the other day Jaycee, Jan's nephew, found a heart-shaped green pepper in the yard. They all think that Jan was there looking after John. I believe so; Jan loved her Daddy very much. Came into bedroom at 11:53 p.m., said goodnight to Jan. Lights flashed at 12:08 a.m.

Oct 19 – Tuesday

2:55 p.m. lights flashed.

3:05 p.m. Lisa called to tell me that John is not feeling well. I talked to Jan to go take care of John. Lights flashed.

Came in bedroom at 11:08 p.m., said goodnight honey and lights flashed at 11:28 p.m.

Oct 20 – Wednesday

7:39 a.m. lights flashed, still in bed. Good morning Jan. 2:03 p.m. called Lucy. John feeling much better, lights flashed. 4:39 p.m. lights flashed. 4:57 p.m. lights flashed twice. Came into bedroom at 12:28 a.m. Lights flashed at 12:42 a.m., said goodnight Jan.

Oct 22 – Friday early morning

Lisa is leaving Las Vegas to be home with John & Lucy, a decision she made. It's the proper time for her to go home to find her own happiness. I guess Lisa belongs in South Dakota with the Forgeys. Lisa's friend Bob is a trucker who owns his own moving van. He did all the work to move Lisa's belongings. Lisa, Toni and Dakota all rode with the truck. Lisa's jeep went into the truck also. What a perfect setup. Cannot imagine Jan didn't arrange for all this. It's just perfect for Lisa's move back home.

Lisa left work early, as Lisa's jeep pulled into the driveway, the lights flashed 12:29 a.m.

Drove Lisa, Toni, and Dakota to Wild Wild West where the truck was parked. Came home and went to bed at 3:20 a.m., lights flashed at 3:34 a.m. All is well, goodnight my Love. A nice ending to Lisa's chapter in Las Vegas.

Oct 24 – Sunday

8:24 p.m. lights flashed. Vikings played but lost the game.

Came into bedroom at 11:21 p.m., said goodnight and lights flashed at 11:47 p.m.

Oct 25 – Monday

Lisa went to visit our headstone after arriving home and she texted a picture of the headstone to Susan. It had rained overnight. Lisa went back to the cemetery this morning. The rain had stopped. The headstone was dry except for a rain stain inside Jan's heart – it was the shape of a person! There was no stain on my side or anywhere else. Lisa took a picture and texted it to Susan. She texted, "Nobody can tell us she is not here!" I will ask Susan to print the photo. People who love and miss each other should see this. Your soul mate never left, and if she had a pure soul, God will grant her the ability to visit her love ones anytime, anywhere. The many and regular events over the more than two years since Jan's passing should convince everybody that their soul mate will be around to take care of them and their loved ones. Came into bedroom at 11:37 p.m. and said goodnight. The lights flashed at 11:39 p.m. Goodnight, honey, and thank you for the sign on the headstone. It brought a lot of comfort to your loved ones.

Oct 26 – Tuesday

Bought two rocker recliner chairs for the living room. Laid the cell phone on the arm rest of the recliner. Lights flashed at 7:26 p.m. while watching TV in the living room. The lights flashed again at 8:10 p.m.

Came into bedroom at 10:50 p.m., said goodnight honey; lights flashed at 11:03 p.m.

Oct 27 – Wednesday

Cleaned and rearranged the garage. Came back into the house tired! The lights flashed at 10:41 a.m. 6:40 p.m. lights flashed while watching NBA in living room. Came in bedroom at 11:56 p.m. Said goodnight love and the lights flashed at 11:57 p.m.

Oct 28 – Thursday

4:24 p.m. lights flashed while talking to Vic. 6:04 p.m. lights flashed while watching football in living room. Came into bedroom at 12:28 a.m., lights flashed at 12:35 a.m., goodnight Jan.

Oct 29 – Friday

6:24 a.m. woke up and the lights flashed. Good morning honey. 6:44 a.m. lights flashed again. Better get up.

3:56 p.m. lay down in bed after cleaning the house and yard. Lights flashed, Jan must be saying, "Honey, don't work too hard." She always said that when I am tired. 6:09 p.m. lights flashed. 6:35 p.m. lights flashed as Susan pulled into the garage.

Oct 30 – Saturday

Lights flashed at 3:04 and 8:00 p.m. Came into bedroom at 11:58 p.m. Said g.n. Lights flashed at 12:05 a.m. – g.n. Jan.

Oct 31 – Sunday

Came into bedroom at 12:15 a.m. Lights flashed at 12:33 a.m. Goodnight Jan.

Nov 2 – Tuesday

Election Day. Lights flashed at 7:24 a.m., good morning Jan.

4:40 p.m. lights flashed while watching election returns. Flashed again at 5:48 p.m.

Came into bedroom at 11:40 p.m. Said goodnight to Jan, lights flashed at 11:49 p.m.

Nov 3 – Wednesday

7:01 a.m. lights flashed. Good morning Jan. 7:25 p.m. lights flashed while watching TV in living room. Came into bedroom 11:13 p.m. Lights flashed at 11:25 p.m. Said goodnight to Jan.

Nov 4 –Thursday

6:57 a.m. woke up, lights flashed. Good morning Jan.

10:32 a.m., before going out, stood in front of cell phone; told Jan "I'll be home shortly, honey." Lights flashed.

Came into room at 11:45 p.m. Said g.n., lights flashed at 11:50 p.m. G.n. honey.

Nov 5 – Friday

Lights flashed at 4:29, 4:59 and 5:39 p.m. Came into bedroom at 11:03 p.m. Said g.n., lights flashed at 11:04 p.m. G.n. Jan.

Nov 6 – Saturday

Woke up at 6:42 a.m. Still dark, said good morning Jan. Lights flashed in the dark at 6:44 a.m.

1:33 p.m. lights flashed, watching football in living room.

Came into bedroom, said goodnight to Jan at 10:59 p.m. Lights flashed at 11:08 p.m. G.n. honey.

Nov 7 – Sunday

Woke up in the dark, went to the bathroom. Came back to bed, the lights started flashing nonstop between 2:52 – 3:03 a.m. I counted 116 times within 11 minutes. It hasn't done that since I was in Manila for Mama's cremation. What was Jan trying to tell me? Maybe I will know in due time.

11:20 a.m. talking to Susan on the phone, mentioned that Lucy had told me this morning that Aunt Georgie doesn't recognize her son anymore, the lights flashed at that moment.

2:22 p.m. lights flashed, watching football in living room.

Came into bedroom at 10:13 p.m.; said goodnight. Lights flashed at 10:17 p.m.

Nov 8 – Monday

Woke up in the middle of the night; lights flashed in the dark at 1:08 a.m.

12:15 p.m. just struck me that last year at this time Mama was rushed to the hospital on 11/7 and passed away the next day, today. Is this why the lights flashed nonstop the morning of 11/7, when Jan met Mama again on the other side?

Nov 9 – Tuesday

8:17 a.m. took the cell with me into the computer room, lights flashed while I was reading the morning news on the computer.

Came into bedroom at 10:36 p.m. and said goodnight. Lights flashed at 10:46 p.m. – g.n. honey.

Nov 10 – Wednesday

Watching TV in bed. Lights flashed at 9:43 a.m.

1:35 p.m. alone at home. Watched a video on the internet – a lovely video about life. The thought of Jan came in that was so overwhelming I started crying. Cannot control myself. Went into the bedroom and started crying out loud. Told Jan I missed her so much over and over. The lights flashed right then. Thank you Jan for acknowledging my feelings.

The video I watched was, "If I had my life to live over," made by Andie – **www.andiesisle.com**

2:18 p.m. came into bedroom. Thoughts of Jan still overflowing. Knelt down in front of our bed. Said to Jan aloud, "I love you so much, can you hear me?" The lights flashed instantly, Jan heard me!

4:02 and 4:30 p.m. lights flashed while I watched NBA Magic/ Jazz in the bedroom.

Nov 11 – Thursday

4:30 p.m. watching news in bedroom. I was eating grapes. Asked Jan if she cares for some grapes? Jan loved grapes, the lights flashed. I put some grapes for her on her altar. 5:03 and 5:26 p.m. lights flashed while watching football in living room with Susan.

Nov 12 – Friday

4:46 and 5:15 p.m. lights flashed while watching TV in living room.

Nov 14 – Sunday

1:15 p.m., lights finally flashed. Flashed again at 1:35, 2:37 and 8:05 p.m.

While feeling lost because the lights hadn't flashed since Friday afternoon, I opened up the cell phone, pressed the button to check calls. Why did I do it? The cell has had no service for a long time. To my surprise, there were calls registered on the phone! I listed down the calls:

Date	Number	Person Called	Events Associated with the Day
3/3/10	xxx-9734	Jan	Lisa was in turmoil. I asked Jan to guide her.
12/16/09	xxx-8316	Susan	(Cannot recall)
12/14/09	Voice mail		Photos of headstone decorated for Xmas sent to us by Lyn
11/15/09	xxx-8316	Susan	I was in Manila during wake of Mama
10/18/09	Voice mail		I was in Colome viewing the headstone
10/18/09	xxx-xxx-3112	Lucy's cell	
10/18/09	xxx-xxx-3112	Vic & Lusing	
10/16/09	xxx-0787	Susan	We were on our way to South Dakota
10/16/09	xxx-9734	Jan	
10/16/09	xxx-1234	Jean	
10/16/09	xxx-4816	Lisa	
10/16/09	xxx-9734	Jan	

I have asked Susan to take pictures of these calls on the cell; don't know if it will be visible.

Why? How? – I will know one day.

Nov 15 – Monday

So much to write today.

7:16 a.m. just got a call from Lisa; John is in the hospital. He was in a lot of pain and was undergoing tests to find out what may be the problem. I lit incense, telling Jan about her Daddy.

7:21 a.m. called Lisa. Lisa said Lucy swore that somebody was at home last night, that she heard footsteps in the hallway.

9:27 a.m. the lights flashed, and Susan called to say that Doctor didn't find any major problem with John.

I have been smelling the smell of cookies the last two days. Jan baked the best cookies. She often baked cookies for her friends at work, and they liked them very much; I do not like cookies. So I decided to call Lucy at 3:24 p.m. Lucy answered the phone. They had just gotten home. I told Lucy that Jan wants her to bake some cookies for John, John loves cookies. Well, John said that Lucy had promised to bake him cookies but didn't. Lucy said she will today, and she again told me that she heard footsteps in the hallway last night.

4:00 p.m. told Jan that Lucy is going to bake cookies for John and the lights flashed instantly at 4:01 p.m.

Nov 16 – Tuesday

6:48 p.m. John called to place some football bets, told me that he is feeling fine. Jan didn't flash me the whole day. Must be with John in Colome.

Nov 17 – Wednesday

6:08 a.m. woke up, turned on TV and said good morning to Jan. Lights flashed right away.

6:30 a.m. still in bed, lights flashed again, better get up.

5:05 p.m. Susan was on the phone with Toni, talking about Dakota; that Lisa took him to the Vet. His butt gland was full and he could not wag his tail. The lights flashed.

Came into bedroom at 11:58 p.m. and said goodnight. Lights flashed at 12:11 a.m.

Nov 18 – Thursday

5:25 a.m. woke up, opened my eyes, the lights flashed instantly in the dark, very comforting. Good morning honey.

3:50 p.m. waiting to see the lights flash the whole time since 5:25 a.m. Sitting alone in the living room watching TV, I said aloud, "Honey, are you busy? Are you home?" Within 5 minutes, the lights flashed.

5:45 p.m. lights flashed again.

Came in bedroom at 11:02 p.m., said goodnight. Lights flashed at 11:25 p.m. – goodnight Jan.

Nov 19 – Friday

7:15 a.m. lights flashed. Good morning Jan.

7:41 a.m. lights flashed again. Told Jan that I asked Susan to drive us to the WorldMark – Indio resort for the weekend.

Arrived at Indio 8:25 p.m. Went to turn on the TV in the living room. Susan said that the light above me just turned off. There were many lights in the room, I didn't notice it. I looked up, the light was off. So I flipped the switch a couple of times. Nothing happened. I went into the bedroom to unpack. When I came out, I noticed the light is now on! The lights turned on and off the last time Susan and I came to Indio Resort – one week after Jan's passing. I must have logged it in my journal in 2008.

8:36 p.m. the light above the TV went off again. 8:41 p.m. the light turned on again. I decided to get up on a chair a few minutes ago to rotate the light bulb to see if the light bulb was loose. It wasn't loose and the light didn't come on. Now it came on by itself!

9:37 p.m. chatting with Susan while watching TV. We talked about Lisa going home to South Dakota to be with John and Lucy. I said Jan knew that I, a city man since childhood, would not be comfortable in a small town like Colome. This is why Jan stated in her last writing that she wants to be with me until the time I pass, and then we will both go back to Colome to be with John & Lucy. And this is also the reason Susan and Lisa were with me all this time to make sure they both understand our wishes. I jokingly said, "What if Jan had asked me to go back to Colome? I guess I might have to open a Chinese restaurant there and name it the Sitting Duck Restaurant, since everybody knows Sitting Bull. The lights flashed instantly after I said it. Just like old days when Jan and I would laugh heartily with each other's jokes. Susan saw the lights flash also, and she said, "Jan, you are here!"

11:00 p.m. Susan and I went to the spa. Came back to the room; I sat in front of the TV with the cell phone in front of me. I had brought Jan's urn with me. I said, "Jan, goodnight and thank you for coming here with me." The lights flashed instantly.

Nov 21 – Sunday

Home from Indio. Came into bedroom at 10:23 p.m., said goodnight. Lights flashed at 10:43 p.m. – goodnight Jan.

Nov 22 – Monday

My allergies are bad today. Came in bedroom and lay down to rest at 1:26 p.m. Lights flashed at 1:29 p.m. The lights flashed again at 4:00 p.m.

Came into bedroom at 11:47 p.m. Said goodnight, lights flashed at 11:56 p.m. Goodnight Jan.

Nov 23 – Tuesday

8:33 a.m. lights flashed while I was talking to Lusing in the computer room.

3:42 p.m. gathered dried leaves in the yard; got tired. Came and lay down in bed. Lights flashed.

4:14 p.m. lights flashed, still in bed.

12:06 a.m. came into bedroom. Lights flashed instantly, goodnight Jan.

Nov 25 – Thursday (Thanksgiving)

First Thanksgiving at home for Lisa in the last 20 years. Such are the sacrifices for people working in the casinos.

Lights flashed at 7:45 a.m. Said Happy Thanksgiving to Jan. Told Jan it is alright for her to be with her family for Thanksgiving, I will be okay. John, Lucy, Lisa, Danny and family are gathering at Aunt Marilyn's house in Springview, Nebraska today.

Nov 26 – Friday

12:27 p.m. all alone at home watching TV, lights flashed. Jan is home,

Came in bedroom at 12:25 a.m. Said goodnight, lights flashed at 12:39 a.m. Goodnight Jan.

Nov 27 – Saturday

10:25 a.m. lights flashed while I watched football in the living room.

Nov 29 – Monday

Getting a bit anxious to see the lights flash. It flashed at 3:45 p.m.

Dec 1 – Wednesday

6:43 a.m. lights flashed.

Dec 2 – Thursday

Feel lonely these days when I do not see the flashes for some time. Jan must be busy on something.

1:34 p.m. feeling lonely I looked at Jan's picture. Told her that I am lonely and missing her. Lights flashed after that.

Dec 3 – Friday

Susan left for Florida to visit her parents. Lights flashed at 12:22 noon, then flashed again at 10:15 and 10:45 p.m.

Dec 4 – Saturday

Lisa and Lucy are having their Xmas Tea Party in Colome this morning. So I don't expect Jan to be home with me.

5:44 p.m. the lights flashed. The Tea Party was over. Lisa said that they had so much fun with the ladies of Colome; old friends. Jan must have had fun there with them.

8:03 p.m. flashed watching football in living room. Well, said goodnight to Jan. Lights flashed at 11:13 p.m. Goodnight Jan.

Dec 5 – Sunday

Not feeling well the whole day. Lights flashed regularly at: 3:29 watching NFL in living room, 5:05 watching NFL in living room, 7:29 finished dinner, 7:36 watching TV, and 9:19 p.m. in bed. Lights flashed after I said, "Jan, I miss you so much."

10:32 p.m. I dozed off for a while. Lights flashed after I woke up. Said goodnight and went back to sleep.

Dec 6 – Monday

I was going through Jan's collection of quotes last week. Came across a page where she had written a line for John. It was a page about destiny. It is the only page in the whole book where she wrote something. She had dated it May, 2002. I cut out the page, laminated it and sent it to John.

Lisa called to tell me that John had tears coming down when he saw it.

Last night I woke up a couple of times. I felt so warm. The space outside of the place where I was lying felt cold. Once I woke up feeling a pinch on my wrist.

I recall every time Jan's presence was strong, my blood pressure went up. So I tested my blood pressure this morning. It was high – 169/90. I really don't mind as long as Jan is with me.

9:19 a.m. sitting in front of the computer screen and reading about the passing of Don Meredith, the lights flashed.

8:10 p.m. lights flashed watching TV in living room.

10:29 p.m. lights flashed; in bed, called it a night.

Dec 8 – Wednesday

Not feeling well today. Lights flashed at 8:02, 9:28 and 9:59 p.m.

11:03 p.m. lights flashed. Goodnight Jan.

Dec 9 – Thursday

Feeling very lonely. Lights flashed at 6:10, 8:18, 9:03, 9:23 and 11:02 p.m. – goodnight Jan.

Dec 10 – Friday

6:10 p.m. lights flashed watching TV in living room.

Came into bedroom at 9:34 p.m. Lights flashed at 9:35 p.m.; goodnight Jan.

Dec 11 – Saturday

Lights flashed at 3:29 p.m. watching NCAA basketball in living room.

Dec 12 – Sunday

11:40 a.m. lights flashed.

11:59 p.m. lights flashed. Goodnight.

Dec 13 – Monday

The desire to see the lights flash has become a daily habit. I guess it is the sign that my Jan is still watching over me. I feel lonely and low when the lights do not flash for an extended time. But I know that the holiday seasons have always been busy for Jan. She was always happy and busy doing things to spread happiness to others. I think she still does.

The lights flashed at 12:53 p.m. while I was in the computer room. The lights flashed again at 5:05, 5:35 and 6:11 p.m.

Dec 14 – Tuesday

4:40 p.m. the lights flashed while I was talking to Jean. Jean was telling me about the robbery at Bellagio early in the morning. It happened at the Craps table next to where Dane was working.

5:25 p.m. lights flashed. Came into bedroom at 11:12 p.m.; said goodnight and the lights flashed at 11:30 p.m. Goodnight Jan.

Dec 15 – Wednesday

5:15 p.m. lights flashed.

Dec 16 – Thursday

Lazy in bed, tired. Thoughts of Jan were overwhelming. Opened my eyes, the lights flashed, it was 8:58 a.m.

4:00 p.m. lights flashed, and again at 5:25, 6:24 and 8:08 p.m. Came into the bedroom at 11:50 p.m. Lights flashed at 12:03 a.m. – goodnight Jan.

Dec 17 – Friday

9:24 a.m. still in bed when the lights flashed. Have to go to see my dentist at 11 a.m.

3:50 p.m. lights flashed.

Susan was home early, cooked dinner for me. When she served me dinner, while I was in the rocking chair, the lights flashed right after she turned around. Jan must be acknowledging her taking care of me.

The lights flashed again at 5:32, 5:52 and 6:12 p.m.

Dec 18 – Saturday

Lights flashed at 1:03 p.m. and at 1:30 p.m. watching TV in living room.

Dec 19 – Sunday

7:55 a.m. fragrance strong while reading newspaper in computer room. Lights flashed at 10:21 a.m. and 2:25 and 3:06 p.m.

Came in bedroom at 12:12 a.m.; said goodnight, lights flashed at 12:22 a.m. – goodnight Jan.

Dec 20 – Monday

8:48 a.m. lights flashed while I was still in bed thinking about Jan.

1:52 p.m. received a video email from Karen. It is a very well written and touching poem about our soldiers who sacrifice for this country. The cell phone was in front of the computer screen. I said to Jan, "Isn't this a touching video?" The lights flashed instantly. Jan was watching it with me.

Lights flashed today at 5:05 and 6:00 p.m. Came into bedroom at 12:13 a.m., lights flashed goodnight at 12:39 a.m.

Dec 21 – Tuesday

No signs.

Lisa called Susan this morning that she had gone shopping alone in Mitchell. She was sure that Jan had been with her. She was trying to find something for a neighbor, going around the store, her eyes caught a vase with a favorite quote of Jan's – the right gift! If Jan was shopping with Lisa, then I don't expect any flashes today.

Dec 22 – Wednesday

7:00 a.m. lights flashed. Jan is home. Got up from bed and went into the computer room, gathered up yesterday's newspaper, then went into the living room to light up the Xmas tree. While bending over to press the light switch, a small brochure fell out of the newspaper. I picked it up. The big print on the front page is "SHOPPING." Jan is telling me that she was with Lisa yesterday – shopping!

The lights flashed at 3:40 p.m. while I was watching TV in the living room.

Susan came home. I was telling and showing her the brochure that says "shopping." Right then the lights flashed at 4:40 p.m.

The lights flashed again at 5:02 and 5:23 p.m. Said goodnight to Jan at 11:00 p.m. Lights flashed at 11:34 p.m. – goodnight Jan.

Dec 23 – Thursday

12:35 noon lights flashed while I was in the computer room reading Drudge Report.

Lights flashed at 6:20 p.m. Came in bedroom at 12:23 a.m. Lights flashed at 12:30 a.m. – goodnight Jan.

Dec 24 – Friday

Day before Xmas. Lights flashed at 7:42 a.m. Jan is home for Xmas – just as she promised before she passed. I told Jan that I wouldn't mind if she goes to Colome to spend Xmas with John, Lucy, Lisa, Danny and family. It's been a long 20 years since they are able to get together for Xmas. How happy will Jan be? Very!

Lisa had made some of her home-made noodles for me. She called to say that when she opened the cloth used to cover the noodles for drying, the noodles appeared in a heart-shaped arrangement. She sent me a picture thru the phone. This happened on the day Lisa went to Mitchell shopping. Amazing!

Dec 25 – Saturday

Xmas Day. 7:42 a.m. lights flashed Merry Xmas from Jan!

Lights flashed again at 7:58 and 9:45 a.m.

Susan showed me a picture sent to her cell phone by Lisa. They had put two baskets of flowers at our headstone. As I looked at the picture and asked, "Jan, you see the two lovely flower baskets at our headstone?" The lights flashed right away. It was 10:35 a.m. I asked Susan to print out the two pictures; the heart shaped noodles and the flower baskets. Susan gave me the pictures. I looked at them, the lights flashed in front of me at 1:35 p.m.

The lights flashed again at 4:05 p.m.

Dec 26 – Sunday

Didn't feel good the whole day. Watched TV, football in living room most of the day. The green lights flashed many times today. Jan was staying with me today.

The lights flashed at: 10:10, 10:55, 11:15, 11:37 and 11:58 a.m. and 1:40, 3:25, 3:46, 4:07, 5:33, 6:17, 6:40 and 8:10 p.m.

I was watching the Florida International game. Susan was in her room and she knew that I had bet on FIU. They just made a good play. Susan shouted loudly in her room. I pointed towards the room, smiled and in my mind saying to Jan, "Honey, you heard Susan?" The lights flashed right away!

Dec 27 – Monday

Feeling better today. The lights flashed at 3:10, 3:41, 4:35 and 4:45 p.m.

Susan came into the living room at 6:01 p.m. She just saw the picture of little new born baby Valerie, Melissa's baby, and Susan said, "Valerie looks just like baby Jan." Susan turned back to go into her room, the lights flashed.

The lights flashed again at 6:50, 7:30, 7:50 and 8:31 p.m. At 12:45 a.m. the lights flashed. Goodnight Jan.

Dec 28 – Tuesday

Lusing called this morning saying that they might come to Vegas on Super Bowl weekend. The lights flashed right then at 8:26 a.m. Jan is happy that her "partner" is thinking about coming to Vegas.

The lights flashed at 8:47 and 9:07 a.m.

Susan called at 10:00 a.m. Lucy and Lisa were at Winner Hospital; Lucy was feeling sick. They were running tests on her to make sure it was nothing serious. Jan must have gone to be with them since the lights haven't flashed since 9:07 a.m. until 4:16 p.m. when it flashed again. I called Lisa and was told that the tests indicated nothing serious and that Lucy was playing cards with friends. The lights flashed again at 4:40, 5:07, 6:40 and 7:10 p.m.

Went to bedroom at 12:16 a.m.; lights flashed at 12:33 a.m. Goodnight Jan. Glad Lucy is all right.

Dec 30 – Thursday

9:50 a.m. flashed, I was on the computer. 2:49 p.m. flashed watching basketball, Kansas/Syracuse in the living room. Lights flashed at: 3:12, 3:39, 4:19 and 4:41 p.m.

5:01 lights flashed when I was telling Susan about a nice email Clarice sent me. It was about showing kindness to others.

Lights flashed at: 6:00, 7:20, 8:08, 8:40 and 9:02 p.m.

Dec 31 – Friday

Last day of 2010.

After 9:02 p.m. last night, the lights flashed again at 4:03 p.m. Happy that Jan is here to spend New Year's Eve with me. We used to stay up the whole night to wait for the New Year.

4:34 p.m. lights flashed.

5:01 p.m. Susan was going thru her collection of Disney T–shirts. I commented about Jan's collection of Beanie Babies. The lights flashed right then.

Went to have dinner with Susan and came home to watch football. Lights flashed at: 6:49, then 7:17 and 7:37 p.m.

Came into the bedroom at 1:12 a.m.; it's the New Year. The smell of fragrance filled my senses before I went to sleep.

YEAR 2011

Jan 1 – Saturday

3:04 p.m. watching Rose Bowl in the living room, the lights flashed, then again at 4:22, 5:31, 6:13 and 7:06 p.m.

Jan 2 – Sunday

10:47 a.m. watching football Pitt/Cleveland (NFL) in the living room. Lights flashed then again at 11:11 a.m.

Jan 4 – Tuesday

Lisa called early 7:27 a.m. to inform me that Aunt Georgie, Lucy's eldest sister, had passed away yesterday in Oklahoma. Aunt Georgie was Jan's favorite Aunt. Jan must be with her as the lights haven't flashed since 11:11 a.m. on Sunday and there were no flashes yesterday.

Good news though, Teneil had a baby, Jan's new grandniece or nephew? Didn't ask Lisa.

3:36 p.m. on the phone with Susan asking her to get an address for William, the son of Aunt Georgie and the lights flashed.

Lights flashed again at: 3:55, 4:20, 4:40, 7:52 and 8:14 p.m.

Jan 5 – Wednesday

The lights flashed at 9:36 a.m. when I was on the computer. I started entering my Jan's journal into the computer file last week. As I was on the Feb 22 entry, the lights flashed at 3:50 p.m.

6:15 p.m. lights flashed while watching NBA Bulls/Nets in the living room.

Jan 6 – Thursday

Lights flashed while I was entering Jan's file in the computer room at 10:24 a.m.

Jan 7 – Friday

Lights flashed at 6:53 a.m. when I woke up. It's been some time since Jan greeted me good morning when I woke up; the last time was on Xmas day.

Came back from the Las Vegas Athletic Club. Stayed in the steam room too long, temperature was too high. I may have suffered dehydration or a mild heat stroke, almost fainted. Came home; went to bed early. Lights flashed at 10:11 p.m. Told Jan if she flashed me again I will go to sleep. The lights flashed at 10:31 p.m. – goodnight Jan.

Jan 8 – Saturday

Feeling much better this morning. The lights flashed many times today. Jan must be watching over me. The lights flashed at: 9:27, 10:05, 10:40, 11:00 and 11:25 a.m., and 12:04, 2:45, 3:06, 6:05, 6:37 and 7:22 p.m.

Jan 9 – Sunday

Lights flashed at 11:55 a.m. – watching Ravens/Chiefs in the living room.

I went browsing at a discount furniture outlet on Decatur/Sahara last week. Caught a glimpse of a Chinese screen, but didn't even take a closer look. The only thing I remember was it was oriental with drawings of flowers. The image of the screen kept coming into my mind for many days. Susan has been redecorating the guest room. It suddenly entered my mind that Jan wants the screen, John and Lucy will be here around Super Bowl weekend. So I went with Susan to get it. After it was setup in the guest room, I sat down to watch football in the living room, the lights flashed at 2:38 and then 2:58 p.m. Jan is happy.

The lights flashed again at 4:13 p.m.

An ad for AT&T was on TV. It is advertising their new "4G" system. I looked at the cell phone and said, "Look, honey, they are now using 4G. Remember you always told people to park at level 4G – 4th floor, G spot at the Treasure Island?" The green lights flashed instantly! Jan is laughing.

Jan 10 – Monday

Cleared some dried leaves and pulled weeds in the backyard. Got tired out; sat in rocker to rest. The lights flashed at 4:39 and 6:56 p.m.

Jan 11 – Tuesday

4:39 p.m. lights flashed watching basketball UConn/Rutgers in living room.

Came into bedroom at 10:20 p.m. Both Susan and I appeared to be catching a cold. Said goodnight to Jan. Lights flashed at 10:29 p.m.

Jan 12 – Wednesday

Woke up with a sore throat at 5:26 a.m. Turned on the TV, lights flashed at 5:42 a.m. Good morning Jan. I sound like a frog.

It was in the 30's (temperature), cold for Las Vegas. Sat down to enter the journal into the computer. Lights flashed at 8:55 a.m.

Have a slight bout of cold and cough. 6:22 p.m. lights flashed while watching TV in the living room. Lights flashed again at 7:35 and 8:11 p.m. At 8:36 p.m. the fragrance came to me strong, followed by the lights flashing. Jan is here taking care of me. The smell of fragrance stayed with me until 9:00 p.m. I had gone into Susan's bedroom to watch TV. Susan said she didn't smell anything.

Went into my bedroom at 10:38 p.m. The smell of fragrance still persisted. At 10:56 p.m. the lights flashed. I said goodnight to Jan.

Jan 13 – Thursday

Woke up, went out to get the newspaper in the driveway; decided to go back to bed. The lights flashed as I lay down in bed at 7:06 a.m. – good morning Jan. My cough has disappeared although my throat still feels itchy. 9:34 a.m. lights flashed as I was entering the journal into the computer.

Went back to bed after a while. At 12:14 noon, the smell of fragrance came on, followed by the lights flashing.

3:37 p.m. I rested in the rocker in the living room, the lights flashed. Shortly after the flash, the TV showed an ad for AT&T using system 4G. I looked at the cell and said, "Honey, you were ahead of them, now 4G is on every now and then on the TV. You are the greatest!" The lights flashed at that instant. It was 3:56 p.m. The lights then flashed again at: 4:39, 5:22, 5:50, 6:15, 10:22, 10:48 and 11:08 p.m. I was still not well and decided to say goodnight to Jan.

Jan 14 – Friday

Woke up at 5:56 a.m., coughing slightly. Went out to get the newspaper and came back to bed. Lights flashed at 6:36 a.m. Good morning Jan. "I don't like this cough," I said to Jan.

8:40 a.m. lights flashed while I was talking to Lusing. Jean called me at 2:25 p.m. informing me of her date for the hip replacement on her left hip. She was crying on the phone lamenting that she has become a burden to everybody. I told her that anyone who loves her doesn't mind taking care of her and that she deserves the care because she is a good person. Right then the lights flashed. I told her that Jan has just responded and was agreeing with what I told her. "Bless my angel!" was what Jean said. The lights flashed at: 4:40, 5:40 and 6:04 p.m.

Jan 15 – Saturday

10:00 a.m. fragrance came on strong while watching TV in living room. 10:10 a.m. lights flashed.

Dawn and Tom came to visit, and we had lunch at Dim Sum with them. Had nice time talking about her Aunt Jan. The first time I met Dawn was when she came to Vegas to attend Lisa's wedding some 18 years ago. Time flies. Only happy memories remain to be cherished.

2:16 p.m. flashed watching Steelers/Ravens in living room.

2:40 p.m. flashed. 4:24 p.m. flashed. 5:03 p.m. flashed. Steelers won!

7:03 p.m. flashed watching Atlanta/Green Bay in living room.

Jan 16 – Sunday

11:28 a.m. lights flashed, watching Bears/Seahawks in living room.

1:51 p.m. flashed watching NE/Jets. Tom Brady just threw an interception.

4:20 p.m. flashed. 4:42 p.m. flashed.

Came into bedroom at 11:51 p.m. after watching a movie, "Warlords," with Susan; had a bad headache. Meditated and wished to see a sign from my Jan. Lights flashed at 11:56 p.m. Goodnight Jan.

Jan 17 – Monday

A holiday – MLK day. 11:00 a.m. lights flashed watching TV in living room.

2:14 p.m. flashed watching Clippers/Pacers in living room.

2:54 p.m. – flashed. 5:16 p.m. – flashed. 6:36 p.m. – flashed.

Jan 18 – Tuesday

Went out to the library; the place was crowded. No parking spaces were available. So decided to come home and clean the driveway. The fence was dirtied with paw prints of wildcats that climb over the yard fence. Cleaned them off and cleaned the driveway of dried leaves. Came into the bedroom and said aloud, "Honey, I love you!" Instantly the lights flashed. It was 12:21 p.m. Coincidence? It's happened too many times over these last 2 years and 7 months. My Jan is here with me. She watches and protects me, and she will until the day I join her.

4:40 p.m. lights flashed just when I was thinking of Jan.

5:55 p.m. flashed. 6:15 p.m. flashed when I was just telling Susan that Rachel thinks I am a funny guy. The lights flashed. Jan must be laughing.

6:43 p.m. – flashed. 7:03 p.m. – flashed. 7:27 p.m. – flashed.

Came into bedroom 11:56 p.m. Said goodnight to Jan. Fragrance came at 12:05 a.m. and the lights flashed at 12:06 a.m. Goodnight Jan.

Jan 19 – Wednesday

Opened my eyes. 6:28 a.m. turned on the TV, said good morning to Jan. The lights flashed at 6:32 a.m.

Last night while watching a movie, "A Foreign Field," Alec Guinness portrayed a WWII British veteran who became mentally damaged while trying to save a fellow soldier. He played a harmonica. I told Susan that I use to play a harmonica in high school. Susan went to her drawer and gave me a harmonica. She said she had it but never knew how to play it. Today I picked up the harmonica and started playing, "Amazing Grace," and the lights flashed at 9:42 a.m. The lights flashed again at 10:02 a.m. when I was playing, "Onward Christian Soldiers," and then at

10:36 a.m. when I played, "You Are My Sunshine." I felt both happy and sad. Happy that Jan heard me, but sad that I never played the harmonica for her in our 18 years together.

5:15 p.m. lights flashed while watching basketball in the living room. 12:20 a.m. lights flashed – goodnight Jan.

Jan 20 – Thursday

Allergies bothering me. 3:46 p.m. lights flashed while resting in the rocker. Then flashed again at 4:17 and 5:10 p.m.

I came into the bedroom at 12:05 a.m. Said goodnight. Lights flashed at 12:15 a.m. Goodnight Jan.

Jan 21 – Friday

Got up at 3:22 a.m. to go to the bathroom. Got back in bed. The lights flashed in the dark at 3:24 a.m.

Today is Jean's 83rd Birthday. Went to Chinatown to get a birthday cake for her. Also picked up some of Jean's favorite port buns. Just so happened that there was only one pink decorated cake in the bakery.

Susan gave me a red colored turtleneck sweater. I told Susan I won't be wearing it until after June 5th of this year. I had made a promise to myself that I will not wear anything red colored until after three years of Jan's passing; a Chinese tradition – 3 years of mourning for someone you love.

The lights flashed at 5:18 and 6:39 p.m.

Got into bed at 12:24 a.m. lights flashed 10 minutes later. Goodnight Jan.

Jan 22 – Saturday

Lights flashed at 5:22 p.m.; last at 11:27 p.m. – goodnight Jan.

Jan 23 – Sunday

Woke up at 5:30 a.m. Wanted to see a flash badly; stayed in bed. The lights finally flashed at 8:53 a.m. Jan must be saying, "You are getting spoiled!"

Today is championship day for NFL football. Positioned myself in the rocker ready to watch football. Lights flashed at 10:25 and then at 11:37 a.m. Game started at 12:30 p.m. Lights flashed at 12:50, 3:12, 3:30, and 4:05 p.m. – Steelers/Ravens. At 4:06 p.m. – fragrance came on. Lights flashed at: 4:30, 5:20, 6:08 and 6:49 p.m. A nice day of football, my two favorite teams won.

Jan 24 – Monday

Went to the gym with Susan last night after the Steelers game. Got dehydrated and possibly a heat stroke by staying in the overheated Jacuzzi too long. Came home and was feeling so bad. Tried to sleep but had a horrible night sleeping. Still feeling bad today. Rested in the rocker. The lights finally flashed at 4:22 p.m.; just seeing the lights made me feel so much better. The lights flashed again at 4:51and 5:46 p.m. – smelled the fragrance and the lights flashed 4 minutes later. They flashed again at 6:54, 7:16, 7:36 and 8:18 p.m. Felt a lot better when I came into bed at 11:16 p.m. and said goodnight to Jan. Lights flashed at 11:32 p.m. Goodnight and thank you Jan.

Jan 25 – Tuesday

Nothing notable. Lights flashed at: 4:40, 5:24, 6:05, 6:25, 6:45, 7:07 and 7:27 p.m.

Went to bed at 11:52 p.m. As usual said goodnight to Jan at 12:15 a.m. Jan said goodnight and go to sleep.

Jan 26 – Wednesday

Lights flashed at 2:01 p.m. while I was entering the journal into the computer.

Lights flashed again at 7:46 p.m. Went to bed at 11:48 p.m., Jan flashed goodnight at 11:54 p.m.

Going to the Grand Canyon and Sedona for Susan's birthday tomorrow. Hopefully, Jan will be with us. I am bringing the urn with us as I have been doing on our out of town trips that do not require customs inspection. I cannot imagine Jan being disturbed by the current TSA inspection.

Jan 27 – Thursday

Before leaving for Arizona, received an email from Shirley. The email explains it all. Amazed is what I felt. Almost 23 years and my Jan still brings memories to her loved ones. Shirley was her favorite sister-in-law.

TRIP TO THE GRAND CANYON AND SEDONA

I positioned the cell phone in the glove compartment in front of my seat so that I can see the lights if they flash.

While on US-93 the CD was playing, "I'll Miss You When You Go." I was about to tell Susan that was the song playing when Jan and I were vacationing in Solvang. Before I said it, the lights flashed at 11:21 a.m. Memories, Jan still treasures them!

The lights flashed 27 times starting at 11:27 a.m. while we traveled on US-93.

11:31 a.m. Susan said she wonders what Jan will do when we reach the energy vortexes in Sedona. Right after that, the lights flashed continuously 42 times. The flashes stopped for a minute, then started again. I showed the flashing cell to Susan.

At 1:53 p.m. the flashes stopped when I told Susan about what Lisa felt at the time of Jan's passing. I always feel sad and lost when this thought enters my mind. I guess Jan feels the same way.

It is 3:23 p.m. and we are heading to the Grand Canyon on AZ-64. The flashes stopped at 1:53 p.m. The song, "Bridge Over Troubled Waters" came on. I told Susan that I was Jan's bridge when we met. Then she became my bridge later on. I must have told Susan many times about this; the lights flashed instantly at 3:23 p.m.

3:52 p.m. the CD was playing Elvis, I sang along with the line, "If you ever go darling I'll be oh so lonely," right then the lights flashed.

4:49 p.m. Arizona time went to eat in the basement bar of the Best Western Hotel. The lights kept flashing until we got back to the Holiday Inn Express.

5:21 p.m. in our room watching TNT basketball game where Kenny Smith and Charles Barkley are the commentators. I told Susan, "Kenny and Charles were Jan's favorite sportscasters." Right then the lights flashed. Jan was saying, "You are right!"

I know people might say that the flashes are just flashes; maybe electronic or telecommunication glitches, etc. I have lived for these flashes the last 2 years and 7 months. They have become a big part of my life. There are the flashes that just occur regularly these days without my thoughts, actions, or words. I regard them as Jan's messages to me that she was here with me. Then there are the flashes that responded to my thoughts for her, and then the flashes that respond to my questions to Jan, and last but not least, the flashes that occur instantly to circumstances involving our past lives together. After the last 31 months, to me and others who love Jan, there are no more doubts that my Jan is with us and watching over us, more than she ever did before her passing.

Jan 28 – Friday

It's Susan birthday. We went to the lobby for breakfast at 8:14 a.m. I placed the cell phone on the table in front of Susan. The lights flashed continuously in front of Susan. Jan was wishing Susan a happy birthday.

The tour guide picked us up for the Grand Canyon tour. The lights were flashing when we were at the first viewing stop – I think it was Mather point, at 10:14 a.m. It stopped and started again when we got to Grandview, where the first hotel at Grand Canyon was built in 1898. It was 11:11 a.m., then again at 11:44 a.m. when we got to the tourist cabin.

While driving us backed to the Holiday Inn Express, the tour guide asked where we are heading after Grand Canyon. Susan told her Sedona. The tour guide said "Oh! You are going to Oak Creek Canyon." Right then the word "creek" stood out in my mind. I remember having a dream months ago where Jan told me she was going to a place with water, a place with the word "creek." Could it be Oak Creek Canyon? Sedona? The energy vortexes? I will have to check my journal when I get home.

2:52 p.m. entering the winding road to Sedona, the sign, "Oak Creek Canyon" showed up and the lights started flashing. The mountain road was only two narrow lanes. It was a very winding road. Susan was driving only 15-20 miles per hour. The lights flashed all the way. It stopped only when we got off the winding road into Sedona. I counted 53 flashes during the 18 minute drive.

Jan 29 – Saturday

No flashes since entering Sedona yesterday afternoon. After breakfast, we set out for the Boynton Canyon Vortex. While searching for the Vortex, the driving instructions said to look for a "T" sign. We arrive at a "T" sign, and the lights flashed twice. We are on the right track. The lights flashed 3 times when we got to the parking lot to start hiking up the trail to the Vortex. I told Susan, "Don't let anyone tell us she is not here with us," and the lights flashed instantly.

As Susan and I walked uphill on the trail, half way up, I was worried about Susan not being able to complete the trail. It was uphill and a red dirt trail, not even easy for me, more so for Susan. I asked Susan if she wanted to turn back because the downhill could be even more difficult on her knees. Susan said without hesitation, "I am here with Jan, I can make it!" She did. We placed a red rock on the tree limbs at the peak of the Vortex. When Susan placed hers, the lights flashed 3 times. I asked, "Jan is this where you came to?" The lights flashed.

Rock tree in Boynton Canyon, Sedona, Arizona

Rock tree in Boynton Canyon, Sedona, Arizona

While coming down the trail I told Susan, "Jan would have loved to walk this trail with us." I remember when we were walking on the hills at John's ranch with John. It was getting late in the day. Jan was just so happy, her "simple happiness of life," as she coined it. The lights flashed right then.

We got back into the car. I said, "Thank you Jan for coming on the trail with us." The lights flashed at 11:18 a.m.

Jan 30 – Sunday

The lights stopped flashing after leaving the Boynton Vortex. It flashed twice again at 11:34 a.m. when we were on US-40 on the way home.

At 12:04 p.m., the CD was playing the Everly Brothers song, "Dream, Dream, Dream." I started singing along with it. When the song reached, "And I love you so, and that is why whenever I want you all I have to do, is dream," the lights flashed right then three times.

We stopped at Popeye's Chicken for lunch. The lights flashed continuously starting at 12:34 up to 2:35 p.m. when we were 50 miles from Las Vegas.

Arrived home. Came into the bedroom at 10:24 p.m. Meditated and said goodnight to Jan. The lights flashed within a minute at 10:34 p.m. Goodnight my love. Thank you for a very nice trip.

Jan 31 – Monday

4:07 p.m. the lights flashed. I was resting in the rocker.

The walking in Grand Canyon and at the Vortex trail is catching up to Susan and me. Retired to the bedroom early. The lights flashed at 8:37 p.m., seven minutes after I got into bed. I dozed off and woke up at 9:35 p.m. and the lights flashed shortly after I opened my eyes. Thoughts of Jan filled my mind and the lights flashed at that moment, at 10:54 p.m. Miss her so much. Goodnight Jan.

Feb 1 – Tuesday

Was in the computer room and suddenly remembered to check out the dream I had months ago about Jan telling me that she was going to a place with water with the work "creek" in it. I went back thru the diary. Found it on August 12, 2010, where Jan said she was going to a place where there is water and a place with the word "creek" in it. This was five months ago. Sedona is in "Oak Creek Canyon." There is water around Sedona. The Boynton Vortex is on "Old Creek Road." Coincidence?

Another interesting thing, when we stopped at Kingman for lunch, Susan bought two apple pies. She didn't eat any. She brought them home and left it on the dining table. I asked Susan as she was leaving for work this morning if she is going to eat the apple pie or throw it away? She said, "Oh!" took one of them, and then said, "They taste good when reheated." I reheated one and took it in the computer room. As I was reading the entry of August 12, it was the day Jan made me go to McDonald to buy apple pie, and I bought two on sale for $1. Coincidence again?

The lights haven't flashed since 10:54 p.m. last night. I normally don't open up the cell phone to check. At 4:50 p.m., however, something compelled me to open the cell. Surprisingly it was off. I didn't do anything to the phone since 10:54 last night. Why did it turn off by itself? I recall this happened once a long time ago. So again, I went back thru the journal to check my recollection. Yes, this happened on Jan 18, 2010. In fact, I was just typing in the diary of that particular month this morning that is why I remembered. Again, coincidence?

The lights flashed at 7:15 p.m. and 12:00 a.m. Goodnight Jan.

Feb 2 – Wednesday

Feeling extremely tired. The temperature outside had dropped to the 20's. I was either catching a cold or allergies were getting to me. I took a nap at noon. Woke up and the lights flashed at 2:30 p.m. and again at 3:10, 3:29, 4:30 and 5:52 p.m.

Feb 3 – Thursday

Chinese New Year – Year of the Rabbit.

Lights flashed at 5:01 and 5:57 p.m.

6:56 p.m. Susan was coughing badly, the lights flashed and flashed again at 7:22 p.m.

Came into the bedroom at 11:25 p.m. Anxious to see the lights, meditated and asked for Jan to show me a sign. When I opened my eyes, the lights flashed very shortly. It was 11:41 p.m. Goodnight my love.

Feb 4 – Friday

Feeding a bit light headed, went to rest in bed. The lights flashed while I was watching TV. It was 9:16 a.m. Watching the chaos in

Egypt, snow storms in most of America, financial crisis in the US, can't help but feel sad for the next generation. Hope things will get better. 9:59 a.m. lights flashed again. 5:02 p.m. lights flashed when I was resting the rocker.

At 8:32 p.m. I was watching NBA games in Susan's room. I started smelling the fragrance. This time I decided to go into my bedroom right away. I looked at the cell phone on the bed, and asked, "Honey, are you calling me?" and the lights flashed instantly. A very comforting experience, something I cannot find words to describe.

Susan finished making the DVD of our trip to Grand Canyon and Sedona. We watched it and it was lovely. I went into my bedroom to rest for the night. The lights flashed as I got into bed. Jan must love the DVD also. It was 8:57 p.m. Said goodnight to Jan at 11:48 p.m. and the lights flashed at 12:13 a.m. Goodnight Jan.

Feb 5 – Saturday

A special note about the apple pies Susan bought at Kingman's Popeye's. I asked Susan tonight what made her buy the two apple pies when we stopped at Kingman. She said that the cashier told her they are for sale; it was $1.29 for 2. So she bought it, although she didn't feel like eating it. On August 12, I bought two apple pies at McDonald when told the same thing – on sale. Coincidence?

Susan decided to do a scrapbook for her trip to Grand Canyon. There was a time when scrapbooking was a pastime for Jan. I remember having to drive her to scrapbook sessions at night.

When Susan came home with her scrapbook material from Michael's, the green lights flashed at 5:20 p.m. Then the lights flashed again at 5:47 and 7:45 p.m. when Susan was working on the scrapbook.

At 12:29 a.m. the lights flashed, signaling goodnight.

Feb 6 – Sunday

The lights flashed several times today. There was nothing in particular to note except that Susan has been working hard on her scrapbook. The lights flashed at 5:54, 6:24, 7:04, 7:29, 8:27, 8:47 and 9:59 p.m. Could Jan be watching Susan doing her scrapbook?

Feb 7 – Monday

The lights didn't flash goodnight last night. No signs the whole day until I said goodnight at 10:56 p.m. I didn't turn off the TV, and it flashed again at 11:17 p.m. It's goodnight from Jan.

Feb 8 – Tuesday

I have been inputting my handwritten diaries into the computer file. As I was typing, I can't help but be amused by how crude my English was – spelling mistakes, tense errors, bad English. At any rate, my intent was, and still is, to have an honest and truthful record of events. A true description of my inner feelings, and a refuge for me when I feel sad, lonely, or bored. There were no exaggerations or distortions, for such would be an insult to Jan's love for me.

At 7:35 p.m. when I asked Susan, "When is the bull sale auction for Danny and John?" Susan replied, "Next Tuesday," the lights flashed. I am sure Jan will be there with Danny and John. The lights flashed again at 7:55 p.m.

I came into the bedroom at 10:26 p.m.; said goodnight and the lights flashed at 10:55 p.m. Goodnight Jan.

Feb 10 – Thursday

John and Lucy delivered beef to Casper for Steve and others. I didn't expect Jan to be home. She should be with John and Lucy. There were no flashes since yesterday.

The lights finally flashed at 12:21 a.m. Jan had come home and I should be sleeping.

Feb 12 – Saturday

Missed Jan yesterday. Woke up at 6:57 a.m.; the lights flashed almost instantly, brightening my day. Thank you Jan.

Feb 13 – Sunday

In the living room watching the Celtics/Heat game, the lights flashed at 11:00 a.m. and 11:42 a.m. I dozed off. No sooner did I wake up, the lights flashed again at 12:32 p.m.

Decided to go to the 2:55 p.m. show of the movie, "Eagle" with Susan. Brought the cell phone with me to the Orleans. The cell lights flashed once during the movie. Jan was enjoying the popcorn, just like old days.

7:22 p.m. lights flashed.

10:33 p.m. went to bed, said goodnight. Lights flashed at 10:43 p.m., goodnight Jan.

Feb 14 – Monday

It's Valentine's Day. Before I went to sleep last night, I was hoping, deep inside of me, that my eternal Valentine would greet me happy Valentine's today.

I got up at 6:23 a.m. to go to the bathroom. It was still dark. As soon as I entered the bedroom, the lights flashed. Thank you Jan for the blessing. I meditated, mentally told Jan how much I missed her today. That I am very glad the whole Forgey clan are doing well. I opened my eyes, the lights flashed. It was 6:52 a.m. I put on Jan's favorite songs, the lights flashed again at 7:17 a.m.

Tonight the lights flashed at: 6:19, 7:23, 7:54 and 8:21 p.m. No goodnight flashes.

Feb 15 – Tuesday

Susan had a stress test appointment in Henderson. Drove her to the doctor at 10:30 a.m. When I came home, decided to cut a banana for Jan, haven't done this for some time. I put the banana on Jan's altar. Came into the computer room, put the cell in front of the computer screen. The green lights started flashing. It was 11:33 a.m. It must have flashed continuously at least 40 times! I started wondering why? Is there something that made Jan flash this many times?

Suddenly remembered that Danny and John were having their bull sale at the auction this morning. I called John's home, no answer. Lucy's cell, no answer. Lucy finally called me back at 2:10 p.m. She was very happy. She told me that Danny and John sold their entire herd. Neil was also home. Now I know why Jan was so happy. I told Lucy about the flashes. Lucy giggled, "Oh! That girl of mine!" Jan, you are the greatest!

Feb 16 – Wednesday

Went back to bed after having breakfast. Felt a bit tired. Looking at Jan's picture, the memories of Lisa's wedding day rushed into my mind. I can see Jan running around like a bumble bee. She kicked off her heeled shoes and was laughing so contagiously. She was so happy. She had arranged for all her brothers and sisters-in-law, and aunties/uncles to be here in Vegas for the wedding. The lights flashed right then. It was 8:34 a.m.

I went into the computer room to enter the diaries into Jan's file. The lights flashed at 10:07 a.m. when I was on Dec 15, 2009.

I was doing the entry again in the afternoon. The lights flashed at 2:48 p.m. when I was entering Dec 29, 2009. Both dates had diaries laden with heavy recollections of the last days of Jan and Mama. I felt like crying. The lights flashed again at 5:20 p.m.

Feb 17 – Thursday

Pulled some weeds in the backyard. Got tired and dizzy. Cannot fight old age. Came into bed to rest. Lights flashed at 10:53 a.m.

Slept in the rocker in the afternoon. Woke up, the lights flashed instantly at 5:15 p.m., then at 5:57 p.m. The lights flashed tonight at 12:07 a.m. Goodnight Jan.

Feb 18 – Friday

Opened my eyes at 5:56 a.m., the lights flashed. Then again at 6:36 and 7:08 a.m. I was watching TV in bed. Better get up.

Feb 19 – Saturday

A day for NCAA basketball games. The lights flashed many times while I was watching games: 10:40 watching Notre Dame/W. Virginia, 11:00 and 11:41 a.m. and 12:02, 12:31 and 12:56 p.m.

Watched a movie with Susan tonight, "High Winds in Jamaica." At 10:50 p.m. a feeling of loneliness and being lost sank in. Went into the bedroom to be with my Jan. The lights flashed at 11:05 p.m. Jan must know that I was feeling lonely. If I were a ship moribund on the open seas, I wish Jan could guide me to my eventual destination. A safe harbor where I could be with my Jan again. I miss Jan dearly tonight. The lights flashed at 12:00 midnight. Jan wanted me to rest my weary mind. Goodnight my love.

Feb 20 – Sunday

Woke up at 7:14 a.m., turned on the TV to see what the politicians are doing to mess up the country. The lights flashed. Didn't get out of bed. The lights flashed again at 7:34 a.m., time to get up said Jan.

The lights flashed many times today: 1:22 p.m. watching "Bugsy" on Encore in the living room, 2:17, then at 3:08 watching NBA all-star pregame show, 4:50, 5:12, 6:52 – all-star game, 7:59 and 8:33 p.m.

Feb 21 – Monday

John, Lucy and Lisa left this morning for Casper. They arrived at Steve's house around 6 p.m. The lights didn't flash the whole day. It flashed at 7:08 p.m. Jan must have been with them on the way. My angel watches over everybody she loves.

Feb 22 – Tuesday

The lights flashed at 9:26 a.m., then at 3:06 and at 3:36 p.m. the lights flashed as I was talking to Jan.

The lights flashed again at 4:38 p.m. John, Lucy and Lisa arrived around 6:30 p.m. 8:04 p.m. I was talking to John in the living room, the lights flashed.

9:03 p.m. the lights flashed as John and Lucy went to bed to rest. Came into the bedroom at 12:00 midnight. After watching a movie, "Train" with Burt Lancaster, the lights flashed at 12:05 a.m. Goodnight Jan.

Feb 23 – Wednesday

The lights flashed at 5:19 p.m. John and Lucy spent the day at the Orleans. Jan must have been with them like old times.

Lisa, Lucy, and Susan were playing cards in the dining room. John said goodnight; the lights flashed as John walked into their bedroom to rest.

The lights flashed at: 9:15, 9:35, 9:56, 10:17, 10:37 and 11:09 p.m. The girls were playing cards nearby all this time.

Feb 24 – Thursday

Missing Jan badly. How happy she would have been with John and Lucy here at home. On another thought, she is happy. The lights flashed at 4:33 p.m., I was watching TV with John. They flashed again at: 5:00, 6:09, 6:31, 6:51, 7:12, 7:41, 8:01 and 8:24 p.m. Felt a bit light-headed; went into the bedroom to measure my blood pressure. I suspected it must be high because I feet Jan's presence so strongly. My blood pressure reading was 175/101.

The lights flashed again at 9:07 p.m. I went to bed at 11:30 p.m. Said goodnight to Jan and the lights flashed at 11:39 p.m. Goodnight my love.

Feb 25 – Friday

Woke up at 6:50 a.m. Measured my blood pressure, it was 159/83. The lights didn't flash the whole day until 6:42 p.m. when I was watching an NBA game.

At 11:30 p.m. I said goodnight to Jan, the lights flashed instantly. Went to sleep.

Feb 26 – Saturday

Woke up at 9:20 a.m. Measured my blood pressure, it read 117/73.

The lights didn't flash until 10:25 and 11:30 p.m. when I said goodnight.

Feb 27 – Sunday

7:05 a.m. my blood pressure reading was 122/75.

John, Lucy and Lisa planned to leave for Wyoming early morning at 5:00 a.m. The lights flashed at 10:54 p.m. John, Lucy and Lisa all rested early.

Feb 28 – Monday

John and Lucy asked to be awakened at 4:30 a.m. I set the alarm but woke up at 4:10 a.m. anyway. The lights flashed at 4:16 a.m. Jan is here to see them off.

John, Lucy and Lisa left at 5:15 a.m. I went back to bed. The lights flashed at 6:22 a.m.

The lights didn't flash the whole day until 6:07 p.m. Lisa had texted Susan at 6:02 p.m. informing us that they had arrived at Steve's house. Jan had come home to be with me. The lights flashed at 10:25, then at 11:26 p.m. Goodnight Jan.

March 1 – Tuesday

Had a good night's sleep. Woke up at 6:20 a.m.; went out to get the newspaper. Came back to bed, turned on TV to watch Fox Business News with Varney. Lights flashed at 6:28 a.m., then again at 6:53 a.m.

Lucy called to tell me that everything is fine and that they are heading home. The lights flashed at 10:27 a.m.

Susan came home around four p.m. – the lights flashed at 4:26 p.m. I told Susan that John, Lucy and Lisa must have arrived in Colome because Jan just flashed me. Sure enough, Lucy called to say they were home. The lights flashed again at 5:47 p.m.

Watched a movie, "Tell No One" (French); a good movie. Came into the bedroom at 12:08 a.m., said goodnight, lights flashed at 12:09 a.m. Goodnight honey.

March 2 – Wednesday

Woke up at 6:25 a.m., said good morning to Jan. Lights flashed at 6:28 a.m.

4:22 p.m. lights flashed while watching NBA Bulls/Hawks in the living room.

12:32 a.m. lights flashed – goodnight Jan.

March 3 – Thursday

Not much to write about. Lights flashed at 5:06 p.m. while watching NCAA Seton Hall/St. John. Then flashed again at 6:18 and 7:10 p.m. Said goodnight to Jan at 11:51 p.m., lights flashed at 12:05 a.m. Goodnight my love.

March 4 – Friday

Miss Jan very much. Had the urge to play the harmonica for her. When I played, "How Great Thou Art," the lights flashed. It was 11:04 a.m. Jan heard me and she acknowledged it.

The lights flashed at 4:21 and 6:38 p.m. while I watch NBA Minnesota/76ers.

March 5 – Saturday

Lights flashed regularly at: 4:03, 5:16, 5:43 (NCAA Duke game), 6:06, 6:31, 7:13 (NCAA Texas/Baylor), 7:33, 8:20 and 9:01 p.m. Thank you Jan for keeping me company.

My left side of my stomach has been hurting since this afternoon. Felt like a pulled muscle. Hurts every time I bend.

Watched a movie with Susan, "Moliere," an entertaining French movie. Came into bedroom at 12:25 a.m.; still aching. I told Jan, "When the time comes for me to join you, promise me that you won't let me suffer." Jan asked me the same when she was last rushed to the ER at Summerlin Hospital. The lights flashed instantly. It was 12:27 a.m. Thank you Jan, my eternal love.

March 6 – Sunday

Jan accompanied me the whole day while I watched basketball: 11:23 a.m. flashed – NBA Bull/Heat, 12:26, 2:25 p.m. – NCAA Ohio State/Wisconsin, 5:05, 5:25, 5:50 and 6:10 p.m. – NBA Oklahoma City/Suns.

Came into bedroom at 11:05 p.m. Lights flashed at 11:25 p.m. – goodnight Jan.

March 7 – Monday

Susan visited Jean on her way home. The lights flashed when she was telling me about Jean's surgery on Wednesday. It was 4:44 p.m.

March 8 – Tuesday

Had a hard time sleeping last night. Still awake a 2:59 a.m. Asked Jan to please come into my dreams; haven't dreamt about her for a long time. Fell asleep after that. Woke up at 7:40 a.m. and remembered clearly that I dreamed about meeting Jan in a park. I looked at her; held her heavenly face in my hands and asked, "Is this true? I am so happy!" Jan replied, "Don't you think I am happy too?" I woke up feeling happy; been a long time since I woke up this way. Thank you, Jan.

I was on the phone with Susan talking about Jean's surgery tomorrow. She has to be at the hospital early at 5:30 a.m. I told Susan I offered to take Jean to the hospital but Jean said that Dane had already told her he will drive her. The lights flashed. It was 3:30 p.m.

By the way, my aches and pains of the last few days had disappeared this morning after I woke up feeling happy. The lights just flashed while I am writing this at 4:01 p.m.

Lights flashed at: 5:29, 6:14 and 6:37 p.m. At 7:14 p.m. Marquette was playing. I shouted to Susan to come quick and look at the coach of Marquette. "He looks like one of the 3 stooges!" Susan laughed and the lights flashed. Jan was laughing too!

Watched a movie, "From Here to Eternity." Came into the bedroom at 11:52 p.m. and said goodnight. Lights flashed at 12:09 a.m. Goodnight Jan.

March 9 – Wednesday

Jean's hip surgery took place at 7:30 a.m. The lights flashed at 8:52, 9:10 and 9:19 a.m. I dozed off to sleep while watching NCAA basketball St John vs. Rutgers; dreamed about Jan. With her lovely smile still in mind, I opened my eyes, the lights flashed instantly; it was 11:57 a.m. The lights flashed again at 1:03 p.m. Jean called a short time later at 1:37 p.m. to let me know that she was already resting in her room at the hospital. The lights flashed last at 4:56 p.m.

March 10 – Thursday

The lights flashed many times today. I woke up at 6:46 a.m., turned on the TV to watch news. The lights flashed at 6:56 a.m. Good morning Jan. The lights flashed again at 7:22 a.m.; got out of bed.

The lights flashed again at: 9:31 a.m., I was watching NCAA Pittsburgh vs. UConn. 10:07, 10:36 and 11:54 a.m. (St John vs. Syracuse), 1:05, 1:25, 1:45, 3:25 (NCAA Arizona vs. Oregon St), 4:12, 4:32, 5:23, 5:52 (NBA Lakers vs. Heat) and 6:37 p.m.

March 11 – Friday

Lucy called at 12:36 p.m. to ask about Jean. The lights flashed when I finished talking to Lucy.

The lights flashed again at 1:25 (NCAA Ill vs. Michigan), 4:50 (NBA Charlotte vs. Portland), 5:30, 5:58 and 6:22 p.m.

Came into the bedroom at 12:20 a.m. and bid Jan goodnight. Lights flashed at 12:29 a.m. Goodnight Jan.

March 12 – Saturday

The lights flashed at 10:18 a.m. (NCAA Memphis vs. UTEP), 5:08, 5:54 (NBA Jazz vs. Bulls), 6:20, 7:10 and 7:36 p.m.

March 13 – Sunday

Uneventful day, maybe because I was not doing anything except watching basketball – what's new these days for me?

The lights flashed at: 11:25 (NCAA Duke vs. N. Carolina) and 11:45 a.m., 1:20 (NBA Magic/Suns), 1:40, 2:16, 2:36, 2:40 – fragrance came, 3:06 lights flashed and 8:12 p.m.

March 14 – Monday

Another basketball game day. The lights flashed at: 5:05, 7:37, 8:06 and 8:46 p.m.

Came into bedroom at 11:40 p.m., said goodnight to Jan. Lights flashed at 11:45 p.m. Goodnight love.

March 15 – Tuesday

The lights flashed at 9:14 a.m. while I was watching news. The world is in chaos – turmoil in the Middle East, earthquake in Japan, and economic problems in America. What's next? Glad Jan doesn't have to go through this.

Lights flashed at: 4:07, 4:54, 5:21, 6:17 and 7:32 p.m.

Came into the bedroom at 11:11 p.m. Said goodnight, lights flashed at 11:20 p.m. Goodnight Jan. I kept watching TV, lights flashed again at 11:49 p.m.; had to go to sleep.

March 16 – Wednesday

Lights flashed at 4:09, 5:35 and 6:52 p.m. – all during basketball games.

March 17 – Thursday

Today is the first day of "March Madness." Jan was always happy during March Madness. Lots of people at the casino; everybody was happy, full of energy and plenty of laughter. I took the cell phone with me to the Arizona Charlie's and watched the games in the Sports Book. The lights flashed at 11:32 a.m. Jan was with me at the casino.

The lights flashed again at: 3:56 (Florida vs. UCSB), 4:16, 6:06, and 8:21 p.m. Came into bedroom at 12:03 a.m., lights flashed at 12:21 a.m. Goodnight Love.

March 18 – Friday

John was delivering some cattle to Wyoming for Neil. So I was not expecting to see the flash this morning. The lights didn't flash. It was not until 9:49 a.m. when the lights flashed, then again at 1:49 and 5:26 p.m.

March 19 – Saturday

Lights flashed at 10:23 a.m. when I was watching NCAA (Kentucky/W. Virg). Got tired, shut my eyes, Jan came into my mind. When I opened my eyes, the lights flashed – 12:46 p.m. (NCAA Florida/UCLA). The lights flashed again at 1:18, 5:12 and 5:57 p.m. (Pitt/Butler).

March 20 – Sunday

Wind was blowing hard; a day for allergy pain. Stayed at home watching basketball. The lights flashed at: 10:21, 10:52 and 11:13 a.m., and 12:55, 2:24, 2:47, 3:07, 3:27, 3:49 and 7:16 p.m. – Kansas/Illinois. TV just flashed the news for a Tsunami warning in Hawaii; sad to hear so much bad news. Lights last flashed at 7:36 p.m.

March 21 – Monday

Wind still blowing. Mowed the lawn this afternoon. Needless to say, felt bad because of my allergies. Sat down to watch basketball. The lights flashed at 6:10 p.m. (NBA Pacers/Nets). My mind wandered off to be with Jan. At 7:19 p.m. I opened my eyes and the lights flashed immediately. Lights flashed again at 7:39 and 8:09 p.m.

March 22 – Tuesday

Lights flashed at 6:44 p.m. (NBA Bulls/Hawks). I told Jan that I am happy even if I just saw the lights flash once a day because that gives me strength to go on. The lights flashed right after I said it – 7:15 p.m.

March 23 – Wednesday

The lights flashed twice today at 5:14 and 6:31 p.m.

March 24 – Thursday

Stayed in bed watching news, lights flashed at 8:41 a.m.

Called Lucy at 1 p.m. to inform her that Susan's Mother is having surgery on Wednesday for a lump on her breast. Lucy told me that the smell of banana was all over the house this morning. Chad and Melissa and the "little Viking," Vincent, were visiting. No wonder Jan is with them.

Fragrance filled my senses at 4:10 p.m. and the lights flashed at 4:15 p.m. From there, the lights continued to flash at: 4:47, 4:59, 5:06, 5:47, and 7:10 p.m.

At 7:52 p.m. I was wondering if I will see another flash tonight, the lights flashed two minutes later at 7:54 p.m. Jan must have read my mind.

March 25 – Friday

The lights flashed several times when I was watching basketball in the living room: 5:01 NCAA basketball – UNC/Marquette, 6:36, 7:53 and 8:22 p.m. – Ohio State 42/Kentucky 41.

Came into the bedroom at 11:39 p.m. and said goodnight to Jan. Lights flashed at 12:00 a.m. Goodnight Jan.

March 26 – Saturday

Lights flashed when I was watching basketball in the living room, 12:46 p.m. – women's college hoops Oklahoma/N. Dame.

1:45 p.m. – Butler/Florida men, 2:09, 2:43 and 3:25 p.m.

The lights flashed at 4:05 p.m. when Susan was talking to Lucy about her Mother's surgery on Wednesday.

The lights flashed again at: 6:07, 7:10 and 7:37 p.m. No goodnight flash tonight.

March 27 – Sunday

As usual, the lights flashed during my watching basketball games: 9:56, 10:21, 11:07, 11:33 and 11:59 a.m., and 1:01, 1:21, 4:40, 5:40, 7:39 and 7:59 p.m.

Susan's back was aching. I rubbed some muscle pain cream on her and told her to go to sleep early. Got into the bedroom, the lights flashed right away at 11:38 p.m., then again at 12:05 a.m. Goodnight Jan.

March 28 – Monday

Jan greeted me good morning at 7:21 a.m. Lights flashed again during the basketball games: 5:37 – with the score Magic 37/Knicks 42, 7:02 – Magic 90/Knicks 96. 7:34 p.m. – Magic 106/Knicks 111.

Entered the bedroom at 10:53 p.m. Stood in front of her urn, told her I loved her, the cell lights flashed instantly. I do love you Jan.

March 29 – Tuesday

While I was shaving in front of my bed (I shave with an electric shaver), I said, "My baby," and the lights flashed right away.

My allergies were acting up this afternoon; decided to rest. Got into bed at 2:45 p.m.; talked to Jan. Lights flashed at 2:53 p.m., Jan heard me. Lights flashed again at: 3:13, 4:57, 5:24, 6:19, 6:39, 8:02 and 8:22 p.m.

No goodnight flash.

Susan came into the bedroom to talk to Jan. She asked Jan to take care of her Mother having breast surgery for a cancerous lump on Wednesday morning.

March 30 – Wednesday

No good morning flash this morning. Susan called to tell me that she had talked to her Father at 10 a.m. Surgery was smooth. Her Mother was already resting in her room.

I got into bed to take a nap, relieved that Susan's Mother was okay. Decided to put in the CD. The lights flashed after the song, "Wonderful World," then again after, "I'll Never Find Another You." It was 12:04 p.m.

The lights flashed again at 5:22 p.m. No goodnight flash.

March 31 – Thursday

The lights flashed at 5:02 p.m. during NIT basketball Wichita State/Alabama at halftime. Susan's Mother is going home tonight. Came into bedroom at 12:08 a.m. and said goodnight. Lights flashed at 12:28 a.m. Goodnight Honey.

April 1 – Friday

My birthday – April's fool day. I have to be the luckiest fool – having Jan in my life. Lazy in bed thinking about my life with Jan. The lights flashed at 9:49 a.m. Jan is here with me.

3:20 p.m. the lights flashed.

Cheri called from Chicago to greet me happy birthday. The lights flashed while I was talking to Cheri, it was 3:40 p.m. Cheri adores Jan. The lights flashed again at 4:03 and 4:23 p.m. Fragrance came on strong at 5:30 p.m.

Lights flashed at 12:18 a.m. Goodnight Jan.

April 2 – Saturday

Going to Mt. Charleston to spend a night on the mountain. Lights flashed at 7:34 a.m.

Got to Mt. Charleston, 40 miles from Las Vegas. Snow is still visible on the mountain. Finished lunch at Mt Charleston Lodge. Lights flashed while I walked out to the car. Like always, Jan is here with me.

Didn't feel good in the evening; didn't even finish eating dinner. I came back to the room. Lights flashed at 6:18, 6:45 and 6:58 p.m. Jan must be worried about me.

The wind was howling the whole night. My sinus headache was bad. On top of that, the air conditioning system didn't work properly the whole night. A miserable night.

April 3 – Sunday

Left Mt. Charleston first thing in the morning. Got home. Sat down later to watch NBA Lakers/Nuggets. Lights flashed at 2:42 p.m.

April 4 – Monday

Couldn't gather myself to do anything; decided to go to bed. Lit incense for Jan. Turned on the CD, the lights flashed shortly into the first song, "Wonderful World" – Jan's message for me to enjoy life on this world?

My mind has been on "to do something." Enjoy yourself by doing something. I said to myself, "What should I do?" I cannot do heavy yard work anymore. Paint the wall? No, it would be taxing on me to paint in the yard. But it just seemed that Jan was telling me to paint. But I have disposed of a lot of my painting materials. The thought kept coming back. Paint something. So I went into the garage. Sure enough, there was no paint left from the early years. It could have dried up already anyway. As I was walking back into the house, I saw this plastic bag sitting on the rack where Susan and Lisa stacked their things. I opened it, they were paints purchased by Lisa and Susan last Xmas for their décor. But again, the question, "What am I going to paint?"

I only used acrylic paint once – at the behest of Jan to paint a storage cabinet for a friend to be auction off in their church. The theme was the medieval times of knights and castles. I guess I must have done a decent job. The cabinet was bought for $1,500. So I told myself, let Jan tell me what to do. As she always told friends, "He paints what I dream."

The lights flashed at 10:58 a.m. and then at 6:25 p.m.

I was telling Susan about the paint and that Jan must want me to paint again, the lights flashed, it was 8:18 p.m.

Entered my bedroom at 12:23 a.m., said goodnight. The lights flashed shortly at 12:24 a.m. Goodnight Jan.

April 5 – Tuesday

The lights greeted me good morning at 7:15 a.m.

I have written Yong-Yong a letter telling her about Jan's scholarship I set up at Colome High. I sent a copy of the letter to Vic and Lusing. I had not told them about the scholarship before. Lusing called to tell me that they think the scholarship is a great tribute to Jan. Vic emailed me calling it a, "Good job." While Lusing was on the phone, the lights flashed. Jan must be happy.

Worked in the backyard a little; felt tired. Went into the bedroom, lit incense and put on the CD. Told Jan I love her and that is these moments alone with her that keeps me going. The lights flashed halfway into the first song, "Wonderful World." It was 12:15 p.m.

The lights flashed later at: 5:29, 5:49 and 7:35 p.m.

April 6 – Wednesday

Muscles are aching from yesterday's yard work; cannot fight old age. I looked at Jan and told her, "The good thing about getting old is that I am getting closer to seeing her, holding her, and laughing with her." Burned incense, clicked on the CD. On the third song, "My Cup Runneth Over," the lights flashed; it was 8:54 a.m. It flashed again at 9:14 a.m.; a confirmation from Jan.

The lights flashed at 7:40 p.m. during an NBA game, Dallas 92/ Denver 94.

Said goodnight to Jan at 11:25 p.m. Lights flashed at 11:45 p.m. I didn't turn off the TV. Lights flashed again at 12:04 a.m.; have to go to sleep.

April 7 – Thursday

In front of the computer, the lights flashed at 8:43 a.m. Jan is late greeting me good morning. I went back to the bedroom, lit incense, put on the CD, turned on TV to watch developments on the earthquake disaster in Japan. At 9:03 a.m. the lights flashed when the CD was playing, "You're Simply the Best." To Jan, I was "the best." That's how much Jan loves me.

At 6:03 p.m. the lights flashed while Susan was talking to Lucy, then flashed again at 6:23 p.m.

No goodnight flash tonight.

April 8 – Friday

My allergies are bad. Came back into the bedroom after Susan left for work. Lit incense, clicked on CD, the lights flashed at 8:56 a.m. on the song, "Power of Love." The smell of fragrance was strong before the lights flashed. Lusing called shortly, the lights flashed again while I was talking to Lusing at 9:16 a.m. The fragrance remained strong.

I started working on the plywood cutout for the "Happi Hearts Home." I brought the cutout into the bedroom and asked, "Honey, you like it?" The lights flashed right away. It was 10:44 a.m. Jan was happy.

The fragrance came on at 4:45 p.m. while I was watching NBA, and the lights flashed at 4:53 p.m. with the score, New York Knicks 53/New Jersey Nets 40.

I asked Susan to order flowers for Lusing's birthday next week. The lights flashed at 6:21 p.m.

Said goodnight to Jan at 11:20 p.m. Lights flashed at 11:37 p.m. Goodnight my love.

April 9 – Saturday

The news coming out of Washington DC every day is like a perpetual dark cloud hanging over the country. My refuge from this darkness has been the lights flashings which brings comfort to my mind that my Jan is watching over me. I woke up at 7:28 a.m., turned on the TV, the lights flashed at 7:29 a.m.

I finished painting the "Home of Happi Hearts," except for the angel, and showed it to Jan. The lights flashed at 12:18 p.m.

The lights flashed at 4:18 and 4:46 p.m. while I was watching NBA.

Susan was not feeling well tonight. We didn't watch any movie, so I went to bed early. Said goodnight to Jan at 10:12 p.m. The lights flashed good night at 10:24 p.m. Goodnight Jan.

April 10 – Sunday

The lights flashed at 12:34 p.m. during the Bulls/Magic game with the score at 102/99.

April 11 – Monday

The lights flashed at 7:11 a.m. while I was watching morning news in bed. Good morning Jan. Soon after, I lit incense, clicked on the CD, the lights flashed on the third song, "My Cup Runneth Over" at 9:04 a.m.

Said goodnight to Jan at 11:50 p.m. The lights flashed goodnight at 12:00 midnight.

April 12 – Tuesday

Lusing received the birthday flowers, called to say thank you. Had a nice long talk reminiscing childhood days and the current lives of brothers and sisters. We talked about Jan. After hanging up, my mind was full of memories of life with Jan. Went into the bedroom, lit incense, clicked on the CD. Into the fifth song, Tina Turner's, "You're Simply the Best," the lights flashed at 9:24 a.m.

I finished putting on some finishing touches on the "Happi Hearts Home." Note that the left arm of the angel is holding a harp. Since I started on the sign, I had no problem with the right hand pointing to Jan, but was never quite sure what to do with the left arm. Last night the thought that the angel should be holding a harp popped into my mind while I was watching a movie with Susan. I turned to Susan and said, "Okay, Jan just told me that the angel should be holding a harp." Susan said, "What are you talking about?" I said, "Never mind." So the finished sign has the angel holding a harp in her left arm.

Liong's painting "Happi Heart Home"

I brought the final work into the bedroom. I lit incense, clicked on the CD. I was feeling that Jan will give me an acknowledgment. On the fourth song, "The Power of Love," the lights flashed; it was 2:16 p.m. Jan did give me an acknowledgment.

The lights flashed several times thereafter: 4:25, 5:55, 6:46, 7:06 and 7:51 p.m.

Said goodnight to Jan at 11:55 p.m. Lights flashed goodnight at 12:08 a.m.

April 13 – Wednesday

Woke up at 6:28 a.m., fragrance came on at 6:42 a.m., and then the lights flashed at 6:48 a.m. Good morning Jan.

I went to the library this afternoon, and then passed by Smith's to get a pot of yellow tulips for Jan. When I came into the bedroom with the tulips, the candle appeared to look different. I took a close look at the flame, and the wick had split up into three heart shapes. I remember the same happening some time before – going back to check on the journal. Yes, it did happen on 11/27/09, the day after Thanksgiving in 2009. I am glad that Jan is happy with the sign.

Wind was blowing very hard tonight. Susan and I were both affected. We didn't watch a movie tonight. Said goodnight to Jan at 10:22 p.m. Lights flashed good night at 10:30 p.m. Goodnight Jan.

April 14 – Thursday

Lights flashed good morning at 6:49 a.m. I didn't get up; just enjoyed my time thinking about the fun times I had with Jan. The lights flashed again at 7:12 a.m., then again at 9:33 a.m. Cannot describe the feeling whenever the lights flash and I feel her close presence. So, what is the purpose of my existence now? I don't know. Maybe Jan will let me know in time.

Came into the bedroom, lit a candle, clicked on the CD. The lights flashed at 1:46 p.m. during the song, "You're Simply the Best."

The lights flashed again at 5:18 and 6:02 p.m. No goodnight flash tonight.

April 15 – Friday

Woke up at 4:56 a.m.; pitch dark. Can't go back to sleep; turned on TV to watch Imus. The lights flashed at 5:06 a.m. After the flash, I fell asleep. No other flashes today.

April 16 – Saturday

The lights flashed good morning at 7:23 a.m. Talked to Lucy; Colome had 10 inches of snow yesterday, in April?

The lights flashed at: 12:43, 1:15, 2:28, 5:52 and 6:18 p.m. (during NBA game). The flash at 6:18 p.m. occurred when I was telling Susan about the time when Jan took Lucy to the movie, "Waiting to Exhale." Lucy wanted to see it. I said during the movie, Jan was just, "waiting to exit." The lights flashed. Jan must be laughing!

The lights flashed again at: 6:38, 7:07, 8:17, 8:37 and 9:09 p.m.

Said goodnight to Jan at 11:52 p.m. Lights flashed goodnight at 11:59 p.m. Goodnight Jan.

April 17 – Sunday

Woke up, went to the bathroom, and then went out to pick up newspaper in the driveway. Came back to bed, turned on the TV. The lights flashed good morning at 6:33 a.m. and then flashed again at 6:53 a.m.

The lights flashed many times during the NBA games: 11:20 and 11:49 a.m., and 12:34, 12:54, 1:37, 2:37, 5:50, 6:48, 7:15, 8:09 and 8:31 p.m.

No goodnight flash tonight.

April 18 – Monday

The lights didn't flash the whole day. It finally flashed at 7:36 p.m.

April 19 – Tuesday

The lights flashed good morning at 7:25 a.m. Susan left to serve jury duty. I came back to bed. Missing Jan badly. Clicked on the CD, the lights flashed on the fourth song, "Power of Love" at 9:45 a.m. I miss her smile, her laughter, her love for fun, and especially at times like now when America is going through so many difficulties – politically and economically. America is too good a country to deserve this.

Felt tired this afternoon; came into the bedroom to rest. Clicked on the CD. The lights flashed during the second song, "I'll Never Find Another You" at 1:31 p.m. Dearest Jan, we both know we will never find another "You."

I let the music play thru "The Blue Danube." The lights flashed again on the following song, "My Cup Runneth Over" at 1:43 p.m. How many times had I watched my Jan sleeping like a baby next to me? My cup runneth over every time I watched her smiling in her sleep.

No goodnight flash tonight.

April 20 – Wednesday

Lights flashed at 5:27, 5:54 and 6:39 p.m. during the NBA games. Said goodnight to Jan at 12:02 a.m.; lights flashed at 12:21 a.m. Goodnight love.

April 21 – Thursday

Lights flashed good morning at 5:28 a.m.

Started sketching the next project, "Baby Jan with Tusk and Friends." The lights flashed at 4:43, 5:03 p.m. and then 5:23 p.m. It appears that 20 minute intervals are the most frequent between flashes. I don't know why it is so. I had thought about this many times; still waiting to find an answer for it.

Liong's paintings of the Tusk characters

The lights flashed again at 6:04 p.m. Said goodnight to Jan at 10:20 p.m. Lights flashed goodnight at 10:42 p.m. Goodnight honey.

April 22 –Friday

Lucy had called several times asking me to fly to Sioux Falls on May 27 to watch Skylar runs in the South Dakota State track meet. At the same time, to attend the memorial of Aunt Georgie in Springview. I said yes. However, after saying yes, the thought that I would be leaving Jan behind kept bothering me. Jan loved to go home. She went home twice every year. Mostly alone because she knew that I am a city person.

The lights flashed good morning at 5:34 a.m. The thought of going to South Dakota without her kept bothering me. I put in the DVD Susan made – Remembrance – A chronicle of Jan's life. Tears began flowing after the first view of baby Jan. The pain of missing her is still deep. After watching the DVD, I simply collapsed mentally. Clicked on the CD. The song of Perry Como, "And I Love You So" came on! I had clicked on the CD countless times. This is the second time this happened. The last time was when it played The Three Bells; had to check when that happened.

I turned and looked at the disc indicator. It showed disc #1, the first song is, "Wonderful World." The Perry Como song is the first song on disc #2. Puzzled, I let it play thru the song, turned off the player, and then restarted it. This time the song, "Wonderful World" came on. I turned to the cell phone and asked, "Honey, did you do this?" Right then, the lights flashed at 9:13 a.m. Dearest Jan, I will go home with you for the Forgey family reunion in Deadwood come July.

The lights flashed at 3:53 p.m. when I finished cutting out the sketches for, "Baby Jan, Tusk and friends."

The lights flashed again at 5:51 and 7:03 p.m. No goodnight flash tonight.

April 23 – Saturday

No good morning flash. Lights flashed at 1:54, 2:25, 5:41 and 6:51 p.m.

The smell of banana fragrance came on at 9:10 p.m., the lights flashed at 9:25 p.m. At 9:47 p.m. the lights flashed when Susan came into the bedroom and asked, "Do you want any coffee?" Jan must be giggling. She always did before, because Susan would ask her so many times during the day.

Fragrance came on strong at 12:08 a.m. I fell asleep without seeing the goodnight flash.

April 24 – Sunday

No good morning flash. Jan must be home in South Dakota or Wyoming having Easter fun with Family.

The lights flashed at 11:00 a.m.; then 20 minutes later at 11:20 a.m. I recall the lights flashed when Susan and I reached the "T" sign while looking for the Energy Vortex at Boynton Canyon in Sedona. So is this why the 20 minute interval occurs more frequently? "T" is the 20th letter in the alphabet?

The lights flashed again at 12:23 p.m. I finished sketching Aki and Kita. Then I asked, "Jan, do you want more characters from Tusk?" The lights flashed at 2:12 p.m. I will work on adding more characters then.

Susan came home at 2:38 p.m. She saw the sketches. I asked her, "What is the name of the Kitty? I forgot the name." Susan said, "Puffy." The lights flashed. Jan must be saying "Honey how could you forget Puffy!"

I was in the bathroom tonight. The fragrance came on very strong. Sensing that Jan is here close by, I rushed into the bedroom and got hold of the cell phone. The lights flashed with the cell phone in my hand.

I went out to water the lawn. Suddenly the wind started whipping up, and the temperature dropped. I started getting the chills. The fragrance came despite the wind blowing so hard. Jan was telling me to go back to the house. I went back into the house and the fragrance hung with me for some time until 8:04 p.m.

No midnight flash tonight.

April 25 – Monday

First flash today occurred at 5:20 p.m. while I watched NBA SA/ Memphis and then at 7:12 and 7:32 p.m.

Said goodnight to Jan at 11:27 p.m. Lights flashed goodnight at 11:29 p.m. Goodnight Jan.

April 26 – Tuesday

Lights flashed this morning at 6:59 a.m. after I got the newspaper and came back to bed. I continued watching news on TV. Lights flashed again at 7:06 a.m.

I started painting Baby Jan on the cutout board. Lights flashed at 5:45 p.m. and then at 7:10 p.m.

No midnight flash.

April 27 – Wednesday

Lights flashed at 7:18 a.m.; then at 4:49 and 7:36 p.m. while I was watching the NBA playoffs. No goodnight flash.

April 28 – Thursday

Lights flashed good morning at 6:46 a.m.

Susan left for work. I was standing in front of the front lawn. Suddenly a little hummingbird appeared out of nowhere. Looked at me then flew away. It's been a long time since a hummingbird came to me. Jan loved hummingbirds. A message from Jan? There are no red flowers in the front lawn.

I went back into the computer room and started writing down this incident. The lights flashed in front of the screen at 8:53 a.m.

The lights flashed again 6:23 and 7:26 p.m. Said goodnight at 11:49 p.m.; lights flashed at 11:54 p.m. Goodnight Jan.

April 30 – Saturday

Didn't feel like getting up this morning. The lights finally flashed at 7:29 a.m. Jean is coming for lunch today; first time since she had her hip surgeries.

Lights flashed at 10:36 a.m. Jean arrived at 12:30 p.m. and had a nice visit with her. As Jean got into her car to leave, and Susan and I were in the driveway, a little hummingbird flew in front of me and Susan. Susan quickly told Jean. Jean had tears in her eyes. She believed her darling Jan had sent her a message.

May 1 – Sunday

Good morning flash at 6:49 a.m. No flashes today after the morning flash.

May 2 – Monday

The only news on every TV channel was Osama Bin Laden's death. A reason to rejoice. Hope it doesn't distract the country from the reality of pressing problems – energy costs, food costs, inflation, etc.

Miss Jan so much. This world is really a difficult place to live in, and any happiness one can have is a blessing. Jan lived her life with smiles, laughter, care, and love. When a life passes, these are the only memories worth remembering and cherishing.

I lit a candle, clicked on the CD, hoped to share some moments with my Jan. The lights flashed at 9:05 a.m. when the song, "My Cup Runneth Over" was playing. This is a heavenly moment in my life these days. The CD kept on playing. The lights flashed again at 9:28 a.m. on the song, "Unchained Melody." Jan always said, "Honey, they are playing our song!"

I decided to check on the times this happened lately. These are the times and the songs:

Date	Time	Song Title
3/30	12:04 P.M.	"Wonderful World," then "I'll Never Find Another You."
4/4	10:58 A.M.	"Wonderful World"
4/5	12:15 P.M.	"Wonderful World"
4/6	8:45 A.M.	"My Cup Runneth Over"
4/7	9:30 A.M.	"You're Simply The Best"
4/8	8:56 A.M.	"Power of Love"
4/11	9:04 A.M.	"My Cup Runneth Over"
4/12	9:24 A.M.	"You're Simply the Best"
	2:16 P.M.	"Power of Love"
4/14	1:46 P.M.	"You're Simply the Best"
4/19	9:45 A.M.	"Power of Love"
	1:31 P.M.	"I'll Never Find Another You"
	1:43 P.M.	"My Cup Runneth Over"
4/22	9:13 A.M.	"Wonderful World"
5/2	9:05 A.M.	"My Cup Runneth Over"
	9:28 A.M.	"Unchained Melody"

Interestingly, the lights didn't flash on the other songs on the CD like, "The Blue Danube," "It's Just My Funny Way of Laughing," "Bridge Over Troubled Waters," and "I Will Miss You When You Go."

I used to call our Condo, "our little corner of heaven on earth." I don't know what it is when life passes, but I do love my Jan for bringing me that heaven on earth feeling thru these occurrences. She wants me to keep enjoying life – "Wonderful World." She still feels the same way we do about each other – "I'll Never Find Another You." She watches over me when I sleep – "My Cup Runneth Over." She wants me to keep believing in love – "The Power of Love." She still dances to the song, "You're Simply the Best," and today, for the first time, she told me that she will be waiting for me – "Unchained Melody."

I went to the library. Stopped by Smith's and got a pot of lovely pink flowers for Jan. After that, I went to Arizona Charlie's, decided to play a few hands of video poker. No sooner did I sit down to play when I heard, "Honey I am home." I turned and looked around; there was nobody within 15 feet of me. I cashed out and came home.

The lights flashed at 8:13 p.m. during the game with Dallas Mavs 23/Lakers 21.

Said goodnight to Jan at 11:50 p.m. Lights flashed goodnight at 11:59 p.m. Goodnight my love.

May 3 – Tuesday

No good morning flash.

Cut some bananas for Jan and lit incense. The lights flashed instantly at 11:15 a.m.

May 4 – Wednesday

No good morning flash today.

I mowed the front lawn, then took a shower. Cut some bananas for Jan, then got into bed to watch TV. Nothing on the news except all about the death of Bin Laden. Got tired and bored about the same thing over and over again. Jan came into my mind. So I clicked on the CD player at 11:38 a.m., the lights flashed on the song, "I'll Never Find Another You." The lights flashed again at 11:58 a.m. when the song, "Bridge Over Troubled Waters" was playing. To think that I wrote on 5/2, just two days ago, that the lights have not flashed on this song. Okay Jan, you got me again.

While watching NBA Hawks/Bulls game, the lights flashed at 4:46 and 5:34 p.m.

Said goodnight to Jan at 12:03 a.m. Lights flashed 20 minutes later at 12:23 a.m. Goodnight Jan.

May 5 – Thursday

Good morning flash at 7:06 a.m. The lights flashed twice at 10:09 and 10:19 a.m. when I was in the computer room entering into the journal.

May 6 – Friday

Didn't see any flashes since 10:19 yesterday morning. Felt a bit low and lazy. Came back to bed after the morning routine of getting newspaper, coffee, reading news, clicked on the CD player. At the end of the first song, "Wonderful World," the lights flashed at 9:06 a.m. Thank you Jan for lifting my spirits.

Went to Arizona Charlie's for a while. Still cannot get over missing Jan. Decided to come home and be with Jan. Clicked on the CD player. At 12:48 p.m. the lights flashed at the song, "You're Simply the Best." Love you Jan.

Did some house work, came back into the bedroom, stood in front of the bed. Stared at Jan's photos, mind full of memories and the lights flashed at 1:35 p.m.

May 7 – Saturday

Saw a good morning flash at 7:14 a.m. The lights flashed many times during the day when I was watching NBA basketball.

2:29 p.m. game between Oklahoma City/Memphis

3:52 p.m. lights flashed as Susan came into the living room and sat down to watch the game with me. Jan said, "Hi" to Susan.

4:22, 5:39, 6:24, 7:23 and 7:50 p.m. game between Heat/Celtics just ended. I was on the phone with Lusing.

May 8 – Sunday

Mother's Day. No flashes the whole morning. Jan must be with Lucy for Mother's Day. Expect her to be home later.

Fragrance came at 12:40 p.m. I told myself that Jan must be home now. The lights flashed at 12:46 p.m.

The lights flashed again during NBA games: 1:29, 2:04, 2:24, 2:55 and 5:40 p.m.

Said goodnight to Jan at 11:36 p.m. Lights flashed at 11:54 p.m. Goodnight Jan.

May 9 – Monday

Lights flashed at 6:57 and 7:19 p.m.

May 10 – Tuesday

Saw the morning flash at 7:00 a.m.

Came home at 3:00 p.m.; cut a banana for Jan, lit incense and then clicked on the CD player. The lights flashed at 3:41 p.m. on the song, "You're Simply the Best." Borrowing a line in the song, I now, "hang on to every flash I see." Jan, to me, you will always be, "The Best."

Lights flashed at 5:41 p.m. with NBA, the Hawks playing the Bulls and then again at 6:35 p.m. during halftime.

Saw the lights again at 7:09 p.m.

Got into bed at 11:35 p.m. Saw the goodnight flash at 11:54 p.m. Goodnight honey.

May 11 – Wednesday

Starting at 6:51 a.m. with the good morning flash. The lights flashed many times today.

9:22 a.m. – while I was entering the diary into computer file. Then again at 9:42 a.m.

4:31 p.m. – lights flashed at the end of 1st qtr. game between Celtics/Heat.

5:01, 5:48, 6:08, 6:34, 6:55 and 7:40 p.m. – all during NBA games.

Got into bed at 11:37 p.m. Lights flashed goodnight at 11:49 p.m. Goodnight love.

May 12 – Thursday

Felt a bit low because I didn't see my morning flash. How spoiled can I get? Since I cannot get myself up to do anything, I decided to click on the CD player. The lights flashed at 9:11 a.m. on the song, "You're Simply the Best." Thank you. You always thought of me as a strong-willed person, but I feel weak these days without you. The times when I feel a surge of energy is when I see the lights flash; it is a feeling that I cannot control.

Lights flashed again at 9:38 a.m. I was still in bed. Better get up. Jan wouldn't like for me to feel this way.

Lights flashed at 6:01 p.m. during the game between Chicago Bulls and Atlanta Hawks.

Came into bedroom at 11:59 p.m. Saw the goodnight flash at 12:27 a.m. Goodnight Jan.

May 13 – Friday

Lights flashed good morning at 6:45 a.m. Today is Mama's birthday. I misread her birthday more than a week ago. Her birthday was lunar April 11; I misread it for Lunar 4/1. So I celebrated it again. I always said that there is no overdose of love for your Mother; the one who gave you life. I was lucky to have Mama live with us after the passing of Papa. Mama got to know and love Jan so much. They chatted on the long distance phone regularly after Mama decided to go back to Manila to live in the house Papa built for her.

I came home after buying Chinese medicine for Lucy. I also bought some of Jean's favorite pork buns and passed by Jean's house. Jean was not home. When I came into the bedroom, I asked, "Honey, are you home?" and the lights flashed right away. The comfort that it brought was indescribable. It was 1:32 p.m. The thought of taking the pork buns over again to Jean came into mind. So I called Jean to find out if she had come home. Jean answered the phone and the lights flashed. I told Jean that she cannot refuse me because it was Jan's wish that I bring them over to her. Visited with Jean. Had a nice visit.

Came home and decided to cut a fresh pineapple for Jan. Jan was always so happy to see me cutting up a fresh pineapple for her. She bragged about it to John all the time. Giving her the freshly cut pineapple, I saw the lights flash right away at 3:43 p.m.

Got into bed at 12:15 a.m. Lights flashed goodnight at 12:33 a.m. Goodnight Jan.

May 14 – Saturday

The morning flash came at 9:01 a.m. No other flashes during the day.

Got into bed at 12:22 a.m. Lights flashed goodnight at 12:36 a.m. Goodnight Love.

May 15 – Sunday

Lucy called. They went to Radar Hill Casino yesterday, and were on the way to Rosebud Casino today. No wonder I didn't see flashes yesterday during the day and none also this morning. Lights started flashing after Lucy's call: 3:34, 4:15, 4:35, 5:29 and 5:50 p.m.

Watched a movie, "Just Like Heaven" on TNT with Susan. At 11:48 p.m. the smell of fragrance came on very strong. I told Susan she should be sleeping. Came into my bedroom, the movie had me thinking about the last days of Jan on earth. The lights flashed instantly at 11:49 p.m. I continued to watch the movie. Told Jan I will go to sleep after the movie. The lights flashed at 12:20 a.m. when the movie was about to end. The flashed again at 12:28 a.m. when it ended. Goodnight Jan.

May 16 – Monday

No good morning flash today. Wind was blowing hard. It was a cold, 50° F day. Susan left for work. I was feeling tired, low, and lonely. When I feel this way, I seek refuge with my Jan. Clicked on the CD player. The lights flashed at 9:10 a.m. at the song, "Unchained Melody."

Still not feeling happy, I clicked on the CD player again this afternoon. Midway into the first song "Wonderful World," the lights flashed at 4:30 p.m., not only once but twice. Jan wanted me to be happy. She always wanted me to be happy. But Jan, it just isn't the same without you. As the CD played on, the lights flashed twice again at 4:34 p.m. on the second song, "I'll Never

Find Another You," and the lights flashed again on the fourth song, "The Power of Love" at 4:39 p.m.

After that I started talking to Jan. I talked about renewing the Rapid City Journal for John; Jan always did that. I told her all the Forgeys are fine. I told her how I missed our lives together and how sad Las Vegas has become. The lights flashed at 4:50 p.m. I took a walk out to the front yard. I felt a sense of loss. Came back in the house. The thought of preparing a gift for Lucy this Xmas came in. One of Jan's Xmas cards stared me in the eyes. It was the one that shows a little girl, Jan, on the hill waiving to her Mother, Lucy, asking her to come home. Lucy loves that card. She said it was so, "Jan." I said, "Jan, I will paint it for Lucy." The lights flashed when I said it at 5:06 p.m. I went into the bedroom, looked around and said to Jan, "Honey, this is now my little corner of heaven on earth." The lights flashed at 5:10 p.m.

Went to bed early, not feeling well. However, tired as I was, just could not get to sleep. Still watching TV passed one o'clock. The lights flashed in the dark at 1:41 a.m. Turned off the TV, was able to sleep after that, but did wake up in short intervals; very uncomfortable.

May 17 – Tuesday

Woke up at 7:34 a.m. a bit later than usual and still feeling unhappy. After the morning routine, sat down to read my emails. Surprised to see an email from Barbara; haven't heard from her for some time. She said she is now working for the state of Texas. However, the bad news was that her daughter, Emily, was diagnosed with cancer two months ago and is currently undergoing chemotherapy. My heart felt for Barbara. Now I know why I was so uncomfortable. Life is so unpredictable. Feeling sad, I went into the bedroom, clicked on the CD player. The lights flashed at 9:26 a.m. on the song, "The Power of Love."

Came into the bedroom at 11:30 p.m.; lights flashed goodnight at 11:58 p.m. Goodnight Jan.

May 18 – Wednesday

I finished cutting the board for Lucy's Xmas gift. The lights flashed at 5:11 p.m. while I was waiting for the NBA game Heat/ Bulls.

May 19 – Thursday

Started painting, "Baby Jan picking up pinecones." Lights flashed at 7:14 p.m.

Said goodnight at 11:35 p.m. Lights flashed at 11:45 p.m. Goodnight Jan. Promised to finish the painting tomorrow.

May 20 – Friday

Finished painting, "Baby Jan picking pinecones." After that, I clicked on the CD player. The lights flashed at 1:23 p.m. on the song, "Simply the Best." Jan loved the painting. She always said that when she liked a drawing.

Liong's original watercolor of "Jan Picking Pinecones"

Liong's painting of "Jan Picking Pinecones"

Said goodnight at 11:53 p.m. Lights flashed goodnight at 12:13 a.m. Goodnight Jan.

May 21 – Saturday

Have had a bum stomach since yesterday. Decided to go to the movie, "Pirates of the Caribbean" with Susan. Lights flashed good morning at 7:19 a.m.

Came home after the movie. My stomach still playing a bum game with me. Very irritating. So I got into bed, clicked on the CD player. What came on wasn't, "Wonderful World," it was Perry Como, "And I Love You So." I turned and looked at the player; it indicated disc #1 – 101. It was Jan again. I restarted the player, this time, "Wonderful World" came on, and the lights flashed at 4:01 p.m. during, "Bridge Over Troubled Waters." My Jan, my bridge over troubled waters. The lights flashed again on, "Unchained Melody" at 4:09 p.m. Yes Jan, "I'll be coming home, wait for me."

May 22 – Sunday

Lights flashed good morning at 8:01 a.m. and flashed again at 9:13 a.m.

Mary, our neighbor, came over to visit with Susan. I stayed in the bedroom watching TV. The lights flashed many times while Mary was with Susan, at: 3:49, 3:53, 4:00, 4:27, 4:28 and 4:54 p.m. I told myself what a way to spend an afternoon with Jan.

After Mary left, Susan told me that Mary liked the paintings. Now I know why Jan was so happy flashing me. She was always so happy when people liked my paintings. "He draws what I dream." She always said that when people liked the paintings.

Said goodnight at 11:30 p.m. Lights flashed goodnight at 11:43 p.m.

May 23 – Monday

Good morning flash at 6:30 a.m. No flashes after that.

May 24 – Tuesday

No good morning flash; cannot help it, clicked on the CD player, the lights flashed at 12:55 p.m. on the song, "Bridge Over Troubled Waters." The lights flashed again at 7:55 and 8:17 p.m.

Said goodnight at 11:30 p.m. Lights flashed goodnight at 11:39 p.m. Goodnight Jan. I keep bothering you, but I cannot help it. I miss you.

May 25 – Wednesday

Lights flashed good morning at 9:19 a.m.

Miss Jan. Focused on her picture and held the urn in my embrace and told her softly, "Hi Baby." The lights flashed instantly at 3:35 p.m. Moments like this are heavenly to me.

May 26 – Thursday

Lights flashed at 9:19 a.m.

Said goodnight at 11:20 p.m. Lights flashed goodnight shortly after at 11:21 p.m.

Oh, I watched a movie, "Beyond Christmas" tonight. The movie was made in 1941. It is about life and the afterlife; about kindness and about love. A lot of what is in the movie resonates with what I have experienced since Jan's passing; deeply touching.

May 27 – Friday

No flashes today. Lisa called at 5:30 p.m. and she told me that Steve, Neil, Dale and their families are all in Colome for the Memorial Day weekend; a surprise to John and Lucy. No wonder I didn't see any flashes today. Jan wouldn't miss the happy gathering for anything. I am glad Jan was having fun with them.

I stayed up watching TV. The lights finally flashed at 12:48 a.m. past midnight. Jan must have known that I am having a hard time going to sleep. Thank you Jan for coming to let me know that you came to see me. Go have fun with your family. I will be all right.

May 28 – Saturday

No flashes. Talked to Lucy; she was cooking for 24 people. Jan must be happy and with them.

May 29 – Sunday

Saw a good morning flash at 7:04 a.m. Jan had to come and take a look at her "baby."

The lights flashed 20 minutes later at 7:24 a.m., and then at 9:20 a.m.

I knew that John and Lucy and the others are going to Springview, Nebraska for the memorial service of Aunt Georgie. So I was wondering if Jan had decided not to go. I called Lucy at 11:23 a.m. Turned out that they were only getting ready to leave for Nebraska.

The lights flashed at 4:18 p.m. (6:18 p.m. in Colome). The lights flashed again at 4:43 p.m. I called John at 5:07 p.m. They had been home since 4 p.m. The lights flashed one more time at 5:18 p.m., then no more for the night. Jan must have gone back to Colome to spend the night with her family.

May 30 – Monday

Memorial Day. No flashes until 4:07 p.m. I called Lucy, and was told everybody had left for their homes. Lucy and John are both resting after a busy weekend.

May 31 – Tuesday

No flashes last night and no good morning flash, made me miss Jan. After Susan left for work, I clicked on the CD player. The lights flashed at 8:53 a.m. on the song, "The Power of Love." Thank you, Jan. I bothered you again.

I've had an itchy allergic reaction since last night, from eating a mango from Mexico. Decided to get into bed around 1 p.m.; the lights flashed at 1:10 p.m. I dozed off. Woke up at 2:03 p.m. and the lights flashed right after I opened my eyes.

The lights flashed again at 4:55 p.m. while I was waiting to watch the NBA championship game between Dallas and Miami.

June 1 – Wednesday

No goodnight flash last night. No good morning flash when I got up.

After Susan left for work, couldn't help myself but clicked on the CD player. The lights flashed at 9:02 a.m. on the song, "The Power of Love." Shortly after seeing the flash, a thought came into my mind – I never knew the lyrics to the song. All this time

I just sang along, but I really didn't know all the lyrics. But why did I think about this only now? So I wrote a note asking Susan to look up the lyrics for both, "The Power of Love," and "You're Simply the Best."

June 2 – Thursday

Susan gave the lyrics to me last night. After reading the lyrics, I stood in front of Jan's photo and her urn. I whispered to her, "Honey, I got your message." There is a paragraph in the song where it says, "Even though there may be times, it seems I'm far away. Never wonder where I am, 'cause I am always by your side."

I checked the opening statement that I wrote for this journal. It was in June of 2008. I wrote on June 5, 2008 – "I knew then, that I will never travel alone. Jan will always be by my side." Susan cried. Is this a coincidence? Or is it the, "Power of Love?"

THE BEST – Verse
(as performed by Tina Turner)

You're simply the best, better than all the rest. Better than anyone, anyone I ever met. I'm stuck on your heart.
I hang on ev'ry word you say.

I came home from the library in the afternoon and clicked on the CD player. The lights flashed at 3:23 p.m. on, "I'll Never Find Another You."

Said goodnight to Jan at 11:46 p.m. Lights flashed at 11:58 p.m.

June 3 – Friday

Lights flashed at 6:49, 9:12, 3:22 and 3:42 p.m.

June 4 – Saturday

No goodnight flash last night. No good morning flash. A feeling of loss came in. Cannot help it again; clicked on the CD player.

Lights flashed at 8:51 a.m. on the song, "The Power of Love." Although I got her message two days ago, I still want her to let me know.

June 5 – Sunday

It was three years ago today when Jan went "Home." Since I was a child, it has been imbedded in my mind by my parents that we should hold our respect and esteem; I do not like the word mourning, for someone we hold dear for a period of three years. Although Jan left for "Home" three years ago, she has been by my side all this time. She cares for me and takes care of me. Our love has grown over the last three years. Jan comes to my side whenever she feels that I need her. From here on, I will probably not record the flashes that are now an integral part of my life. Three years of seeing the flashes every day now, and on the notable events associated with the flashes, are enough to convince me that we, on this earth, in general, do not understand the permanent existence of souls. I am blessed to have a soul mate in Jan.

John, Lucy and Lisa laid some beautiful flowers on our headstone in Colome. They sent me photos. This is a blessing that I wish everyone could have; loving parents and a loving family. When I look through Jan's eyes, I can see Jan's "Wonderful World." For her, it's all about happiness that emanates from love and care.

So, on this day, I retreat to my corner of heaven on earth to spend a day with my Jan. The lights flashed at 9:28, 10:09, 10:37, 10:57 and 11:46 a.m., and at 12:06, 12:27, 5:47, 6:07, 6:41 and 7:01 p.m.

Said goodnight at 12:52 a.m. Lights flashed goodnight at 1:13 a.m. Goodnight my love.

CHAPTER 17

Fun Statistics

This chapter is for the mathematicians out there who just love statistics. Just for fun, Liong assembled the following data to measure statistically the frequency of certain recognizable patterns.

The first section, for example, identifies the specific songs during which the cell phone flashed, clearly showing that out of the ten songs on her memorial CD, Jan had preferences. This first CD included, in order:

1. Louis Armstrong, "What a Wonderful World"
2. The Browns, "I'll Never Find Another You"
3. Johann Strauss II, "The Blue Danube"
4. Burl Ives, "Funny Way of Laughing"
5. Ed Ames, "My Cup Runneth Over"
6. Celine Dion, "The Power of Love"
7. Tina Turner, "Simply the Best"
8. Simon and Garfunkel, "Bridge Over Troubled Waters"
9. George Hamilton IV, "I'll Miss You When You Go"
10. The Righteous Brothers, "Unchained Melody"

As you will see, Jan consistently preferred songs one, two, six, seven, and ten over the rest. Clearly, song number one, Louis

Armstrong's "What a Wonderful World," was her ultimate favorite. If you recall, that was the song she was listening to when Liong called her the first time. Some songs Jan never flashed on at all, like numbers three, four, and nine. Then again, she also overrode "What a Wonderful World" twice by playing Perry Como's "And I Love You So." Is it a pattern? I think so.

Flashes on Jan's Favorite Songs

Date	Song	Time of Occurrence
Jan 19, 2010	Silent Night – Susan Boyle	3:27 P.M.
Mar 22, 2010	Wonderful World – Louis Armstrong	7:52 P.M.
Apr 11, 2010	Unchained Melody – Righteous Brothers	1:53 P.M.
Apr 22, 2010	Wonderful World	8:54 P.M.
	I'll Never Find Another You – Seekers	8:56 P.M.
	Simply The Best – Tina Turner	9:09 P.M.
	Unchained Melody	9:23 P.M.
Apr 26, 2010	I'll Never Find Another You	7:19 P.M.
Aug 11, 2010	Wonderful World	8:14 P.M.
Sept 11, 2010	Unchained Melody	9:39 P.M.
Sept 15, 2010	I'll Never Find Another You	7:34 P.M.
Mar 30, 2011	Wonderful World	
	I'll Never Find Another You	12:04 P.M.
Apr 4, 2011	Wonderful World	
Apr 5, 2011	Wonderful World	12:15 P.M.
Apr 6, 2011	My Cup Runneth Over – Ed Ames	8:45 A.M.
Apr 7, 2011	Simply the Best	9:03 A.M.
Apr 8, 2011	The Power of Love – Celine Dion	8:56 A.M.
Apr 11, 2011	My Cup Runneth Over	9:04 A.M.
Apr 12, 2011	Simply the Best	9:24 A.M.
	The Power of Love	2:16 P.M.
Apr 14, 2011	Simply the Best	1:46 P.M.
Apr 19, 2011	The Power of Love	9:45 A.M.
	I'll Never Find Another You	1:31 P.M.
	My Cup Runneth Over	1:43 P.M.
Apr 22, 2011	And I Love You So – Perry Como (Indicator showed Disc #1 – Wonderful World	9:13 A.M.

May 2, 2011	My Cup Runneth Over	9:05 A.M.
	Unchained Melody	9:28 A.M.
May 4, 2011	I'll Never Find Another You	11:38 A.M.
	Bridge Over Troubled Waters – Simon & Garfunkel	11:58 A.M.
May 6, 2011	Wonderful World	9:06 A.M.
	Simply the Best	12:48 P.M.
May 12, 2011	Simply the Best	9:11 A.M.
May 16, 2011	Unchained Melody	9:10 A.M.
	Wonderful World	4:30 P.M.
	I'll Never Find Another You	4:34 P.M.
	The Power of Love	4:39 P.M.
May 17, 2011	The Power of Love	9:26 A.M.
May 20, 2011	Simply the Best	1:23 P.M.
May 21, 2011	And I Love You So (Indicator showed Disc #1 – Wonderful World	
	Wonderful World (restarted CD)	4:01 P.M.
	Unchained Melody	4:09 P.M.
May 24, 2011	Bridge Over Troubled Waters	12:55 P.M.
May 31, 2011	The Power of Love	8:53 P.M.
June 1, 2011	The Power of Love	9:02 A.M.
June 2, 2011	I'll Never Find Another You	3:23 P.M.
June 4, 2011	The Power of Love	8:51 A.M.

The second set of data identifies the number of times that Jan flashed either good morning or good evening, by year, and documents the increase in the percentage of occurrences from 2009 through 2011. As was said in the beginning, her communications have increased in both frequency and precision. Is this another pattern? I am leaning toward yes, but all of this is for you to decide for yourself.

Good-night Flashes

The good-night flashes are those that happened at 9:35 p.m. or later, depending on when Liong went to bed and said goodnight to Jan.

Starting Date:	October 17, 2009
End Date:	June 5, 2011
2009:	6 times (2 months 14 days) 8.1%
2010:	157 times (365 days) 43%
2011:	74 times (5 months 5 days) 47%

Good-morning Flashes

The good-morning flashes occurred before 10:19 a.m., depending on when Liong woke up and said good morning to Jan.

Starting Date:	October 26, 2009
End Date:	June 5, 2011
2009:	2 times (2 months 5 days) 2.7%
2010:	93 times (365 days) 25.5%
2011:	57 times (5 months, 5 days) 36.7%

CHAPTER 18

For Your Reference

This section is a listing of the books, movies, and songs which were mentioned in Liong's journal.

Books

1. Allen, Miles Edward. *The Survival Files: The Most Compelling Evidence Yet Compiled for the Survival of Your Soul.* Needham, MA: Momentpoint Media, 2007.
2. Browne, Sylvia. *God, Creation, and Tools for Life.* Carlsbad, CA: Hay House, 2000.
3. Browne, Sylvia. *Soul's Perfection.* Carlsbad, CA: Hay House, 2000.
4. DuBois, Allison. *We Are Their Heaven: Why the Dead Never Leave Us.* New York, NY: Simon & Schuster, 2006.
5. Newton, Michael. *Journey of Souls: Case Studies of Life Between Lives.* 5th ed. St. Paul, MN: Llewellyn, 2008.
6. Newton, Michael. *Destiny of Souls: New Case Studies of Life Between Lives.* St. Paul, MN: Llewellyn, 2000.
7. Northrop, Suzane. *Second Chance: Healing Messages From the Afterlife.* San Diego, CA: Jodere Group, 2002.

Films

1. *Avatar*. Directed by James Cameron Twentieth Century Fox, Los Angeles, CA: 2009. Film.
2. *Beowulf and Grendel*. Directed by Sturia Gunnarsson. Movision, 2005. Film.
3. *Beyond Christmas*. Directed by A. Edward Sutherland. Academy Productions, Los Angeles, CA: 1940. Film.
4. *Breaking Bad*. Created by Vince Gilligan. Sony Pictures Television, Los Angeles, CA: 2008-. Television.
5. *Bugsy*. Directed by Barry Levinson. TriStar Pictures, Los Angeles, CA: 1991. Film.
6. *A Foreign Field*. Directed by Charles Sturridge. British Broadcasting Company/Masterpiece Theatre, London, UK: 1993. Television.
7. *From Here to Eternity*. Directed by Fred Zinnemann. Columbia Pictures, Los Angeles, CA: 1953. Film.
8. *A High Wind in Jamaica*. Directed by Alexander Mackendrick. Twentieth Century Fox, Los Angeles, CA: 1965. Film.
9. *Just Like Heaven*. Directed by Mark Waters. DreamWorks SKG, Los Angeles, CA: 2005. Film.
10. *Living With the Dead*. Directed by Stephen Gyllenhaal. Columbia Broadcasting System, Los Angeles, CA: 2002. Television.
11. *Moliere*. Directed by Laurent Tirard. Fidélité Productions, Paris, FR: 2007. Film.
12. *Never Back Down*. Directed by Jeff Wadlow. Summit Entertainment, Los Angeles, CA: 2008. Film.
13. *Once Upon a Time in America*. Directed by Sergio Leone. The Ladd Company, Los Angeles, CA: 1984. Film.
14. *Pirates of the Caribbean: On Stranger Tides*. Directed by Rob Marshall. Walt Disney Pictures, Burbank: 2011. Film.

15. *Prom Night.* Directed by Paul Lynch. Quadrant Trust, Los Angeles, CA: 1980. Film.
16. *Rock Around the Clock.* Directed by Fred F. Sears. Clover Productions, Los Angeles, CA: 1956. Film.
17. *Spartacus: Blood and Sand.* Created by Steven S. DeNight. Starz Media, Santa Monica, CA: 2010. Television.
18. *Tell No One.* Directed by Guillaume Canet. Les Productions du Trésor, Paris, FR: 2006. Film.
19. *The Expendables.* Directed by Sylvester Stallone. Millennium Films, Los Angeles, CA: 2010. Film.
20. *The Secret in Their Eyes.* Directed by Juan José Campanella. Tornasol Films, Madrid, SP: 2009. Film.
21. *Showdown in Little Tokyo.* Directed by Mark Lester. Warner Bros. Pictures, Burbank, CA: 1991. Film.
22. *The Spy Who Loved Me.* Directed by Lewis Gilbert. Danjag Productions, Los Angeles, CA: 1977. Film.
23. *Train.* Directed by John Frankenheimer. Dear Film Produzione, Rome, IT: 1964. Film.
24. *Waiting To Exhale.* Directed by Forest Whitaker. Twentieth Century Fox, Los Angeles, CA: 1995. Film.
25. *What Dreams May Come.* Directed by Vincent Ward. Universal Studios, Universal City, CA: 1998. Film.
26. *Who Was Jesus?* Directed by Alexander Marengo. Renegade Pictures, London, UK: 2009. Television.

Songs

1. Ames, Ed. "My Cup Runneth Over." By Tom Jones and Harvey Schmidt. *Who Will Answer/My Cup Runneth Over.* BMG Collectibles, New York, NY: 1997. CD.
2. Armstrong, Louis. "What a Wonderful World." By George David Weiss and Bob Thiele. *Louis Armstrong's All Time Greatest Hits.* MCA, Universal City, CA: 1994. CD
3. Baring-Gould, Sabine (lyrics), and Sullivan, Arthur (music). "Onward Christian Soldiers." Traditional hymn, 1865/1871.

4. Beach Boys. "I Can Hear Music." By Jeff Barry, Phil Spector, and Ellie Greenwich. *The Very Best of the Beach Boys: Sounds of Summer*. Capital, Hollywood, CA: 1969. CD.
5. Boyle, Susan. "Silent Night." By Franz Gruber and Joseph Mohr. *I Dreamed a Dream*. Simco/Sony Music, Los Angeles, CA: 2009. CD.
6. The Browns. "I'll Meet You in the Morning." By Albert E. Brumley. *Family Bible*. Step One Records, Nashville, TN: 1996. CD.
7. The Browns. "Three Bells." By Bert Reisfeld and Jean Villard. *Simply the Best of the 50s*. Sony/BMG, New York, NY: 2007. CD.
8. Como, Perry. "And I Love You So." By Don McLean. *And I Love You So/It's Impossible*. BMG Collectables, New York, NY: 2001. CD.
9. Como, Perry. "Only One." By Sunny Skylar, Tom Glazer, and Andrew Ackers. *When You Come to the End of the Day/Saturday With Mr. C.* BMG Collectables, New York, NY: 2001. CD.
10. Dion, Celine. "The Power of Love." By Gunther Mende, Candy DeRouge, Jennifer Rush and Mary Susan Applegate. *Celine Dion: The Colour of My Love*. Sony Music-Canada, Montreal, QB: 1993. CD.
11. The Everly Brothers. "All I Have to Do Is Dream." By Felice and Boudleaux Bryant, House of Bryant Music. *The Everly Brothers*. Madacy Entertainment, Montreal, QB: 1999. CD.
12. Fargo, Donna. "I'm the Happiest Girl in the Whole U.S.A." By Donna Fargo. *The Best of Donna Fargo*. Curb, Universal City, CA: 1997. CD.
13. Hamilton, George IV. "I'll Miss You When You Go." By Baby Stewart and Ernest Tubb. *1954-65*. Bear Family Records, Nashville, TN: 1995. CD.

14. Ives, Burl. "Funny Way of Laughing." By Hank Cochran. *Greatest Hits*. MCA, Universal City, CA: 1996. CD.
15. Jackson, Alan. "How Great Thou Art." By Stuart K. Hine. *Precious Moments*. Arista, Los Angeles, CA: 2006. CD.
16. Mathis, Johnny. "I'll Be Home for Christmas." By Kim Gannon, Buck Ram, and Walter Kent. *Merry Christmas: Johnny Mathis*. Columbia, New York, NY: 1958. CD.
17. Mitchell, Charles, and Davis, Jimmy. "You Are My Sunshine." Shreveport, LA: 1940.
18. Newton, John. "Amazing Grace." Traditional hymn, 1779.
19. The Righteous Brothers. "Unchained Melody." By Alex North and Hy Zaret. *Righteous Brothers Anthology 1962-1974*. Rhino Records, Claremont, CA: 1989. CD.
20. The Seekers. "I'll Never Find Another You." By Tom Springfield. *The Seekers Complete*. EMI Music, London, UK: 1997. CD.
21. Simon and Garfunkel. "Bridge Over Troubled Waters." By Paul Simon. *Simon and Garfunkel: Greatest Hits*. Columbia, New York, NY: 1972. CD.
22. Strauss, Johann II. "On the Beautiful Blue Danube." By Johann Strauss II. *Ander Schönen Blauen Donau, Op. 314*. 1866.
23. Turner, Tina. "The Best." By Holly Knight and Mike Chapman. *Simply the Best*. Capital, Hollywood, CA: 1991. CD.

ABOUT THE AUTHOR

While living with Jan and Liong during the last two years of her life, Susan's world was transformed by their warmth, love, and humor. The blessings Susan received compelled her to share Jan's story in order to bring comfort and inspiration to her readers. Susan resides in Las Vegas, Nevada.